The Uzi And The Stone

Images Of Gaza

Rhona Davies and Peter R. Johnson

Detselig Enterprises Ltd.
Calgary, Alberta

Canadian Cataloguing in Publication Data

Davies, Rhona, 1938
The uzi and the stone

ISBN 1-55059-025-1

1. Gaza Strip—Description and travel.
2. Intifada, 1987- I. Johnson, Peter Richard, 1941-
II. Title.
DS110.G3D38 1991 956.9405'4 C91-091304-8

Detselig Enterprises Limited
P.O. Box G 399
Calgary, Alberta, T3A 2G3

Detselig Enterprises Ltd. appreciates the financial assistance for its 1991 program from
Alberta Foundation for the Literary Arts
Canada Council

Printed in Canada SAN 115-0324 ISBN 1-55059-025-1

In the fall of 1988, **Rhona Davies** took a two-year leave of absence from her job as a teacher in Delta, B.C., to accept a position as an instructor in education and teacher training for a group of young Palestinian men and women in the Gaza Strip. She holds a graduate degree in adult education and has lived and worked in several countries. She has published writing in the fields of education, rehabilitation, and women's issues.

Peter Johnson is a clinical psychologist. In the Gaza Strip, he had a two-year appointment as on-site coordinator of a project which involved training Palestinian teachers and providing consultative services for handicapped children and adults. Dr. Johnson is currently helping to establish a rehabilitation program for the victims of gunshot wounds to the head and spinal cord. He has published widely in the fields of rehabilitation and human sexuality.

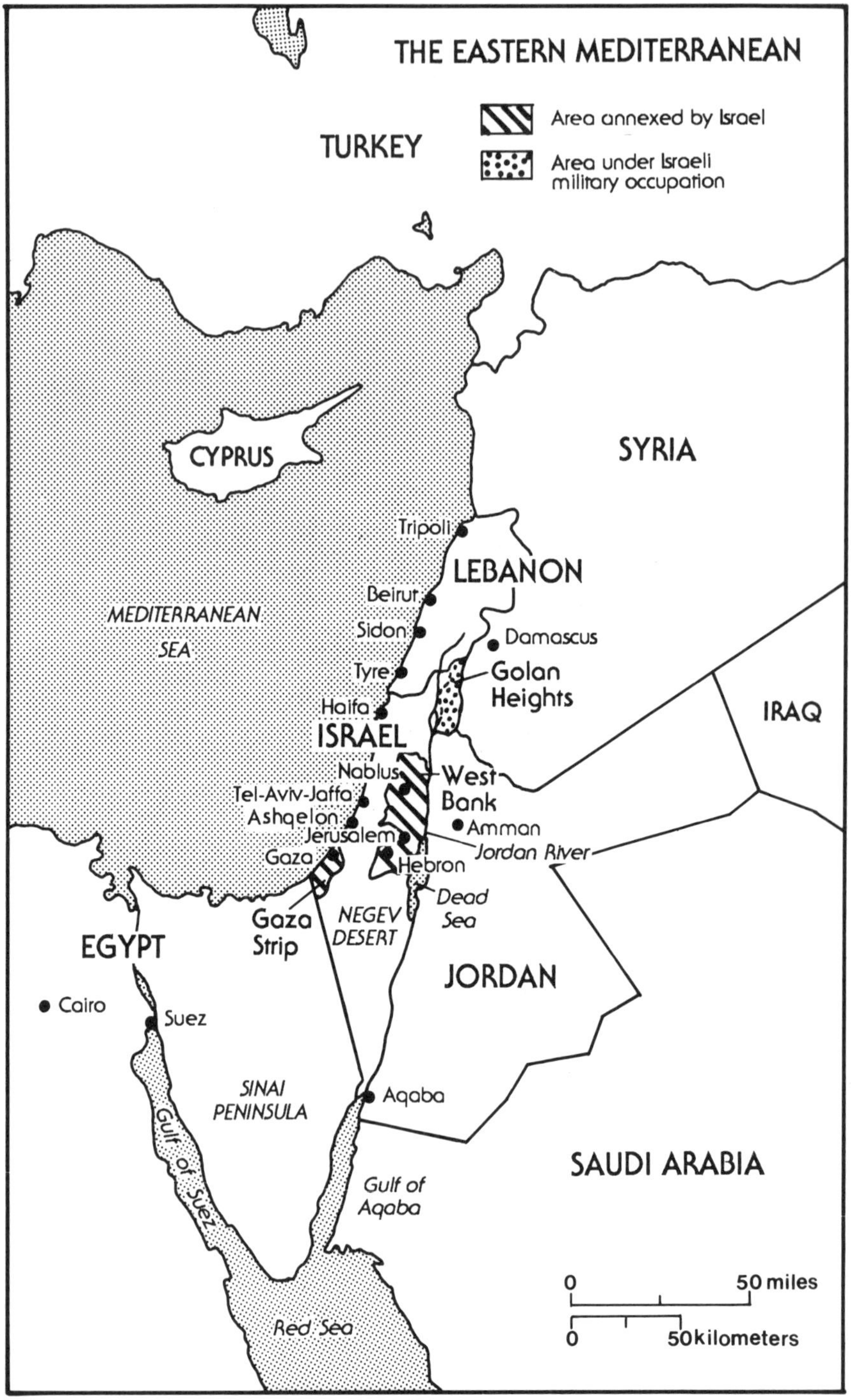
THE EASTERN MEDITERRANEAN
Area annexed by Israel
Area under Israeli military occupation
TURKEY
CYPRUS
SYRIA
Tripoli
LEBANON
Beirut
MEDITERRANEAN SEA
Sidon
Damascus
Tyre
Golan Heights
Haifa
IRAQ
ISRAEL
Nablus
West Bank
Tel-Aviv-Jaffa
Ashqelon
Amman
Jerusalem
Jordan River
Gaza
Hebron
Dead Sea
Gaza Strip
NEGEV DESERT
EGYPT
JORDAN
Cairo
Suez
SINAI PENINSULA
Aqaba
Gulf of Suez
SAUDI ARABIA
Gulf of Aqaba
0
50 miles
Red Sea
0
50 kilometers

Contents

INTRODUCTION

The beginning of the conflict between Israelis and Palestinians goes back to the dawn of recorded history. We know for example that the coastal towns of the area had been trading centres since prehistoric times, and they received a fresh wave of immigrants when the cataclysmic volcanic eruption of Thera destroyed the great Minoan civilization in Crete. About the same time, God was telling Moses to lead his people out of Egypt by crossing the Red Sea, rather than travelling through the land of the Philistines to the north because this would surely result in war between the two nations. The conflict surfaces again in the famous story of Samson and Delilah which culminates in the destruction of the Philistine temple, the ruins of which are said to still lie beneath the foundations of the Great Mosque in Gaza. Through the ensuing centuries of the Old Testament, this enmity remained.

According to the scribes of the Old Testament, the problem with the Philistines was their unwillingness to accept Jehovah as the one true God, and the tenacity with which they clung to their pagan idols. Evidently, these coastal people were also rather half-hearted in their support of Christianity, with the local god, Marnas, retaining quite a following. However, all this ended when the sword of Islam swept through Palestine early in the seventh century A.D. From this time forward, the majority of Palestinians have remained fervent Moslems.

The advent of Zionism in the late nineteenth century marks the start of the modern period of conflict between Jews and Arabs. From 1892, the European followers of Theodor Herzl began to migrate into Palestine. In 1917, Lord Balfour, the British Foreign Secretary, announced his government's pledge to support the creation of a Jewish state in the Holy Land, and shortly after this the League of Nations created the Palestine Mandate to be supervised by Britain. As one might expect, the Arab inhabitants of this region grew increasingly alarmed at these developments and began to fight against the creation of a Jewish homeland in Palestine.

The situation was exacerbated by Hitler's rise to power in Germany and the horrors of the ensuing Nazi Holocaust. Perhaps motivated by guilt at the fate of European Jewry, support for the creation of a homeland gained momentum. Much to the consternation of the Arabs, thousands of Jews fled from Europe and tried to settle within the Mandate of Palestine.

Consequently, as soon as the State of Israel was created in 1948, it was plunged into war with a number of Arab countries. The armies of Israel, Egypt, Jordan, and Iraq waged battle throughout the Mandate of Palestine. Meanwhile, the majority of the Palestinian civilian inhabitants of this country abandoned, or were driven from, their homes as the fighting swirled around them. Most of them fled to Lebanon, Syria, and Jordan, or the small area around the city of Gaza. After the war, they were not allowed to return to their homes in the fertile land they knew, but were confined to the poverty, filth and squalor of refugee camps.

After 1948, the major part of Palestine was under the control of Israel. However, a large tract of land on the West Bank of the Jordan River was occupied by King Abdullah of Jordan and a small strip of land around Gaza was controlled by the Egyptians. In 1950, the United Nations Relief and Works Agency (UNRWA) was created to provide food and shelter for the enormous population of former residents of the land now occupied by Israel. Although the fighting died down, the Arab countries refused to recognize the State of Israel and officially remained in a state of war with the new country.

One cannot over-estimate the effects of history on the Jewish psyche. After centuries of persecution around the world, they had now been subjected to a genocide of inhuman magnitude. Shortly after this, the Arab countries had declared they would not rest until they had destroyed the newly-formed state of Israel. Small wonder that the Israelis were, and remain, overwhelmed by a national paranoia, which has been exploited from time to time by certain power-hungry politicians. This national paranoia was to remain a major factor in subsequent regional events.

After years of relatively minor skirmishes and a more serious international crisis in 1956, another war broke out in 1967. After only a few days, Israel emerged victorious. The Israeli army now occupied the West Bank, the Golan Heights in Syria, and the Gaza Strip. Furthermore, they had pushed as far west as the Suez Canal, thus occupying a large area of Egypt known as Sinai. The major change for hundreds of thousands of Palestinians was that their homes and camps were now occupied by Israel rather than one of the Arab countries.

Some years after another major outbreak of hostilities in 1973, President Jimmy Carter of the United States was instrumental in negotiating a peace agreement between Egypt and Israel. In return for the recognition of its right to exist, Israel gave back the occupied Sinai lands to Egypt. However, the plight of the Palestinian refugees remained unchanged, save that members of a few hundred families were forcibly separated from each other when it was determined that the new Israeli-Egyptian international border ran through the middle of their refugee camp in Rafah, a small town at the southern end of the Gaza Strip.

In 1964, the Palestine Liberation Organization (PLO) was formed to unite the Palestinian factions who were resisting the presence of a Jewish state in their country. By 1969, the Fatah group, headed by Yasser Arafat, gained the leadership of the PLO and remains its dominant faction. In 1974, the PLO was recognized by the United Nations as the sole legitimate representative of the Palestinian people. After being ousted from Jordan in the early seventies, the PLO set up its headquarters in Beirut, Lebanon.

In 1982, there was a serious confrontation between Israel and the PLO. Following a series of guerilla raids on Israel from Lebanon, the Israeli army invaded that country. After being defeated in a bloody battle, Yasser Arafat and the PLO fighters were forced to withdraw from Lebanon. Following the departure of this army, the Israeli commanders allowed their Lebanese Christian allies to enter the refugee camps of Sabbra and Shatilla in Lebanon where hundreds of civilians, including women and children, were murdered. Eventually, Mr. Arafat and his colleagues were allowed to establish their new headquarters in Tunis.

Meanwhile, life remained grim for those Palestinians living in the refugee camps and poor neighborhoods of the West Bank and Gaza Strip. Under the military occupation of Israel since 1967, the factors of grinding poverty and a high birth rate combined with the unsanitary conditions and repressive military laws produced a living hell. The conditions in the Gaza Strip were especially discouraging, earning the area the unenviable title of "the most densely-populated, poorest place on earth."[1] The Occupied Territories were a time-bomb waiting to explode.

The explosion came in December, 1987, when an Israeli vehicle caused the death of four Palestinian day-laborers who were returning from Israel to the Jabalia refugee camp. In response, the young people of the Occupied Territories took to the streets in a spontaneous outburst of pent-up emotion. They barricaded streets, burned tires, flew the outlawed Palestinian flag, and hurled stones at the heavily-armed soldiers. The Palestinian Intifada had begun.

Dr. Hatem Abu Ghazaleh, a Palestinian physician, is the Chairman of the Society for the Care of the Handicapped in Gaza. In 1982, he went to Calgary, Alberta and met Dr. Roy Brown, the Director of Rehabilitation Studies at the University of Calgary, to discuss methods of developing services for the thousands of handicapped children and adults who live in the Gaza Strip. This meeting began a two-year process which culminated in the creation of the Educational Program for Self-Sufficient Services in Gaza.

The main goal of this program is to train Palestinian personnel to become effective special education teachers, vocational workers, and rehabilitation counsellors in their own communities. Although the program is fully funded by the Canadian International Development Agency (CIDA), its day-to-day operations are overseen jointly by the Society for the Care of the Handicapped, the University of Calgary, and Mount Royal Community College in Calgary. In effect, it is an equal partnership, with the college and university being responsible for all academic aspects of the project, while the Society is responsible for its administration. Students follow programs similar to those of their Canadian counterparts, receiving diplomas and degrees which are fully-recognized by post-secondary educational institutions in western countries.

Several program components have been developed since 1984. First, a group of fifteen students obtained graduate diplomas in

---

1 Robin Morgan. *The Demon Lover: On the Sexuality of Terrorism.* Norton, 1989.

Special Education from the University of Calgary. Next, a further eighteen young men and women graduated with Mount Royal College diplomas in Rehabilitation Services, and a second cohort is currently working on the same course. In January, 1990, another graduate diploma program commenced; this one is to train Case Managers for the rehabilitation of those Palestinians who have survived intifada-related gunshot wounds to the brain and spinal cord. To date, approximately 100 Palestinian students have participated in the Educational Program for Self-Sufficient Services.

In the spring of 1988, Peter Johnson and Rhona Davies agreed to join the Gaza project as on-site coordinators and instructors. Peter arrived in Gaza at the beginning of September and Rhona followed two months later. They remained in Gaza for almost two years, leaving in July 1990. This book tells the story of their day-to-day life in Gaza. The journal entries were written by Peter, while Rhona is the author of the essays.

In order to provide protection from possible mistreatment by the authorities, it was considered necessary to falsify the names of many people mentioned in this book.

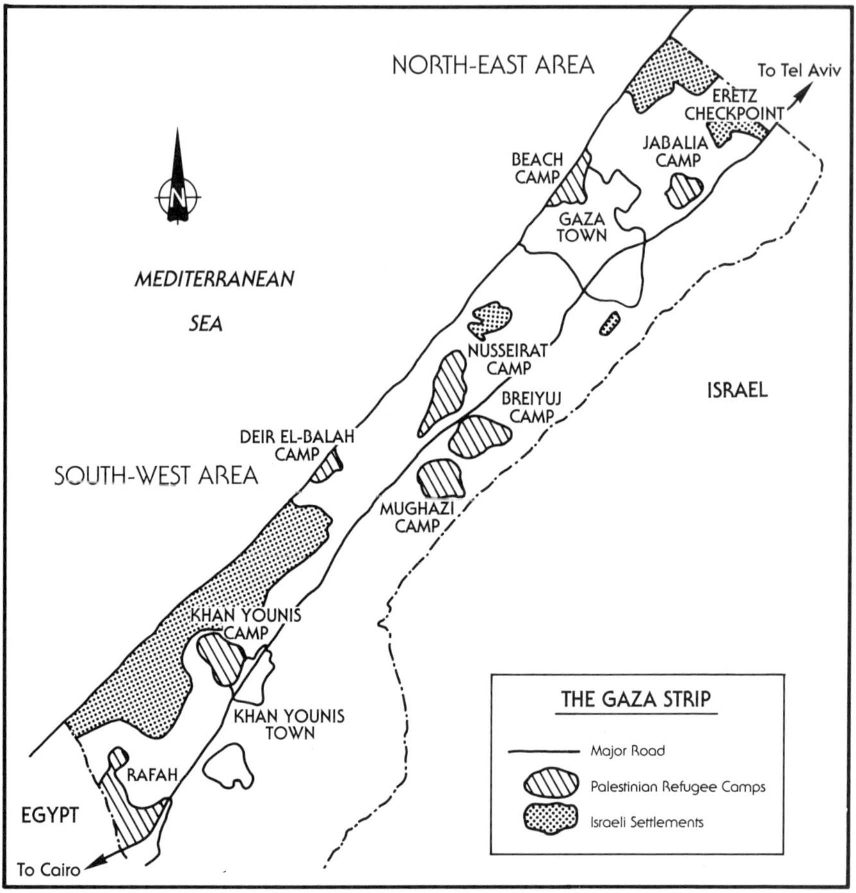
NORTH-EAST AREA
To Tel Aviv
ERETZ CHECKPOINT
JABALIA CAMP
BEACH CAMP
GAZA TOWN
N
MEDITERRANEAN
SEA
NUSSEIRAT CAMP
BREIYUJ CAMP
ISRAEL
DEIR EL-BALAH CAMP
SOUTH-WEST AREA
MUGHAZI CAMP
KHAN YOUNIS CAMP
KHAN YOUNIS TOWN
RAFAH
EGYPT
To Cairo
THE GAZA STRIP
Major Road
Palestinian Refugee Camps
Israeli Settlements

CHAPTER ONE

Retrospect

The snow falls in large soft flakes past the window as I sit writing at my desk. Christmas is only a few days away and Peter and I are both looking forward to the closeness of family and friends, the warmth and security that we no longer take for granted. This year, Christmas has come to mean something extra special, as indeed did Thanksgiving. The traditional words and songs for these occasions now have deeper significance in the aftermath of our two years of living in Gaza.

Our re-entry was not as straightforward as many people might imagine. On the surface everything appeared familiar; the house was exactly as we had left it; the grocery store at the corner was open until midnight; the neighbors we had known were still there and welcomed us home; the ferries and buses ran on a familiar schedule.

We soon realized, however, that many of our responses and perceptions were still trapped in Gaza. The glimpse of a Jeep in the rear-view mirror of the car would produce knots in our stomachs and an impulse to immediately pull over and allow it to pass; I found myself swerving to avoid a group of children I suddenly saw ahead throwing things at each other on their front lawn. They were simply having fun with pine cones. A trip to the theatre to see *Les Miserables* was a disaster. The stage sets reminded us of the barricades we had just left behind, and the electronically-discharged firecrackers simulating gunfire filled us with terror. It will be a long time before we can view as entertainment the real issues for which people have given their lives.

Halloween firecrackers sent us rushing to close windows against tear gas. But the window was not the one I remembered in Gaza, and the only smell drifting into the room was that of the newly-fertilized fields of grain from nearby farmlands stretching away to the water. Gazing toward the ocean, I inevitably contrasted the peacefulness of a stroll to the sea with our abortive picnic the day we were surrounded by armed Jeep-patrols on the beach road in Gaza. Here, we could take Azzad and the Bad Boys down to the beach without threat or hindrance. I longed for them to experience this simple, basic human right.

Images of Gaza intruded into the most apparently insignificant circumstances. A children's choir singing songs of peace and joy, their faces portraying the health and security of a happy childhood, roused me to tears as memories of homes in the refugee camps superimposed themselves.

Then there were the nightmares. We would awaken in the middle of the night sweating with fear, sometimes calling out in panic. Both of us dreamed regularly of being separated, lost in the back streets of Gaza, unable to find each other and being captured or shot by the soldiers, or trapped in a confrontation between them and Palestinians. One especially terrifying night I was convinced I really had been shot and was dying. Even when I awoke, I could feel the pain of the bullets in my spine and, in the darkness, believed I was back in Gaza and alone.

I have also been surprised at the pangs of nostalgia I now experience. It is a nostalgia for the closeness of Palestinian friends, coupled with a feeling that, to some extent, we deserted them, that it was too easy in the end to walk away from it all. At the time, they themselves did their best to make it as difficult as possible for us to leave, telling us that we belonged to them now. But I suppose that is what development, whether international or personal, is all about; there is a time when one has to walk away so that new growth may take place. I doubt it is ever easy.

The Canadian government provided debriefing sessions that were helpful to our process of reintegration. The psychological sessions were especially cathartic. With the skilled guidance of two international counsellors and our substantial collection of photographs, we were able to unburden ourselves of the two years' worth of memories, both happy and painful, and to begin a process of healing and readjustment. Things began to acquire a more manageable perspective, and the nightmares started to fade.

It is impossible, however, to let go completely of our experience in Gaza. Telephone calls and letters arrive each week from friends and students, always with affection and requests for help in some form or other, and always wanting to know when we will return. "Umm Kamal makes us read your letters over and over," writes Salah, our ex-landlord, in the letter accompanying a Christmas card. "Remember you promised to come and see us next year," says Manal, writing from her family home amid the *suk* (market) close to the Swedish clinic. Sana'a sends us a Christmas card in English that plays Jingle Bells when you open it: "This is a simple wish as we hope for a better future," she says. The card, such a simple item to us, may well have taken her weeks of planning and organization to locate in time for Christmas. Someone, somewhere along the grapevine of Gazan communication, would have been assigned the job of finding it somewhere over the Green Line in Israel. Nothing was ever too difficult to be found for us.

I doubt we will ever completely let go of our Gaza experience. Daily news programs cause us a good deal of anguish as we watch the familiar scenes there. We dread seeing someone we know being shot or wounded. Sometimes we see a quick camera shot of masked youths and soldiers in conflict near our home on Ittalatini Street, or the market stalls in the old town, and immediately myriad memories return. The feeling of being part of an extended family refuses to leave us.

The program we were employed to teach has been postponed indefinitely pending the resolution of events revolving around the invasion of Kuwait. Understandably, Canadian colleges are reluctant to send teachers to Gaza during these volatile and unstable times. Therefore the students cannot continue with their diploma work, and are worried that they may never complete the program. Many are asking for assistance in continuing their studies in the West. Others write to say that they have no hope. The letters are always full of loving messages and apologies for asking for assistance.

As I watch the lawn turning to a carpet of white, I remember everyone back in Gaza, and know that while I, like many Canadians, sit enjoying the warmth of a winter fire, with the lights of the Christmas tree glowing in the late afternoon dusk, the people of Gaza seem to be trapped forever in a twilight zone of unbelievable harshness, devoid of everyday comforts, a homeland and freedoms that most of us in the West take for granted. We gain a small measure of consolation in knowing that Azzad and Iyad will be arriving in two days to share this special time with us, for they did manage to get to Canada to continue their studies.

For us, more than ever this year, we wish for peace on earth and goodwill to people everywhere, especially to those striving for solutions to historically-based problems in the very Holy Land from which these expressions of humanity were first heralded.

CHAPTER TWO

September – October 1988

September 27th 1988

I am now three weeks into my second appointment to the University of Calgary's program in the Gaza Strip. I was first here two years ago and find the place quite different. The popular uprising, or intifada in Arabic, has become a constant presence in my life. It is not the sole focus of my thoughts and feelings, but the backdrop against which I now live.

Daily routines are much changed. Every evening I hear the crackle of gunfire from the Beach Refugee Camp which is situated about 500 metres from my apartment at the Sun Centre. There is always a night curfew imposed on the entire Gaza Strip and people cannot be out on the street after 9 p.m. In addition, the United Leadership of the Uprising has decreed the stores may only open from 9 a.m. until noon. These constants have been punctuated by weekly strike days and regular daytime curfews imposed on the various refugee camps, thus making it difficult for my students to attend class on a regular basis.

Before I left Canada, the University of Calgary promised that we would be able to live in an apartment away from the Sun Centre. We were told that work on preparing the apartment had begun during the time of our predecessors and had only been delayed by the onset of the intifada. It was assumed that we would be able to move in almost immediately.

On my second day in Gaza, I was taken to see the apartment. It was an empty shell, gutted of everything including toilet, bathtub, sinks and kitchen appliances. In the middle of the living room was a pile of sand so high I couldn't see over the top of it. I was told not to worry as everything would be finished in three weeks.

Today I visited the apartment again. Not only had nothing changed, but I believe nobody had even entered the place since we were last there! It seems it will be necessary to badger my hosts every day to ensure there is some action on this project.

September 30th 1988

I was invited to Fahed Lababidi's home for lunch today. Fahed is the Director-General of the Society for the Care of the Handicapped. As it is a strike day and no motorized traffic is allowed on the street, I took a dusty walk through the Rimal suburb of Gaza in the heat of the early afternoon.

Fahed came out to meet me and escorted me into his modest home behind a high wall on a quiet residential street. We passed through an untended yard whose tall palm tree and sandy soil are reminders that Gaza is situated on the edge of the great deserts which cover vast stretches of Sinai, Arabia, and North Africa. On entering the house, we climbed the wide staircase with its white walls and mosaic-tiled floor to where his family was waiting. There I met his wife and four children together with his mother who was introduced as *el-hazja*, the female pilgrim.

The food was simple and delicious. The main dish was roast chicken stuffed with rice and spices. There was a tomato and cucumber salad and a small squash-like vegetable called *fa'ouz* which was also stuffed with rice. Finally, there was a dish of *mulukhiyya* into which we dipped pita bread. *Mulukhiyya* is a local plant which is made into a green paste tasting a little like sweet mint.

After the meal, I sat with Fahed in another room where we ate fruit, drank Turkish coffee, and talked. Mohammed, the eldest son, sat with us, and the women and other children moved freely in and out of the room. I was struck by the very clear division of roles between males and females. For example, while Mohammed seemed very comfortable sitting with the men, his sister Zenab was constantly involved in the preparation and serving of the meal.

We spoke of many things in that cool room while the late afternoon sun and a gentle breeze from the Mediterranean filtered through the open shutters. Inevitably, we talked of politics and the intifada. While the tone has never been strident or unreasonable, I have yet to meet a Palestinian who does not support the PLO and its position on establishing a Palestinian homeland.

We moved easily from politics to religion as Fahed described how Islam is a way of life for him. He usually answers the five calls to prayer each day and is guided by the Koran in every aspect of his life. In a strange way, living in a Moslem culture highlights my Christian beliefs, making me realize the strength of religious education at an early age. Fahed, like many Moslems I know, took great pains to point out the similarities between Christianity and Islam.

October 3rd 1988

This is another strike day, so I was not awakened by the usual sound of buses in the courtyard below my apartment. However, as I was finishing my tea, I heard a voice outside the apartment calling my name. It was Fahed, and he had three of his children with him. They live about one kilometre away so he was able to walk down the hill with Zenab (12), Nimir (10) and Lubna (2).

While Fahed was attending to some business in his office, I brought the children up to my terrace. They speak little English so I asked in Arabic if they would like juice and cookies. We sat around a small table and, as usual, I was impressed by their politeness and good manners. Even two-year-old Lubna sat quietly and listened to the conversation for perhaps 15 to 20 minutes.

After a while, I noticed that each child's glass had about an inch of orange juice left in the bottom, and there were several cookies remaining on the plate. I realized that true to the Arab rules of hospitality, they would neither eat nor drink any more unless it was offered. If these children had drained their glasses, it would have indicated that they wanted more and implied that I was a poor host for not providing it.

After they left, I spent the rest of the day alone, unable to drive anywhere and not knowing many people within walking distance.

This was not particularly irksome for me, as I needed the time to catch up on lecture notes, letters home, and Arabic homework. Although I was occupied, I was aware of the unusual silence in the streets with almost a sense of dormancy and expectation in the lives of the families around me.

The streets were indeed quiet. At one point, I saw a truck filled with Israeli soldiers pass by and later heard the siren on a UN ambulance, but that was all. The stillness of the late afternoon was punctuated only by calls to prayer from the loudspeaker atop the minaret of the mosque down the street. Today the calls seemed louder than usual and I could make out the phrase *Allahu akbar* (God is the greatest) as the muezzin's voice echoed eerily through the empty streets.

October 7th 1988

Progress on our new apartment continues to be incredibly slow. When I visited today two men were putting tiles on the bathroom floor. However little else had changed.

October 9th 1988

As the sun set, I heard the crackle of gunfire. It was coming from the Nasser district — or maybe from Beach Camp. This week the Israeli soldiers began using plastic bullets in addition to tear gas — I wonder what was happening out there in the darkness.

Later, I gradually became aware of a faint sound borne through my open windows on a soft evening breeze from the Mediterranean. To my uneducated ears, it sounded like the noise from a distant stadium hosting a rock concert. It was the sound of many voices.

I went to the window to look out, but could see nothing stirring in the still, dark streets. I thought that something was happening in a distant part of Gaza, but reminded myself that our Rimal neighborhood is usually very quiet.

Gradually, the noise grew until I could understand the words which were being shouted — *Allahu akbar!* echoed through the streets. My neighbors came out on to their balconies and took up the cry. Soon the whole area was resounding to the cries of *Allahu akbar! Allahu akbar!*

Next, I could hear the small explosions of tear gas grenades being fired, and with each shot the cries of the Palestinians increased. A burning tire suddenly appeared in the intersection near my apartment, and emergency vehicles, which I took to be ambulances, were soon hurtling down a nearby main street toward the area where the shouting had first begun.

The noise continued for about an hour until the sounds of shooting died away. However, Rimal did not return to its former calm, for in defiance of the curfew, a few restless teenagers roamed the streets, and there were still occasional choruses of *Allahu akbar.*

This has been my first experience of a community response to the occupation. I had heard of course that devout Moslems wish to die with the words *Allahu akbar* on their lips, and that the phrase's current use originated from a Palestinian's response to being beaten by the soldiers. Now, it had escalated into both a cry of resistance and a warning that the soldiers were coming. It seems that the Palestinians take delight in the fact that the soldiers can do nothing to stop these outbursts. It is one of the few remaining ways in which the ordinary person can resist the occupation.

On reflection, it is the sounds of the individual voices which stay with me. In them, I hear fear and even some enjoyment, but mostly the cries appear to be of pain, frustration, and deep, deep anger. Such community-wide expressions of feeling must be cathartic and help people to live through the seemingly endless frustrations of the occupation.

October 15th 1988

The lack of progress with the new apartment is driving me crazy. Sometimes when I visit, it seems they were further ahead the week before!

Today we are into the saga of painting the living room. Here the walls are to be off-white while the fireplace and chimney are to be brown. But when the walls are painted, so much white paint splashes on to the chimney that it needs to be repainted. When the chimney is repainted so much brown paint splashes on to the walls that they must be done again. The process is being repeated ad infinitum. I can see this project taking the painters' entire working lives and still not being finished!

October 20th 1988

Today Dr. Hatem and Mrs. Aida Abu Ghazaleh returned after a period of four months in the United States. I was in Hatem's office when many of the staff came to greet him. It was interesting that the men kissed him while the women merely shook hands. Later, the teachers prepared a celebratory lunch to mark his return.

This morning I went out to buy gas and took Ahmed (a student in our program) with me. We saw Israeli soldiers blocking a street in the Sheikh Radwan district in order to interrogate people. I was shocked to see a man in civilian clothes carrying an uzi. I don't know if he was an Israeli settler or a member of the secret police.

October 23rd 1988

I have arranged for three students to do a practicum at the Dar es Salaam Institution in the Zeitun quarter of the old city of Gaza. This is a Christian institution operated by the Sisters of Charity under the leadership of Mother Theresa. It provides care for about 20 destitute, mentally and physically handicapped children.

Yesterday there was trouble at the institution. When the students asked to take the children into the small garden behind the institution, they were refused permission. One of the Sisters told them that only the nuns are allowed to use the garden. Also, she was angry because the students had told me that some of the children in the institution have head lice and one has a serious skin condition. Such reactions hardly enhance the reputation of this organization.

I had lunch at Hatem's house today and met two interesting Americans from Boston. Sara Roy has a Ph.D. in International Development and is currently a Research Fellow at Harvard. She has written one book on the economic situation in the Gaza Strip and is currently doing research for a second. Jay Schnitzer has a Ph.D. in Chemical Engineering but has just qualified as a surgeon and will be working as a volunteer at the Ahli Arab Hospital in Gaza.

Later in the day, Abdullah (a student in our program) came to the apartment for a tutorial. Afterwards, I drove him back to his home near Jabalia. He warned me to be careful driving home along Nasser Street in the dark because many cars have recently been stoned in that neighborhood. Fortunately, I had no trouble. But, the United Leadership has announced that cars should not be out on the streets after 6:30 p.m.

October 26th 1988

Today is a strike day, and there has been much intifada-related activity in this area. In fact, all the refugee camps are under curfew and the sound of shooting has been heard for most of the morning. The current outburst may be connected with yesterday's death of a teenage girl in Rafah. There are also rumors of several other people killed and many injured.

This morning I heard several loud explosions. They seemed to come from the area of the Shifa Hospital, some 800 metres away. One explosion was loud enough to rattle the windows of my apartment. I assumed this was from the firing of a tear gas grenade, but I did not see any clouds of gas when I looked out the window.

Later, a boy placed a small container in the intersection of a main street near my apartment. The idea was to make the soldiers think this was some kind of explosive device. Sure enough, the soldiers soon appeared. They were in two Jeeps, each containing four men equipped with uzis and riot protection gear. They examined the container and removed it after deciding it was not a bomb.

One block away, three boys stood watching the soldiers. Two of them were about ten years old and the other perhaps two years younger. As the soldiers removed the container, the boys whistled and shouted. The soldier who was nearest to them turned and fired a single bullet. Fortunately, the boys were not injured and fled down a side street.

The soldiers left and within minutes two burning tires had appeared in the same intersection, but there were no young people in sight. Of course, the soldiers soon arrived to deal with the tires. This time they entered a house near the intersection, pulled out two well-dressed, middle-aged men and forced them to bring out a hosepipe and extinguish the blaze.

They also stopped a young man who was passing on a bicycle, took his identity card and forced him to remove the remains of the burning tire from the street. This was a very messy job. They let him go eventually, but I don't know if his identity card was returned.

October 29th 1988

Yesterday, American consultant, David Shearer, arrived at the Centre. He is an expert in the Portage Program for providing in-home educational services to the mothers of handicapped children. He and I went to Fahed's for lunch. The food was delicious and Fahed, as usual, was warm, kind, and hospitable.

It seems that either the intifada is escalating or the Israelis are bringing more soldiers into the Gaza Strip in anticipation of trouble during the upcoming Israeli elections. There were several incidents at the main intersection near my apartment today. At least twice I noticed that objects had been carefully placed in the intersection so they would look like explosive devices. This evening a truck full of soldiers came along and detonated the remaining device. However, I don't think it was a real bomb.

Earlier today I saw a soldier at the same intersection firing at boys who were standing about 100 metres away and were whistling and jeering. This is hardly an activity which threatened the soldier and necessitated the firing of plastic bullets in self-defence. (On the radio, I have heard that it is the policy of the IDF that soldiers may only fire when their lives are being threatened.)

October 30th 1988

There was a dramatic change in the weather today. During the night, it rained very hard and it has continued this morning in fairly violent showers. My apartment is a little chilly because the wind whistles through the gaps between the window frames and the walls. There is also no hot water as the clouds prevented the sun from heating the solar panels of the water tanks on the roof.

There are rumors that a curfew will be imposed on the Gaza Strip next Tuesday. In addition, the United Leadership has called for a four-day strike later next month to coincide with the upcoming meeting of the Palestine National Council in Tunis.

Today Rhona is scheduled to fly from Vancouver to London. I hope she has arrived safely. Tomorrow, I will try to leave Gaza and head for Tel Aviv where I hope to meet her on Tuesday evening.

Preparations For Leaving

Emotionally, I felt I had been leaving Canada for at least two weeks prior to my departure. Things seemed to intensify as the date approached. I had celebrated my fiftieth birthday in grand style, thanks to the planning of treasured friends and colleagues. It had also been a day to start saying goodbyes to those I would not see again until my return from the Gaza Strip. Then there were the goodbyes to the children at the school where I had worked for ten years. I suppose most teachers worry to some extent about handing over their students to new people. The children invariably seem to adjust while we suffer our private agonies. I was particularly concerned about one little girl who had needed a lot of learning support, whereas another tike from the grade two class took the opportunity to use his final "Talking Time" (counselling session) with me to speak very frankly, describing the day when his classroom teacher had been taken sick and I had taken over.

"We're usually naughty, you know, when there's a sub in," he confessed cheerfully, "but somebody came in and said, 'Guess who the sub's going to be...the toughest teacher in the school: Ms. Davies!!' And you know, we were all amazed by recess time that nobody had a detention and we were having *fun*!" I laughed and understood his way of letting go.

Throughout the day, people dropped by my learning assistance room to give me their best wishes. My two parent helpers gave me small, thoughtful gifts: a cloth-bound journal for writing down my experiences in Gaza, and some body lotion to prevent my skin from drying out in desert-like conditions. My assistant came in for one last hug even though Friday was her day off. The school bell played its little tune signalling the end of the day; I closed my teaching binder, picked up my gloves and briefcase, took one last, nostalgic glance at the little room that had been my working home for those ten happy years, and walked away, telling myself that I'd be back in ten months.

Although my suitcases had been sitting half-packed for at least two weeks, it took several hours to complete the task that Friday night. What do you take to the Gaza Strip? Do they have dental floss and aspirin? Should I pack the can opener (I did) and some

SOS scouring pads? Last minute questions flitted through my head as I packed and repacked to exhaustion. Anything else I needed I would have to either survive without or try to locate once I got over there. I counted on the fact that friends had told us to call them collect if there were things we needed, and they would ship us out a CARE package.

Saturday morning brought more goodbye calls and the last-minute addition of OXO cubes. Lynne, a good friend, arrived with lunch at midday, along with Linda who was moving in to house sit for the year. Then Maggie, our company secretary, arrived with her husband Ted to drive me to the airport. I was intensely excited and keen to accept the challenge that Gaza would offer, yet at the last minute I found it hard to say goodbye to my cozy, familiar home. Lynne walked me to the car as I wept, and then Ted took over, speedily whipping us off on to the highway and emphasizing the fact that I had *wanted* to do this and was going to have an incredible time. I was overwhelmed by all the caring support I had had for the past two weeks.

Air Canada flight 852 took off on schedule with a stop in Edmonton. I slept little on the plane and the ten and a half hours seemed interminable. But once in the hotel at Heathrow in London, I was able to catch up on rest after struggling with the mysteries of the English central heating system which, with the vents being located halfway up the wall, kept your head and neck quite cosy but left your legs and feet freezing cold. Since the flight to Tel Aviv did not leave for a day and a half, I spent the time sleeping, occasionally visiting the restaurant, and calling relatives in England who sounded quite bemused by the whole venture. My sister-in-law seemed to think I was going to Israel for some kind of holiday, while my well-intentioned academic brother, who had just completed a course on how to deal with terrorists, provided intriguing advice on coping with possible hijackers. "Don't do anything to draw attention to yourself, and don't look at them," were his suggestions for survival.

Nobody I talked to seemed to know very much about Gaza except that there were people who threw stones because of some kind of problem. However, I didn't really know a whole lot more myself at that point. The media deal in such stereotypes, and the government briefing we had attended in Ottawa was only able to provide us with one person who had actually been to Gaza, and he was there only for a period of three weeks long before the uprising had started.

I turned on the television and heard news that there would be two strike days in Gaza, called by the intifada leadership to protest the forthcoming Israeli elections. There was also a tragic incident in Jericho involving the firebombing of an Israeli bus in which an Israeli woman and her two young children were burned to death. I wondered what else was happening in Gaza, but was unable to call Peter since all international telephone lines to the Strip had been shut down for months. When I did hear from him it was on those occasions when he had managed to get to a town outside the Gaza Strip and call from the post office. The calls were usually exercises in frustration for we would invariably get cut-off after only a couple of sentences, so that our conversations over the previous two months had amounted to rather desperate inquiries of, "Are you all right?" with an affirmative response from both sides before the line went dead. I knew that Peter had my flight arrival time and contingency plans were in place should he be unable to meet me at the airport, for one never knew when the Gaza Strip would be shut down and no-one allowed in or out for days at a time.

I indulged in one last warm bath, as dawn brightened the sky on the day that would see me ten thousand miles from my home, checked out of the hotel and headed for the airport. Having deposited my two large suitcases into the left luggage office where they had sat for two nights, security procedures required that they both be examined thoroughly. I stood by as two bemused security officials carefully scrutinized a year's supply of sani napkins, kitchen gadgets, staples, felt pens, hypodermic needles in case of emergencies, and a regular Aladdin's cave of other survival items. Since many passengers must go through this procedure, it was not surprising that the flight was an hour late arriving in Tel Aviv.

Dusk was descending as I disembarked in Israel and got on the bus which drives passengers from the aircraft to the air terminal. The air felt soft and warm, and the sky glowed pink with a sunset that bespoke a fine summer day, silhouetting the palm trees scattered around the airport. I still did not know whether or not Peter would be on hand to meet me.

Bags retrieved, I loaded up a cart and pushed through the exit doors. A large number of people were waiting for those near and dear, and I was struck immediately by the apparent homogeneity of their appearance. I suppose I had become so accustomed to seeing a wide variety of ethnic groups within our Canadian mosaic, especially in Vancouver, that I somehow felt strange and "other" among these people with their yarmulkas or stove-pipe hats and long ringlets. It had not felt the same in England or other parts of Europe. At the time, I supposed I would get used to it, but I never did.

It was with a good deal of relief and joy that I saw Peter waving to attract my attention in the midst of the crowd, and we hugged and held each other for several minutes, relieved that all was well after two months of separation. He looked in good shape and had everything supremely organized. Due to the strike I had heard about in London on the news, Peter had left the Strip the previous day, driving the car loaned to us by the Society for the Care of the Handicapped. We would have to spend another day in Tel Aviv until the strike was over, for motorized traffic in Gaza is forbidden on such days and likely to be stoned if seen on the streets.

Once in Tel Aviv, Peter had parked the car and taken a taxi to the airport after checking us into a hotel. The taxi driver was a pleasant young man who reminded me of the sixties' hippie genre, and who had offered to wait despite the hour-long delay of my flight. He seemed quiet and helpful and was a reassuring contrast from the crowd I had first encountered.

The strike gave us time to catch up on news, and for me to recuperate from the emotions of leave-taking and the journey east. We talked until after midnight, and then I fell asleep feeling more relaxed than I had in a long time.

Waking up to what would be a warm summer's day in Canada, it was difficult to believe that this was November. Temperatures were in the seventies, and while I basked in the sunshine on the beach, Peter kept saying, "If it's this hot in November, how hot will it be in Gaza during the spring and summer?" I thought it would be fine, always preferring heat to cold.

There was business to do before we returned to Gaza. We first visited the Canadian Embassy to pick up our mail; then a long stride out to the American Express office to get travellers' cheques so that we could shop for food. Peter knew a supermarket where we bought some supplies that we would not be able to get in Gaza. My expectations were shattered by the contrast with our own supermarkets back home in Canada. This one seemed dirty and crowded, but there were some surprising items: HP Sauce that cost the earth, and a can of cranberry sauce for about seven dollars. Most of the shops I saw on this first foraging seemed to be very expensive. Even the revered Gottex swimwear which is designed and manufactured in Israel turned out to be the same price as in Canada and the U.S. (I guess somewhere in the back of my mind, what with the sunshine and all, I had secretly hoped to spot a bargain!).

The brief interlude began to wind down as the reality of what we now had to do insinuated itself into the Tel Aviv sunshine and freedom. Fahed, the director of the Society, had to be telephoned to let him know that we would be on our way just after six in the morning and hoped to arrive at the Centre by eight-thirty at the latest. I enjoyed a last dinner of familiar food, and felt in good spirits even though I knew that tomorrow was going to be a whole new experience. I took out my Arabic phrase book and listened to the tapes I had tried to memorize, not really believing that any of these strange phonemes would be interpreted as communication when I attempted them. Eventually, I fell asleep with *Salaamu alleykum* still drifting through my thoughts. Tomorrow would be the true test.

Entry into Gaza

As events turned out, we got lost trying to leave Tel Aviv. Somewhere around the old clock tower in Jaffa, a wrong left turn took us on a magical mystery tour that we had not bargained for. We knew no Hebrew, and the road signs within the city were not posted in English. Asking for directions to the highway only seemed to add to the confusion since the people we asked barely knew any English, and surprisingly the first foreign language we had to deal with was not Arabic but French. We were amazed at how much high-school French our frantically-churning brains were able to retrieve, and after one and a half hours of being lost we were finally back on track.

The road to the Gaza Strip runs directly south from Tel Aviv, parallel to the spectacular coastline of the Mediterranean Sea. Sand-dunes sweep away to the ocean and eventually the highway curves east for a while, passing a field of magnificent sunflowers nodding their over-sized heads in the breeze, and enters more arable country where citrus groves abound. Occasionally, between the new-looking towns with their red-tiled rooftops, we see a derelict, grey, cement-block, two-storey dwelling standing ghost-like in the middle of a newly-ploughed field or established citrus grove. Sometimes, nearby is an equally-derelict mosque, or the remains of walls that must once have enclosed a farmer's home and garden. The ruins are the only testimony to their original Arab owners, many of whom now reside in the overcrowded refugee camps of the Gaza Strip.

Winding south once more, railway tracks accompany the route. At one time it was possible to travel all the way to Cairo by train, passing through Gaza, but those exotic, romantic times are long past. The old station in Gaza is now an empty piece of land, the tracks barely visible through the weeds and its neglected house overgrown with bouganvilla.

At the Ashqelon junction, Peter suggested I put on the scarf I had brought to cover my hair. It seemed appropriate because cars from Gaza were becoming more numerous. They were filled with curious males staring at the unusual sight of two foreigners driving a vehicle with Gaza licence plates, and especially at the foreign, bareheaded female. Once covered, I felt more comfortable though cynical about the controls that are placed on women because of the potential delinquent behavior of males.

(Much later, on a day which had produced rather more frustrations than usual, I was to admonish some of our male students that if the visibility of women's hair was so jeopardizing to the morality of males, then the men should wear scarves over their eyes to prevent them from transgression. They found this highly amusing.)

Some twenty kilometres south of Ashqelon, Peter pointed out the Israeli security post at Eretz which marks the entrance to the Gaza Strip. As we slowly approached the inspection point, I realized it was not what I had expected. It was rather a shock to someone who had never encountered a country under occupation. Watching the news back home you think you understand the situation, but the reality makes you realize how little is conveyed in a short newsclip with its truncated, selective camera angles. What I now saw ahead of me, as we waited in line for inspection and questioning, was a scene reminiscent to my mind of H.G. Wells' *War of the Worlds*. Khaki-colored watch-towers were poised like grotesque Martians, their spindly legs intertwined with a lattice-work of barbed wire to discourage potential attackers.

The soldiers perched atop these monstrosities were, like their counterparts at ground level, armed with uzi machine guns. The uniforms, as such, were surprising in their lack of uniformity. I suppose I had expected some kind of tight discipline and boot-camp adherence to standards as opposed to the motley assortment of clothing I now observed. A few soldiers wore hunting jackets and baseball caps, while some sported the reflecting sunglasses popularized by military personnel in movies like *Apocalypse Now*, and others wore dirty sneakers, sunhats, and t-shirts. Many were smoking on duty, one hand on the trigger and the other tapping off the ash from a Lucky cigarette. Their swaggering arrogance made me suspect that they had seen too many war movies which they now had the safe opportunity to emulate. This scene is replicated nowadays in many parts of the world where military repression is the order of the day.

Since our car displayed the white licence plate and blue symbol of Gaza (as opposed to the yellow plates of Israeli settlers who drive past the waiting Arab cars and are waved unquestioned through the checkpoint), we were required to stop for questioning. On this and subsequent crossings over the Green Line, we found some soldiers to be abrupt and some to be rude, while others, seeing foreigners, would try to give a better impression by saying things like "Have a nice day," which left us speculating about their handle on reality. For the most part, they seemed sullen and hostile, caring little, if anything, about the impression of Israel which was conveyed to the rest of the world.

The transformation from the reasonably recognizable world we had left inside the Green Line to the squalid primitiveness of the Gaza Strip was immediate and shocking. The road into the town of Gaza seemed to lose more of its paved surface with each passing kilometre. Bedouin encampments sprawled on both sides, but these were not the sturdy goat-hair tents of the proud, nomadic people we had seen in Jordan. They were a hideous mish-mash of wattle sticks and branches, roofed with scavenged pieces of corrugated metal and large amounts of plastic sheeting. In some instances, a television aerial protruded incongruously from the midst of the dwellings, its electrical source a mystery.

Along the roadside, women and children of all ages herded flocks of goats and sheep, or drove donkey-carts laden with vegetables, fruit, or firewood. The women wore the traditional dress, covering their heads and faces with a black or white flowing shawl. Many of them looked incredibly old and haggard, though I was to learn later that they were often only in their forties. Along with the donkeys, they seemed to be used as beasts of burden, though it might be argued that the donkeys have the better deal since they are not required to cook, clean, and farm as well as haul enormous loads on their backs!

Approaching Gaza town, we drove under the "Welcome to Gaza" archway which spans the road, delivering its greeting in English, Arabic, and Hebrew. Presumably, along with the railway, this was also a relic of earlier, better times. The shops, industries, and homes merged into a strip that led into Shezjiyya Square bounded by a cemetery, the post office, and the police station, while on the narrow sidewalks vendors with donkey-carts and push-carts were selling all kinds of food, clothing, and other merchandise. The whole place seemed a squalid conglomeration. I dreaded to think what the refugee camps must be like if this was the town. Everything I saw gave me the impression of being a refugee camp with its narrow back streets and barefoot children playing among garbage.

A drive down El-Waehda Street took us past an old building once inhabited briefly by Napoleon on one of his campaigns in this part of the world. The disintegrating ruins of old, domed mosques were being nudged into oblivion by clumsily-built apartment dwellings competing with each other for space in the back streets and alleys, trying to accommodate the press of humanity within the town. Army Jeeps appeared from nowhere, causing panic as they hurtled head-on against the traffic down a one-way street, and I was suddenly aware of the heavy military presence.

The Society for the Care of the Handicapped is situated in the "nice" part of town, in the suburb called Rimal (The Sands). Relative to the slums of the older parts of Gaza the houses were larger and had gardens. As there was not such a density of people, it seemed calmer and less hostile after the frantic noise and mayhem of the old town.

I recognized the large entrance gate to the Centre with its sign in Arabic and English, and there was the old *bawaab* (gatekeeper) Abu Salah whom I remembered from photographs Peter had taken on his earlier visit. The old man came forward and greeted us warmly as we stepped through the small door cut into the large main gates. Inside was the school for mentally handicapped children, and the tall building that housed both the Mothers' Home Education Project and our own diploma program.

Here, I met for the first time some of the students I would soon be teaching, for a group had gathered to greet and scrutinize the new *ajnabiyya* (foreign woman). I remember feeling quite intimidated by them, especially the young men. They looked older and bigger than I had imagined, though this was in part due to the sudden transfer from teaching very young children to being face to face with characters whose faces reminded me of so-called

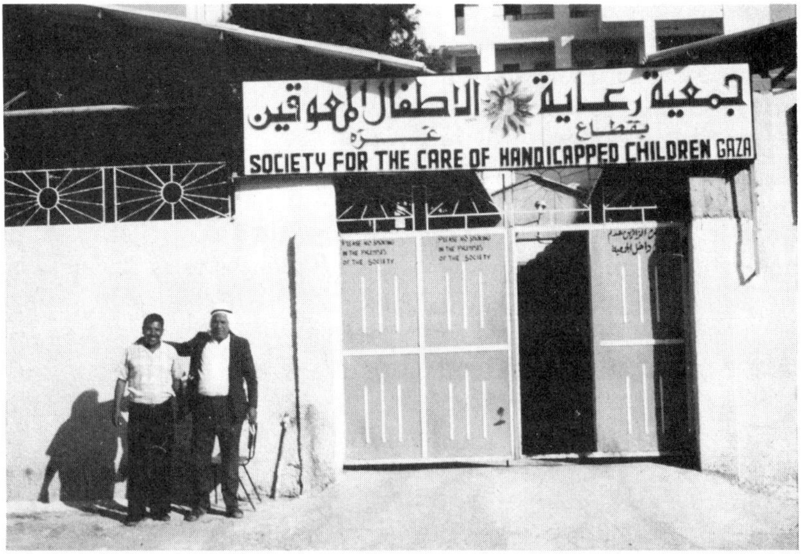

The main entrance to the Society for the Care of the Handicapped in Gaza.

"terrorists" interviewed on television, and whose names I was convinced I would never master. Names like Azzad, Kareem, Samir, and Sabah. At first, I was unable to distinguish names by gender when given a list of the students. For their part, they were equally puzzled by my inability to do so.

But this was the moment; it was time to put my Arabic to the test as I struggled to overcome my shyness and made a half-hearted attempt at a greeting. I was reinforced immediately by their enthusiastic response and proclamations that I spoke Arabic very well. Arab politeness would be difficult to match anywhere in the world, and my first encounter with it was to be the model to which we became accustomed and learned ourselves. Greetings and blessings of welcome are couched in beautiful flowing phrases with correspondingly elegant responses.

Peter gave me a quick tour of the Centre before showing me our temporary apartment on the second floor, overlooking the street which led to the local mosque. It was small but comfortable, with a sitting room, bedroom, tiny kitchen, and full bathroom. Hot water was dependent on the sun, trapped by an ingeniously simple-looking apparatus on the flat roof. We learned to take advantage of the accumulated hot water of the day by taking baths in the late afternoon. By nightfall, which descends early in this part of the world, the water would be cooling off, and by morning, we were lucky if it was still luke-warm. In the kitchen, a separate tap for drinking-water was located next to the regular faucets. After the drinking-water had been cut off on several occasions, we learned to adapt by starting a collection of empty pop bottles which we filled with an emergency supply. (Jewish settlers in the Gaza Strip have unlimited access to water, but the Arab population has its supply cut off for several hours each day. Sometimes, in the case of full curfews, both water and electricity are cut off by the Israeli authorities for days at a time. Since we never knew when these things might occur, we became accustomed to keeping extra bottles and candles on hand.)

There was no time to unpack for we had been invited to lunch at the house of Ali and Na'ela Shawwa, whom we were to come to know and love during our time in Gaza. They had just built a small, new house not far from the beach, and it was always one of our favorite homes to visit. Though deeply loyal to their Muslim faith, they were fully accepting of the beliefs of others, and were not rigid fundamentalists. We always felt more relaxed there than anywhere else we visited in Gaza, and it was here on my very first day that I was introduced to Sara and Jay, two Americans also living and working in Gaza. They were to become our lifeline to sanity in that first year. Sara, an international development specialist, was collecting data for a second book about the economic situation of the Strip, while Jay, a surgeon, was working on a voluntary basis at the local Ahli Arab Hospital. The house was simple but lavish, with high ceilings and an imposing archway dividing the two main sitting and eating areas. Thick, oriental carpets cushioned our feet, and couches were smothered in cushions decorated with small mirrors and beadwork. The principal room was set off by a large arched window decorated with wrought iron.

Here I ate *fatta* for the first time. It is a traditional Palestinian dish of chicken, rice, and roasted pine nuts. In this instance, it had been made by a peasant woman hired for the day. She was strikingly beautiful, her dark skin reminding me of the Nubian people in Egypt. Her as yet unweaned baby had been left in one of the bedrooms while she worked in the kitchen, but the little mite

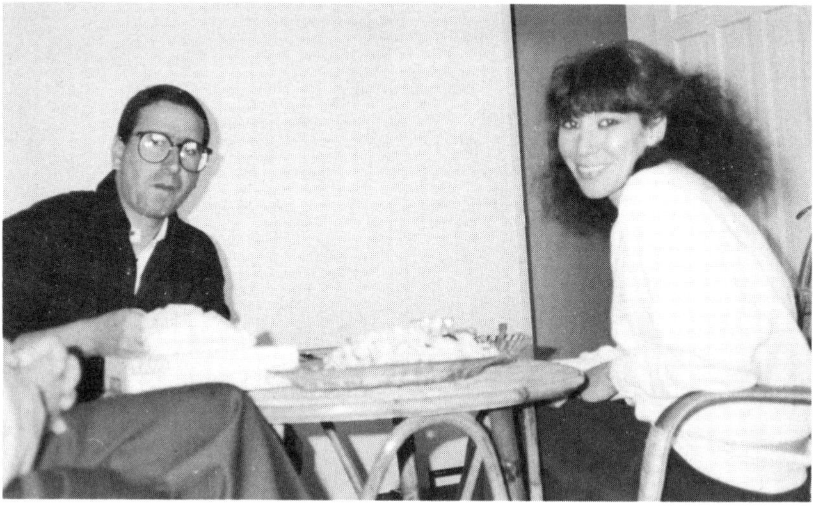

Drs. Sara Roy and Jay Schnitzer, our friends and colleagues

seemed sick and feverish and lay there crying. Jay checked the infant and gave the woman some advice, though whether or not it was ever carried out, we don't know. The woman already had six other children and was pregnant yet again. Large families are the norm, and Na'ela and Ali were unusual in having only one child, their son Fadi who was later to join our college program.

Sipping my Arabic coffee and enjoying the conversation, I realized that in the space of my first day in Gaza I had observed two of its many contrasts: awful poverty and comfortable affluence. It was some months later that such contrasts led us to understand the paradox of life here, for whatever one said or heard about the Gaza Strip would inevitably turn out to be simultaneously true and untrue. It is arguably the poorest, most densely-populated place on earth, and yet there are class distinctions and discrepancies in the levels of poverty and affluence that preclude a clear-cut picture of daily existence.

We returned to our apartment where I unpacked to the sound of the muezzin's call to evening prayers at the mosque. The streets gradually emptied of people and traffic, and fell silent. We were under the nightly curfew.

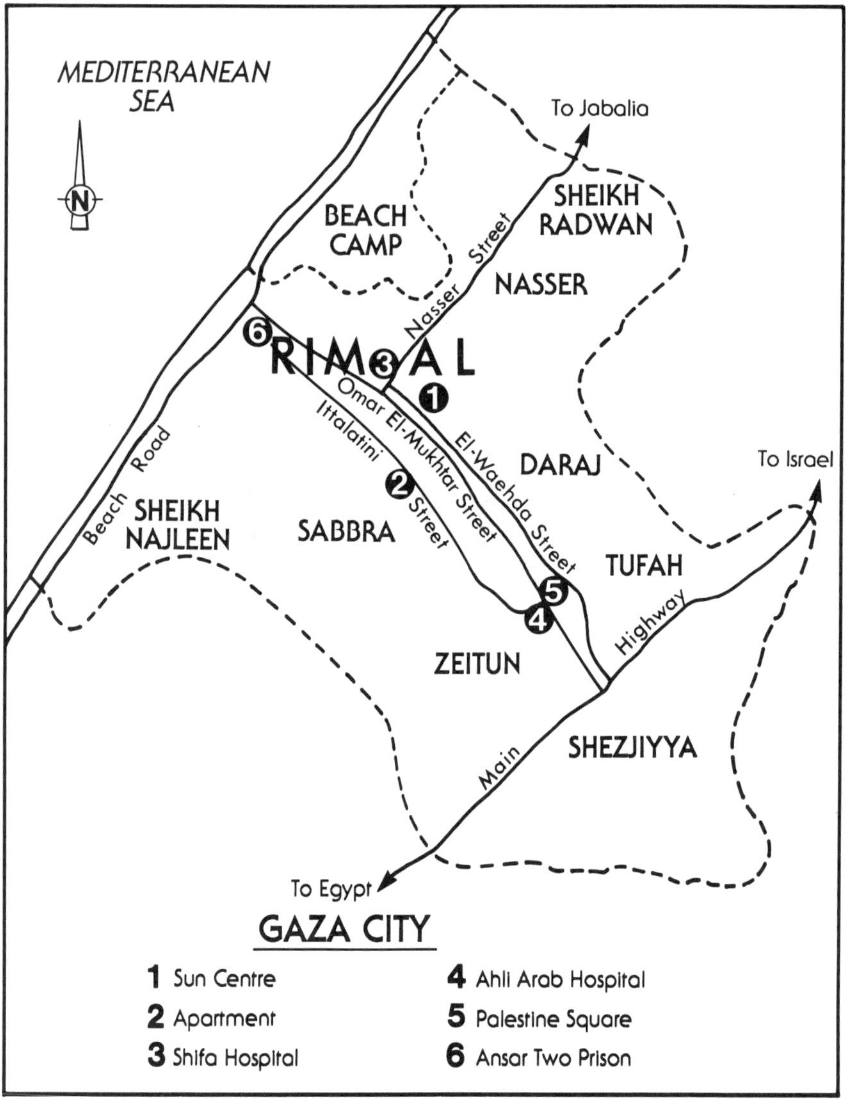
MEDITERRANEAN SEA
N
To Jabalia
BEACH CAMP
SHEIKH RADWAN
Nasser Street
NASSER
RIMAL
Omar El-Mukhtar Street
Ittalatini Street
El-Waehda Street
DARAJ
To Israel
Beach Road
SHEIKH NAJLEEN
SABBRA
TUFAH
Highway
ZEITUN
Main
SHEZJIYYA
To Egypt
GAZA CITY
1 Sun Centre
2 Apartment
3 Shifa Hospital
4 Ahli Arab Hospital
5 Palestine Square
6 Ansar Two Prison

CHAPTER THREE

November 1988

November 3rd 1988

This is Rhona's second day in Gaza. It is Friday so we're able to have a quiet day at home. It's very nice to have her here, as I have missed her a great deal. Fortunately, I don't think we fully realize how much we miss someone until we see them again.

Yesterday we had lunch at Ali and Na'ela Shawwa's home. It's a very beautiful new house situated near the beach. As Hatem is out of the country again, Aida came by herself. David Shearer, Sara Roy, and Jay Schnitzer were also present.

Jay said that at the Ahli Arab Hospital they receive between eight and ten patients a day who are suffering from gunshot wounds. As Ahli is the smallest hospital in Gaza, it is difficult to estimate the daily total of casualties. Jay explained that while plastic bullets travel at a slower velocity than metal bullets, they can still kill a person if they hit a vital organ.

Today, while Mohammed (a student in our program) was making an in-class presentation, one of his relatives came to the door of the lecture room with the message that Mohammed's nephew had been wounded and taken to Shifa Hospital. Mohammed completed his presentation before rushing off to the hospital.

Ali (a student in our program) also went to visit the patient, only to find his own relatives grouped around the next bed. In it lay Ali's cousin who had just been shot in the abdomen with a plastic bullet. This young man was in great pain, so Ali spent the whole night sitting at his bedside trying to comfort him.

November 8th 1988

This afternoon we went for lunch at the apartment of the "Bad Boys." They are a group of our students who have taken the unusual step of moving from their family homes to live in a communal apartment near the Sun Centre. It was very interesting as always. Mohammed's 17-year-old nephew was also there. He had just been released from hospital with the plastic bullet still in his knee. He showed me his X-rays and said that he is not allowed to travel outside the Gaza Strip to get further treatment. This boy is hardly more than a child.

The last few days have been quiet in Gaza, but we may be heading into a further period of unrest as the Palestine National Council begins its meeting on November 11th. It's rumored that they will declare themselves a government-in-exile. People are also saying the Israelis will close the checkpoint on Friday evening and not open it again for several days. We shall see.

November 11th 1988

For two days we have been preparing the students for a curfew. We have given work for each day in lieu of attending lectures and plan, if necessary, to switch to a much more individualized method of instruction for the next few weeks or even months. Our purpose is to ensure these students complete their diploma programs on time.

This morning's class felt quite revolutionary. This was partly due to the weather which was cool and rainy. We held the class on a Friday to make up for a day lost to a strike on Wednesday. Thirteen of the 18 students attended at the early hour of 7:30 a.m., the remainder being under curfew in various parts of the Gaza Strip. However, two of the students managed to escape and came to class. We reviewed our strategy for the next few days (If you can make it, come to class — we will teach anybody who shows up. If you can't get here, do the assignment prescribed on your worksheet). In addition, Rhona gave a three-hour lecture on education systems, comparing Canada and Palestine in what I thought was a very political way. The students were intrigued by her talk.

At lunchtime we were invited to Aida's home for a meal. Hatem is still in Washington, but he is expected to return next Friday. As always the meal was delicious, consisting of a dish called *musaka* which is totally unlike the Greek dish of the same name. Palestinian musaka is made of ground beef, onions, and nuts wrapped in pita bread and fried in olive oil.

While we were there, Aida tuned in to Radio Monte Carlo which gives the news in Arabic. Derisive cheers greeted the announcement that the Israelis have decided to put the Gaza Strip under curfew from 9 p.m. this evening. Rapid plans were made to ensure that everybody would have enough food and companionship for the duration of the curfew.

When we returned to the apartment, Fahed and a group of students dropped by to tell us about the curfew and to ensure we had everything we needed in the way of food. We feel very supported by our Palestinian friends. We could have left the Strip for a quiet and peaceful holiday but decided not to do this as we felt we would be deserting our friends. We have made a commitment to be with them and should honor this in both good times and bad.

Later Iyad arrived to pick up his assignments. He had escaped from his home in the Shezjiyya district which has already been under curfew for two or three days. He told us that the trouble started when a small child was killed by the soldiers. At his funeral there were demonstrations and hundreds of people were arrested; some still remain in detention.

November 12th 1988

This was the first day of the curfew. Our area was incredibly quiet. The streets were not exactly empty, but we saw only a few people walking around, and they seemed to stick pretty close to their homes. Jeeps and trucks full of soldiers passed by on El-Waehda Street, and an army helicopter flew low overhead, obviously monitoring the situation in the streets.

One of the problems in Gaza is that there is no reliable means of communication. There are no Palestinian newspapers or radio stations which can tell everybody what is happening. Our only sources of information are the Voice of Israel and the BBC World Service. Since the Israelis have closed off the Gaza Strip, journalists are forbidden to enter. So, although it is quiet in our area, there might be violent disturbances in other parts of the territory which we are completely unaware of.

November 13th 1988

In spite of the curfew, we were visited by two students who live about 200 metres down the street. I think they were bored with being cooped up in their apartment and wanted a change of scenery. They stayed for a while, and we discussed the current situation. Six people are staying in their apartment, and last night there was no food for supper. Fortunately, a friend who works at a hospital and is allowed to travel back and forth was able to drop by today with some food.

We were very worried about the students going home. If the soldiers caught them on the street, they would be arrested or perhaps even shot. So, we went up on the roof to watch them make their way home. They ran down the street very quickly and disappeared into the doorway of their building. A few seconds later, a Jeep with soldiers appeared on the corner nearest to our apartment. The students had a lucky escape!

Gaza seems very quiet, but from the roof we saw the smoke from many burning tires. There are rumors of trouble in other parts of the Strip and of one person killed in Jabalia Camp. On the BBC news, we just learned that the PNC will declare an independent state of Palestine on Tuesday and recognize UN Resolution 242, which essentially means the PLO accepts Israel's right to exist within secure borders. We feel this large concession will go unrecognized by Israel and the United States.

November 14th 1988

This is the evening of the third day of the curfew. It was not as cold as it has been for the last couple of days, so we were able to go up on the roof to warm up. It was a quiet day, although typically, tires were burned at our nearest intersection and the soldiers responded in the usual way.

Abu Salah cooked us lunch today. It was amazing — eggs and chips! We were very grateful. He also managed to get a couple of scrawny chickens for us. They were purchased from our neighbors with a good deal of shouting and a some rapid sprints across the street.

In addition, Abu Salah arranged for us to visit some people down the street. With neighbors on rooftops watching out for the army, we successfully made the 30 metre dash. Our hosts were Abu and Umm Anton, together with their five daughters and young son. The oldest boy, Anton,[2] is studying in England. As we have come to expect with Palestinians, they were very friendly and hospitable. Other neighbors were invited so there were about a dozen people sitting in the warm and well-furnished solarium. Abu Anton did not speak English, but his wife was able to translate if needed. However, we were able to practise our Arabic and very much appreciated the opportunity. After a polite beginning, the conversation turned serious as we discussed the Palestinian situation. One teenage boy wanted to know if Canada would recognize the new state of Palestine, and if we would let the Palestinian government-in-exile operate from Ottawa. These were intelligent questions from a 15-year-old. We find a great political awareness in nearly all of the children.

This evening we went up on the roof again because there was another outbreak of "*Allahu akbar.*" This one lasted for about half an hour and was accompanied by several fireworks. The Israelis responded in numbers. A convoy of five Jeeps and trucks circled the block. It is impossible to stop these outbursts, but the soldiers persist in trying. Through a loudspeaker, they announced that they would punish any celebrations of the PNC's declaration of an independent country with a fine of $9,000 (US) and a jail term of five years.

November 16th 1988

This is the morning of the fifth day of the curfew, and we are running out of food in spite of our attempts to conserve over the last few days. While we have some large items like the remaining scrawny chicken and some pieces of fish, most of our staples like

2 In the Palestinian culture mothers and fathers are named after their oldest son, i.e., Abu Anton: the father of Anton and Umm Anton: the mother of Anton.

bread, cereal, fruit, and vegetables are gone. On the brighter side, we have discovered a packet of chicken noodle soup at the back of a kitchen cupboard and old Abu Salah appeared at our door with a piece of bread and some freshly made *homous*. No doubt we will survive.

Yesterday there was an almost continuous military presence. Jeeps patrolled the streets, and spotter planes and helicopters hovered overhead, to say nothing of the squadron of Israeli Phantom jets which periodically screamed over the rooftops causing sonic booms which rattled the windows.

Perhaps the incident most symbolic of oppression occurred when a convoy of military Jeeps with loudspeakers toured the neighborbood insisting that if any person wrote slogans on the walls they

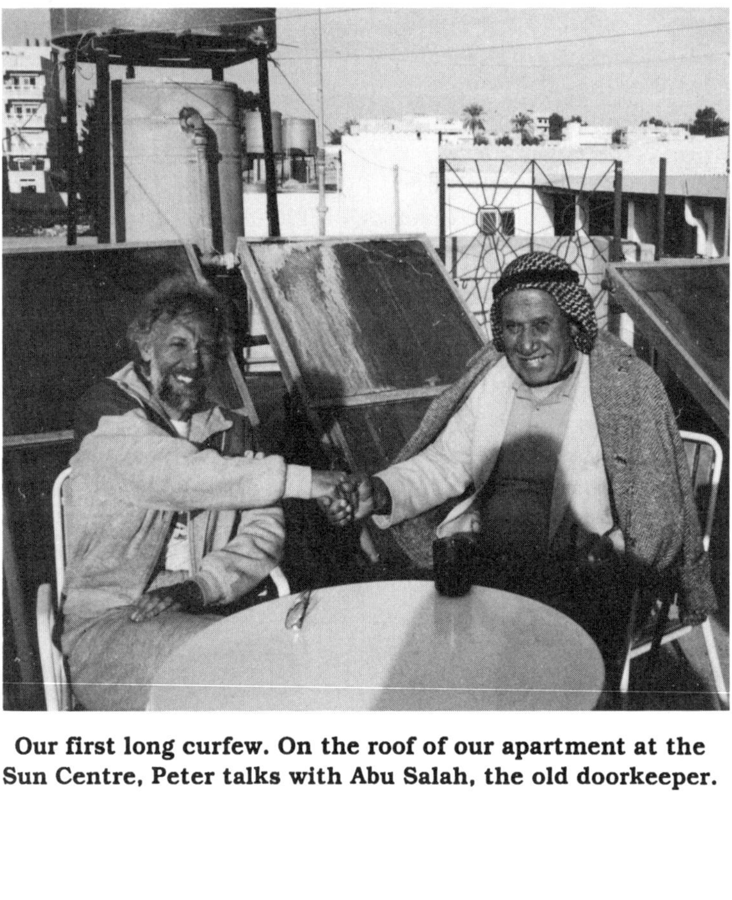

Our first long curfew. On the roof of our apartment at the Sun Centre, Peter talks with Abu Salah, the old doorkeeper.

would be jailed for five years. In addition, if anybody flies the Palestinian flag, they will be fined $12,000 (US). Considering that a teacher's salary is about $500 (US) per month, it seems that few Palestinians would be able to pay such a fine.

Sometimes it is difficult to decide which is the most repressive measure. At 1 p.m. yesterday the Israelis cut off all electricity to the Gaza Strip. We presume this was to disrupt any celebrations coinciding with the declaration of the Palestinian state by the Tunis-based government-in-exile. Power was not restored until the early hours of the morning so we had to go to bed shortly after it got dark at 5:30 p.m. Our area was incredibly quiet during the day, but after dark people started to shout *Allahu akbar* and chant Palestinian slogans. And later several fireworks were set off. I can't help but think that one result of the enforced inactivity and early bedtimes will be the birth of hundreds of Palestinians in about nine months time.

We have heard that the daytime curfew will be lifted at dawn the day after tomorrow.

November 19th 1988

Yesterday was full and interesting. It began at 7:30 a.m. with a lecture for the diploma students, followed by a TOEFL assessment from Rhona, and library tutoring time. In the afternoon, we went to see Tewfik Abu Ghazaleh about the new college building. Then we went to see Hatem who had just returned from a trip to several countries.

The new college building is no nearer to completion than it was two months ago. This new campus, some three kilometres from the Sun Centre, was scheduled to be opened in 1987 but remains inexplicably incomplete. We now hope to provide the workers with a little more motivation, as Fahed and I intend to make a weekly check on the progress. Presently, we are being promised that we can move in next spring.

We were disconcerted to discover that last night some Moslem fundamentalists broke into the Sun Centre and painted slogans on the walls, threatening Hatem. We were in our apartment at the time and heard nothing. They manhandled old Abu Salah, tied him up, and left the message that this was Hatem's last warning. Apparently, they are angry because Hatem has made the staff work on Fridays if there were strikes during the previous week, and this day is the Muslim equivalent of Sunday in our culture. Hatem believes that one of his staff has persuaded the fundamentalists to do this, so he plans to fire or demote the one responsible. We have also been told that all the PLO groups and the Islamic Resistance Movement, Hamas, are fully supportive of Hatem and the programs at the Centre. It is interesting that Hatem is being aggressive rather than conciliatory in his handling of the situation.

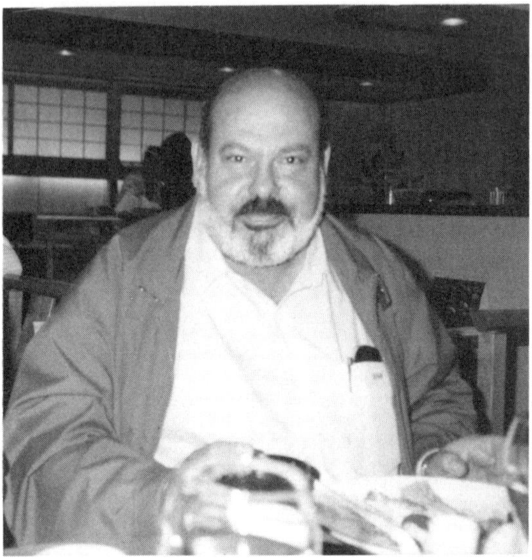

Dr. Hatem Abu Ghazaleh, Chairman of the Society for the Care of the handicapped.

November 22nd 1988

Finally, after being "lost" for two weeks, the man has come and put up the blinds in our new apartment. We plan to move on Friday and are looking forward to living away from the school. It is interesting to note that the refurbishing of the apartment has proceeded much more quickly since the end of October when Hatem and Aida returned from their travels.

Today we went to the Dar es Salaam Institute with Aida. The students put on a puppet show for the children and also played music. They had all the children sitting outside in the sunshine. We were amazed at the improvement in these children. They are sitting up and paying attention to the world around them. This is due to the love and stimulation they are receiving from the students.

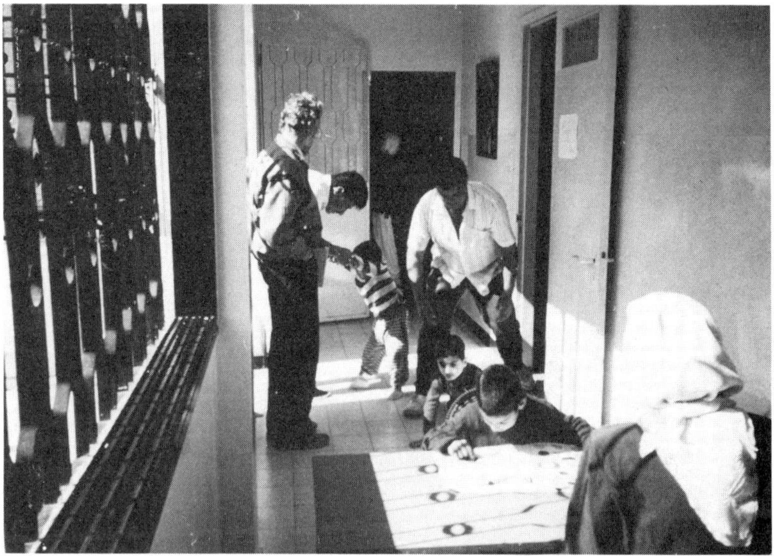

The Dar es Salaam Institution: Peter watches Hanan, Aref and Mohammed as they work with the severely handicapped children.

During this afternoon's break between lectures, I heard a volley of shots fired on El-Waehda Street just outside the Amal Orphanage. When I looked I saw soldiers on the street, and the staff from the orphanage was rapidly bringing the children inside away from the trouble. Once again, I did not see any stones being thrown, nor were there sounds of whistling and shouting.

Judging from their dress and behavior as they drive around in their Jeeps, the soldiers sometimes appear as if they have come to Gaza on a hunting trip.

November 24th 1988

This was a very active day. In the morning there was an assembly for all the students in the school, and I told them a story about Sami the Big Dog. I wrote the story and Rhona taught them an accompanying song which she recently composed. We were both pleased at our success in communicating with the children in Arabic.

The assembly seemed to go well, especially as Rami (a student in our program) produced an excellent set of pictures which illustrated the story. Afterwards, the children went back to their classrooms to draw a picture about the story. It was our intent to use the drawings as the basis for a whole language experience. Unfortunately, the concept of children expressing themselves artistically seems alien to the teachers. They gave each child a small, old piece of wax crayon and did not allow them to use more than one color!

This afternoon Aida put on a special lunch for all the teachers in both the school and the mothers' program. Tables were set up outside in the courtyard. We were at the head table but found it a little disconcerting to be facing about a hundred people while we ate. The main dish was *maftoul*, and Hatem made an appreciative speech of welcome to Rhona and I, and of gratitude to David Shearer who leaves tomorrow to return to the United States.

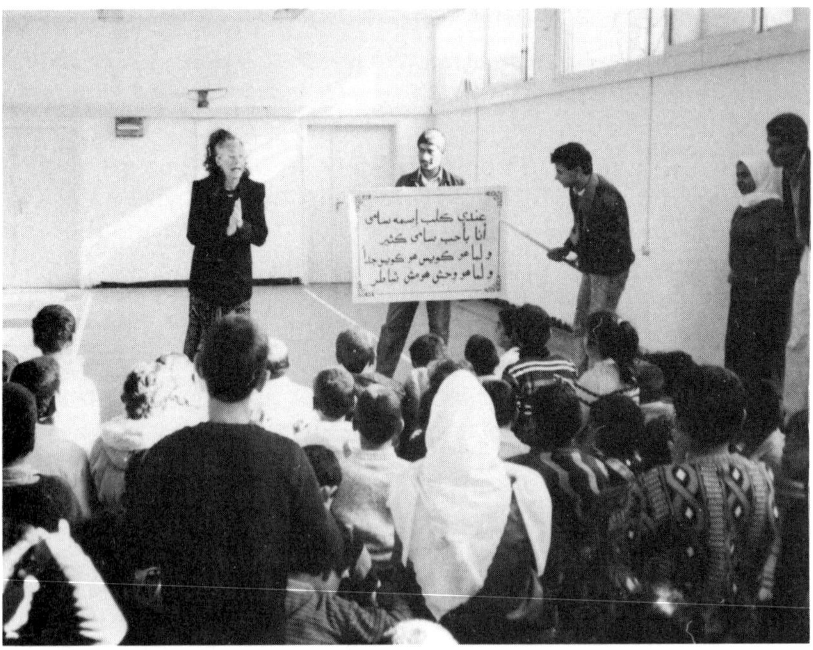

The Sun Centre: Rhona teaching handicapped children with assistance from two diploma students.

After lunch, we went to look at the new apartment. It seems very comfortable and we are preparing to move in tomorrow. While we were packing this evening, David Shearer dropped in to say goodbye. He leaves Gaza at 4:30 a.m. tomorrow. We will miss him as he was our companion during the curfew period. It is surprising how you feel affinity for a person with whom you have shared adversity.

November 30th 1988

Many things have happened since the last entry in this journal. We are now firmly established in our new apartment. Today screens were fitted to the windows and tomorrow the men will begin to lay the carpets. This should make a big difference as the tile floors and high ceilings make the rooms echo. It is much bigger than our other apartment, and we are happy to get away from the school. Our intercom system has been fixed, so we can answer people who ring at the big steel doors which separate the garden from the street. By Gaza standards, the apartment is quite lavish and we are grateful to Hatem and Aida who have gone to an enormous amount of trouble to make us feel comfortable.

We have recently returned from three days in Tel Aviv. We went for a few days' break as a two-day strike had been announced in Gaza. We spent most of our time dealing with business. We had our passports altered so that we can travel more easily between Israel and Egypt. Also, Hatem arranged for us to go to the Egyptian Embassy to obtain visas in preparation for visiting that country. This was an interesting experience, and we met the Second Secretary, Mr. Abdul Ghaffar El-Deeb. We were allowed to enter the embassy and our application was processed very quickly, unlike the people on the street who have to line up in front of a wire-covered window and complete their application forms in the open air. In the Arab culture it is important to know the right people!

This morning we caused quite a disturbance at the Canadian Consulate in Tel Aviv. On entering the building, we were treated very rudely by an Israeli and an American who are employees at the consulate. After being pushed around for several months by the IDF in Gaza without any recourse, we now knew we were on Canadian ground where we had some rights. Consequently, we became very angry and demanded better treatment. This outburst had the desired effect. It was suddenly decided that they didn't need to telex Ottawa before making the required changes in our passports. Later, I called John McNee at the Canadian Embassy and told him about how we had been treated. I said we were concerned about the negative impression of Canada that is projected when the staff is rude. We both agreed that the Consulate employees needed to be reminded to treat all visitors with respect.

Since arriving in Gaza, we have been involved in numerous incidents which illustrate the kind of psychological stress caused by living under military occupation. One evening on the way home to our new apartment, we were passing near the military base on Omar El-Mukhtar Street when we were approached by four military vehicles going the wrong way down a one-way street. Over the loudspeaker they barked something in Arabic which sounded very ominous, so I pulled over and stopped. We were immediately surrounded by the military vehicles whose headlights blinded us so we could see nothing. I wound down the window and said "Good evening" in English. An order was barked, doors were slammed, and all the vehicles roared away into the night. We were left abandoned by the side of the road. They didn't even speak to us!

At 2:45 a.m. the following morning, we were awakened by the noise of soldiers in the street. They announced over their loudspeaker that the nearby Sabbra district was being placed under curfew. They then proceeded to bang on the metal doors of the houses with their clubs to get people out to erase slogans from the walls. We think they deliberately choose these times in order to disturb the sleep of the Palestinian people and to attack them psychologically at their most vulnerable time. There is no reason why these announcements and street cleaning "exercises" cannot be carried out during waking hours.

The Bad Boys

The appellation always puzzled me. Some months prior to our arrival they reportedly had been the instigators of a miniature "uprising" at the Centre. The protest had been directed at the Palestinian administration, for what the "Bad Boys" (as they were thereafter known) perceived to be further transgressions of their rights and freedoms. A demonstration, purportedly organized by Azzad, had been staged outside the offices of the administrators, who had reacted according to Palestinian culture by ordering the families to get control of their offspring or face serious consequences. Azzad was thrown out of the program, but resurfaced later when he was permitted to attend lectures only upon presentation of a courtesy card from the administration office.

Once we had become more accustomed to the rhythm of Palestinian life, we understood how easy it was for young people to provoke outraged responses to what we would consider the normal rebelliousness of youth. Ahmed, for example, achieved exactly what he had planned when he upset the local administrators by slouching in his desk wearing reflecting tear-drop sunglasses with an arrogant smirk on his face. Respect for elders and those in authority is taken very seriously, and he had crossed a cultural line by being so blatantly provocative. When he tried the same strategy in one of my first classes I cheerfully complimented him on his imitation of an Israeli army officer. Throwing back his head, he laughed, removed the sunglasses and settled down to his note-taking. It was no different from scenes we'd encountered a million times at home when our own children were going through their adolescence and youth.

The number of Bad Boys tended to fluctuate as people joined and left the group, mostly according to their economic needs; but there was always a steady core of about four. They shared an apartment next to the mosque down the street, paying about $120 a month. For them this was expensive. Their living arrangement was also unusual for Gaza: four young men sharing an apartment and living independently of their families.

For the first week of my time in Gaza, I had sat in Peter's lectures to observe the class in action, gain some idea of their comprehension of English and become accustomed to their accents which at first I found incomprehensible. I had also started to give some lectures on the development of education, preparing the students for the forthcoming practicum. Although I kept a vigilant ear and eye open for disruptions on the part of the "bad" group, I encountered nothing to cause me any anxiety. The students were respectful and keen to learn and it always seemed to me that the Bad Boys had the most sophisticated sense of humor. They were also the most politically radical, and all but one (a Muslim socialist) believed that Communism was the answer for their beleaguered Palestine. But as far as I could detect, they were no different in their naivete, vulnerability, and behavior than adolescents anywhere in the West.

Anyhow, one way or another the title of Bad Boys stuck, and everyone just accepted it in a half-amused way. In fact, it developed a sort of anti-status of its own, and to become a member of the group meant that you stood up for rights, helped others, and freaked out the administration from time to time.

Not long after I arrived, they invited us to lunch, though Peter had enjoyed their hospitality on previous occasions. The apartment was Spartan in its lack of floor covering and furniture, but it was clean and tidy and run cooperatively, with people sharing chores and expenses. We were impressed by their idealism, gentleness, and mutual support. In response to our questions, they described how they followed a mandate of communal ownership, sharing food, goods, and money.

The rooms were painted white with emerald green doors and window-frames. There were two bedrooms, a dining room and a sort of balcony sitting-room equipped with blinds that could be opened or closed to allow in a cross-breeze from the Mediterranean. There was a rather dirty, smelly toilet, and a sink that looked filthy but which may just have been very old and battered. The kitchen was equipped with an equally battered-looking stove and fridge.

Azzad, whose family home was in the Jabalia refugee camp, was obviously the chief organizer and care-giver. For male students unable to reach their homes after class because of curfews in the camps, there was always a bed and a meal. When transport was needed, Azzad collected money from everyone and shared out the fares. Sometimes there was furniture in the apartment, at other times a table or chair had been sold for badly-needed funds. As guests, Peter and I were given chairs while others sat on broken television sets. On one occasion, however, there were no chairs and even we had to choose from the selection of non-functioning technology. Azzad, knowing my proclivity for Japanese audio-visual equipment, apologized for not having a SONY to offer me as a seat.

After curfew in the evenings, the group would sit around the table until the early hours, studying by the light from a kerosene lamp to save the cost of electricity, sharing their ideas and helping each other complete our assignments.

Their caring treatment was always extended to Peter and me, and as often as not would lead me to quiet distress when we returned to our own apartment. Sometimes I felt that they had spent badly-needed money on meat to serve to us. We suspected that they themselves existed on the more common diet of rice and vegetables and we became concerned during the bitterly cold winter months of that first year when they began to look thin and tired because they didn't have enough food.

And here we made one of our cultural blunders. Our concern prompted us to have them visit us in order to give them some chickens we had bought from the butcher. They accepted gracefully this meagre gift which cost us so little, telling us how generous we were and that really we should not worry about them, it was too much. I felt at least some relief in knowing that they would eat reasonably well for a couple of days.

We realized our mistake when the group later requested a visit to our apartment and arrived with a package that immediately made me uneasy. I suppose that most people unfamiliar with the generosity of Palestinians would view with suspicion a group arriving at the door with a package. Certainly any Israeli would run for cover! My uneasiness had nothing to do with terrorism; it was the fact that our gift of chickens had put them in the position of having to reciprocate according to Palestinian custom. After coffee and conversation, I was handed the package. They had saved money to buy me a Palestinian dress, the long black gown with cross-stitch embroidery on the bodice and skirt. There could be no refusal; the gift had to be accepted, but I was in a state of wretched misery.

I appreciated the beauty of the dress but said that the gift was not necessary, they should have spent the money on more food. His voice quiet but matter-of-fact, Azzad said that it was indeed necessary, that there were Arab ways I did not understand, and Rami would explain why I must accept. Despite rational arguments on my part, drawing on what Communist philosophy I could throw in for good measure, nothing could sway them from their Arab tradition. The dress remains a treasured part of my wardrobe to this day.

Azzad was the most socialist-minded member of the group. He once worked for a day as a cleaner at the local hospital, but when he was paid he distributed all the money to the poor people waiting outside, people he knew from the camps and poor districts of Gaza. On another occasion, after the group had entertained us with a picnic by the beach, he put the remaining food into pots and gave it to the families of the Bedouin farmers who lived in neighboring wattle shacks.

On many a curfew-silent day, confined to the house, I would take out my favorite photograph of the group of them washing up after a party we had given for all the students. I call the photograph *The Terrorists in the Kitchen*, for to most of the world these young men would be viewed that way. But to me they were, and still are, like any group of young people in any society: lively, idealistic, serious, sometimes immature and stupid the way we all are at that age, and despite the social and political situation, able to have fun if the opportunity arises. Their faces reflect innocence and vulnerability rather than anger and callousness. I used to wonder what our own children would have been like if they had grown up only ever knowing the threat of death, or beating, or imprisonment for making a stand for the human rights the Western world takes for granted.

From time to time, I reflect on what has happened to the group since they graduated with their hard-won diplomas and disbanded.

Ahmed, having been in prison for protesting, is refused entry into Israel to work for the meagre wages paid to Palestinian workers. He remains in Breiyuj refugee camp and volunteers at hospitals and clinics.

Mohammed eventually managed to leave his home in Nusseirat refugee camp and reached Abu Dhabi but has had difficulty finding work in his area of expertise. As in most countries, jobs are first given to patriates before others are considered.

Rami ended up selling *fallafel* sandwiches and trying to start a business in constructing iron bed-frames from his home in the Rafah refugee camp.

Azzad was eventually driven by financial necessity to seek work in Israel. In a school for handicapped Israeli children where his diploma reportedly made him the most highly-qualified staff member, he was employed as the janitor and worked fourteen hours a day under the watchful gaze of two armed security guards.

Iyad worked as a health volunteer, giving lectures at clinics, until he was arrested and imprisoned on suspicion of throwing rocks at the soldiers. Each time Iyad's lawyer arranged for a trial, the soldier who claimed to have witnessed the incident failed to appear in court, and Iyad was returned once more to the infamous Ansar Two prison.

For all of them, I see no hope of freedom or identity. The Palestinian tragedy will soon be over-shadowed by more spectacular events that concern Western economic and political interests. I foresee a time when the world will have forgotten that there ever was a Palestine.

My worst fear is that I shall return to Gaza one day in search of the Bad Boys, only to find their names and photographs in the cemeteries dedicated to the martyrs of the uprising.

Children And Politics 1

"So, what is Canada's attitude toward the Palestinians?" asks Ahab, aged fifteen. He leans forward on his upright chair, elbows on his knees, hands folded, looking at us intently to see what our response will be. We are under curfew but have managed to slip out and across the street to the home of a Christian family. Neighbors and their children have climbed over walls and found a myriad of ways to visit without being caught by the soldiers. It is the day the Palestine National Council intends to make its declaration of being a government in exile, and the Palestinians are keen to monitor the reaction of the world.

We do our best to explain that Canada has spoken out against Israeli treatment of the Palestinians in the territories. As we stumble along in our basic Arabic, Ahab's face never changes expression, nor does his gaze falter. He listens in silence. After a pause, he asks, "If your country truly wants to help us, will you allow the PNC to govern from Canada?"

It is not like talking to the fifteen-year-olds we are used to back home in Canada, where the topics might range from the latest rock group to how much hair gel is required to survive the forty-minute rapid transit ride into downtown Vancouver. Ahab has none of the pseudo-sophistication of the middle-class Canadian teenager. From his size, I would have judged him to be no more than twelve years old, but his face shows the expression of a wary thinker, and I'm beginning to feel as if we're in some kind of political seminar that has a lot riding on the impression we make — maybe even our own safety!

Peter thinks quickly and says that of course Canada supports people's human rights, but governing from such a great distance would be impractical and ineffective; it would make better sense to do it from one of the neighboring Arab countries. Ahab remains impassive, looking at us intently, but the reply seems to meet with the approval of everyone else in the room.

Over time, we come to recognize that control of the society is at present in the hands of children and youth like Ahab, who dictate what the population as a whole will or will not do. This leads us to speculate on what might happen in a future autonomous country whose politicized, radical children have had things pretty much their own way. It is doubtful they will return willingly to a daily regimen of school rules, subjugation, and powerlessness.

CHAPTER FOUR

December 1988

December 4th 1988

Last evening we went to Hatem's house. Jay also dropped by for a few minutes to pick up a letter. When we arrived Hatem was speaking with a woman from the U.S. State Department. She made some comments in support of UNRWA and was immediately involved in a heated discussion with the rest of us who consider this UN organization to be a colonial agency without equal. I said I viewed them as the hidden occupiers of Gaza, while Rhona and Hatem were also very vocal on the deficiencies of UNRWA. Jay said that it was a disgrace that after 40 years of UNRWA supervision, there was still no guarantee of clean drinking-water in the camps. Hopefully, we have an effect on the opinions of people who are passing through Gaza.

On the way home, we were again stopped by the soldiers. I was asked to give my name. Answering in Arabic, I said I was a doctor from Canada and I was on my way home. To my surprise, the soldier said, "*Shukran, ma'asalaama.*" (Thank you, Goodbye.) This was the first time a soldier had spoken to me politely.

December 7th 1988

I have just returned from three days in Egypt with Hatem who went on to do some business in Kuwait. We left on Monday afternoon about 2 p.m., with Abed driving us to the Rafah border crossing. It was interesting to get out of Gaza City and see the rest of the Strip which is much as I remembered it from 1986. The exception of course is the increased Israeli military presence.

Because Hatem is a Palestinian, we were treated differently at the border. It took me only 45 minutes to clear both Israeli and Egyptian customs. But, in spite of having all the required official documents, Hatem was detained for more than two hours.

After leaving the customs area, we found one of the waiting cars and the driver agreed to take us to Cairo. First, we drove into the

Egyptian village of Rafah where Hatem phoned ahead to make hotel reservations. (International calls from the Gaza Strip are still banned.) Meanwhile, the driver steered the car into a nearby gas station to change the oil. I went with him and struck up a conversation with two Egyptian teenagers. After a while, they asked me for money. I was surprised and upset by this and supposed the behavior to be a by-product of poor people living in an area frequented by tourists.

It was now getting dark and we drove across Sinai toward the Suez Canal in the gathering dusk. En route, we passed several small towns such as Arish. The Egyptian government has recently spent a good deal of money in establishing a number of tourist resorts along the shore of the Mediterranean Sea in the area formerly occupied by Israel. In the darkness, the lights from the hotels made them seem very attractive.

After two hours, we reached the small ferry which crosses the Suez Canal. A line-up of cars forced us to wait almost an hour before we were able to board the ferry. Luckily, Hatem had brought some *kuftah* sandwiches so we were able to pass the time easily. I was surprised to see people giving bribes to the police so they could jump the queue. But, as I remember, all of this is typical of Egypt.

Once we reached the other side, there was another two-hour drive into Cairo. Although it was 11 p.m. when we eventually arrived at the Ramses Hilton, the lobby was still very busy. No doubt such international hotels are busy day and night.

Our next day was spent in a very leisurely manner. We ate a splendid buffet-style breakfast in the dining room of the Ramses Hilton which overlooks the Nile. Later, we took a taxi down the street and across the river to the Cairo Marriott — a very pretty hotel made of pink stone and enclosing a beautiful garden. I was told that the centre block of the building was originally built by Napoleon III for the Empress Eugenie. Hatem and I sat in the garden and drank an excellent beer, Stella Export, before going in to have lunch at the hotel.

Later in the day, I met some of Hatem's relatives, including Mamdouh who runs a silverware store near the Hilton, and Moussa who has a restaurant called El-Tekia. Among other exotic items on the menu is roast pigeon.

We also visited Hatem's elderly aunt and uncle who live in the Fokky district of Cairo. It seems that this is quite a prestigious area, but the apartment buildings are terribly run down. By contrast, the interior of the apartment is very well kept and decorated in a style reminiscent of Britain in the 1950s. Also on display was the usual large collection of family photographs so loved by Arabs.

The next day I was up at 4 a.m. to take a taxi to the airport to catch the early Air Sinai flight to Tel Aviv. As we drove to the airport through some of the poorer areas of Cairo, I was amazed to find that even at this early hour the mosques were crammed full of praying men who spilled over into the street blocking traffic.

The flight in a largely-empty 737 was uneventful.

December 8th 1988

There is another strike in Gaza today in celebration of the first anniversary of the intifada. The army's reaction to the burning tires was typical — heavily armed soldiers kicked in street doors, confiscated identity cards, and insisted that uninvolved people extinguish the blazes. In addition, two Palestinian flags were flown from telephone wires, and the soldiers forced people out of their homes to pull them down. A little later we saw soldiers fire a shot to disperse some youths who were whistling at them. In Gaza, even symbolic resistance is forbidden.

December 10th 1988

Yesterday the Gaza Strip was under curfew because December 9th is generally recognized as the first anniversary of the intifada. Our area was very quiet except for the massive military presence. Soldiers in all kinds of military vehicles spent the whole day driving up and down our street looking for trouble spots.

Today began quietly at the Sun Centre as all the camps and some parts of the city are still under curfew. I think there were only about 35 children and ten diploma students in attendance.

About mid-morning we heard a volley of shots fired some 100 metres away on El-Waehda Street. We learned later from our neighbors that a 12-year-old boy had been killed outside the orphanage which adjoins the Sun Centre. We were told that he waved the Palestinian flag and threw rocks at the soldiers. He was shot in the back as he was escaping over a wall. Our neighbors said he was dead before he hit the ground, but the soldiers still beat him with their clubs. He was then thrown into a Jeep and driven away.

It is difficult to describe my feelings. Part of me wants to believe that this is just another Arab rumor, but it fits so closely with what I myself have seen and heard that I cannot dismiss the story. On the other hand, I do not want to face the horror of a child being murdered by a so-called democratic state in the name of self-defence.

(The death was later confirmed by United Nations observers. These people also reported that the boy lay on the ground for more than half an hour while the IDF refused permission for Palestinian doctors from the nearby Telashomer Clinic to provide him with medical assistance.)

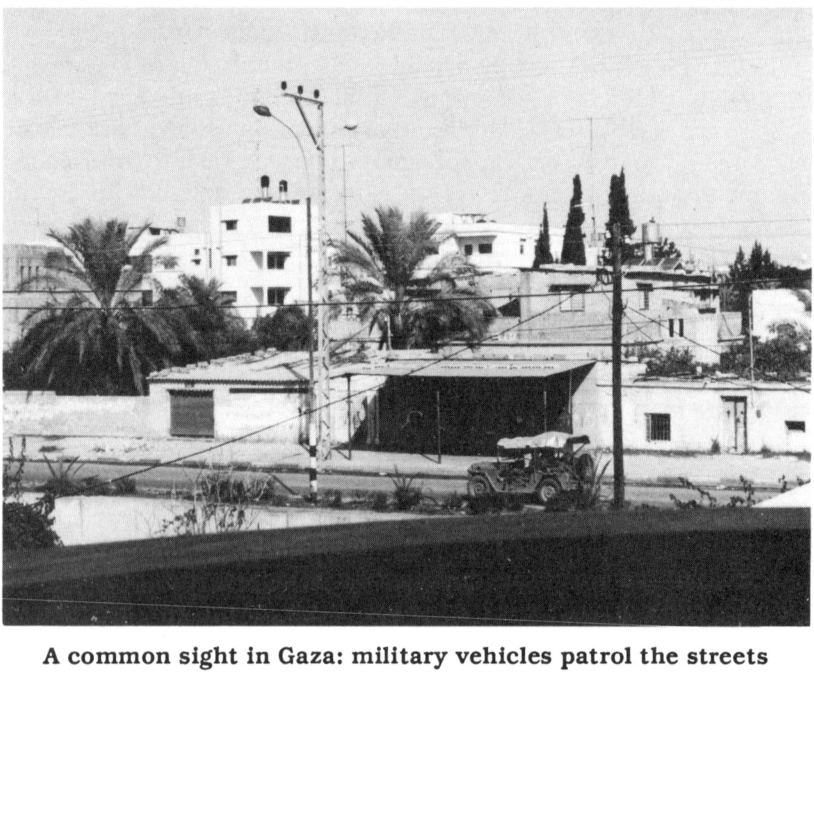

A common sight in Gaza: military vehicles patrol the streets

December 13th 1988

We are under curfew once again. I think this is because Mr. Arafat is addressing the UN General Assembly today, and this may spark trouble in the Occupied Territories.

Today the Israeli media gave the official version of the killing of the boy on El-Waehda Street. It was reported that he had thrown a Molotov Cocktail at the soldiers and thus they had no choice but to gun him down. They have also bulldozed the wall he was trying to hide behind. I suppose the message is that the owner of the wall is an accessory to an act of terrorism and will be punished. It is likely that the Israeli reaction has induced more anger than fear.

A couple of days ago Salah told me that the neighbors were upset because we had taken photographs of an incident which occurred near the house. We had surreptitiously taken pictures of the soldiers making people extinguish a burning tire and pull down a Palestinian flag. Salah said that some members of the secret police have been posing as journalists and taking pictures of people who are later arrested. It is also possible that Salah himself was alarmed by our photography in case it drew the army's attention to his home and family. I quickly apologized and told him we would be more careful in the future.

December 15th 1988

There has been a good deal of excitement in Gaza today because it was announced that the United States will begin a dialogue with the PLO. Many people are hopeful that a solution to the Palestinian problem will be forthcoming. However, the more cynical among them are saying that Israel will do all it can to sabotage this U.S.-PLO dialogue at the earliest opportunity. My prediction is that there will be a terrorist attack somewhere in the world during the next two weeks, and the Palestinians will be labelled as the perpetrators. But, we'll probably never know who is responsible for such a terrorist act.

Rhona and I went into the Beach Camp to visit the school. This is the first day in more than a week that the area has not been under curfew. The place was bristling with soldiers. When we tried to leave the main road out of the camp was blocked by three

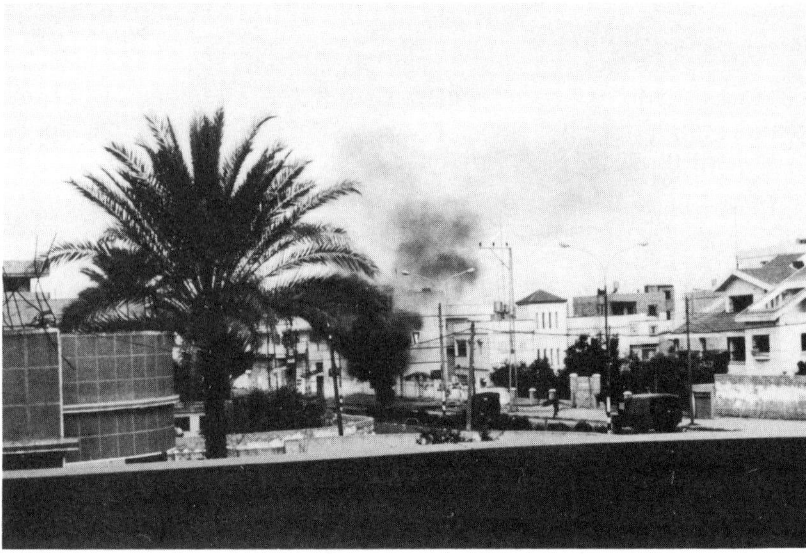

A burning tire incident secretly taken from our balcony

military vehicles, and about 20 soldiers who were parading in front of them. The residents were very tense, and we saw older Palestinians warning young people about the location of the troops.

At one point, we saw two soldiers chasing a group of young men. As the soldiers ran past us, it appeared they were enjoying the chase. The young men, however, seemed to be running for their lives. I don't believe the soldiers were in great danger or gave much thought to the humanity of the Palestinians. Perhaps their social indoctrination and army training teach them that Palestinians are somewhat less than human.

December 16th 1988

Today Rhona went to Tel Aviv to buy equipment for the mothers' program and was able to call in at the Canadian Embassy to pick up our mail. There were many letters. In one from Anna, (Rhona's daughter) we learned that she had won the first prize in a competition for short story writing. She enclosed a copy of "The Twister," which I think is extremely good. We also had a letter from

Bryn (my son) who seems just fine. However, the general effect of the mail was to make me feel a little homesick.

I also went running on the beach with Samir (a student in our program). He is a very kind and patient young man. Just before we got to the beach, we saw a crowd of Palestinians. This is visiting day at Ansar Two, but the visitors must wait about 100 metres from the prison gates. Today only a few were allowed inside to see their sons and the rest were told to go home. The rejected crowd was of course upset, but when they realized their objections were useless they reluctantly drifted home.

Later, I was outside my apartment and saw many soldiers surrounding the apartment block down the street with guns at the ready. It looked like a stake-out. Perhaps they were going to arrest a person inside the building.

The soldiers were still there when I took Samir downtown to get a taxi to Breiyuj Camp. On the way back, I tried to drive along El-Waehda Street but could not move due to a convoy of Israeli military vehicles. In the end, I turned off and came back another way. When I got back to the apartment the soldiers were still staked out around the building. It seems the military presence in Gaza is excessive today.

December 18th 1988

It is the second of a three-day strike in the Occupied Territories. It was called because five people were killed in Nablus. Four of them were shot at the funeral of the first victim. Others were seriously injured and the death toll may now be as high as seven.

The strike started yesterday while we were shopping near Palestine Square in the centre of Gaza. Although it was only 8:45 a.m., the stores were beginning to close. The IDF was present in force and the whole situation was very tense. The soldiers blocked the one-way section of Omar El-Mukhtar Street, and this caused chaos as the drivers were forced to turn around and drive back against the oncoming traffic.

At one point, we were stopped by a patrol blocking all the traffic. Our teaching assistant, Sabah El-Hato, was with us and became frightened when she thought we would end up in the middle of a demonstration. Fortunately, nothing developed except that two donkeys were abandoned by their drivers. Left to their own devices the donkeys began pulling their carts in circles in the middle of the street, much to the consternation of the soldiers who were trying to impose order on the situation. It was rather amusing to see an angry and frustrated soldier shouting in vain at the two stubborn animals who remained immune to his insults.

December 20th 1988

Today was cold, windy, and rainy. We had to visit the Beach Camp School to watch our students teaching. The conditions in the camp were terrible. The homes of the refugees let in the wind and rain which have also turned the streets and alleys into almost impassible morasses of mud. The open drains are flooded, so raw sewage flows out on to the street. "Now is the winter of our discontent made glorious summer." The situation is likely to worsen as winter does not officially begin for another five days.

December 22nd 1988

We have learned that a bomb has exploded aboard a Panam jumbo jet as it flew over the village of Lockerbie in Scotland. Hundreds of people were killed. Although the investigation has only just begun, the PLO is already being blamed for this barbaric act of terrorism. It gives me no satisfaction to have accurately predicted this event, and I still believe we will never discover the true identities of the perpetrators.

December 24th 1988

Today it rained all day. As this is typical Vancouver weather and it is Christmas Eve, we have been feeling depressed and homesick. This evening however, Salah, Wasfia, and their three children came down to wish us a "Merry Christmas." Salah's sister, Mellika, also joined us from downstairs. We were touched by their thoughtful gifts and kindness to us at this time of year.

December 26th 1988

The bad weather continues with tremendously high winds and periods of torrential rain, lightning, and thunder. This morning we were once again in Beach Camp where large areas are now under water. There was a small river running down one of the streets through which we had to pass in order to reach the school. How can people exist in such conditions?

This afternoon we had visitors at home. Sara and Jay came along with Hatem, Aida, and their three children. We served pop, tea, cookies, and chocolates. Although we felt quite nervous because the rituals of hospitality are highly valued by Palestinians, people were kind and tried to make us feel as if it were Christmas. It was very enjoyable for us because such a sophisticated and international group always makes for interesting conversation.

December 28th 1988

Yesterday I witnessed a mini-demonstration. At noon, a group of about 100 children from a school behind the Sun Centre poured into the street. One stood atop a pile of garbage waving a Palestinian flag, while the others chanted slogans and whistled for the soldiers to come. Then suddenly most of the children began running away very quickly. A few braver ones lingered for a few seconds and threw three or four stones before they too ran off. A couple of minutes later five Israeli military vehicles appeared and searched for the troublemakers. I don't know if they found anybody.

There are several points to be made from this incident. One is that this preparatory school only takes children up to the age of 13 years. Another is the quick and formidable military response to a group of naughty children. The final point is that these young people are deeply committed to the intifada — something which is truly local rather than a tactic imposed by the PLO from Tunis.

We received a very nice Christmas gift from Hatem the other day. It was a new Sony Trinitron television set. So, last evening, for the first time in four months, we sat in front of the tube and vegged out. We can get stations from Jordan, Egypt, and Israel all of which show occasional programs in English.

Today was a strike day, but we were invited to the home of Hatem and Aida for a delicious lunch. This meant we had to walk through the quiet streets from our apartment to their house. I was surprised that the walk took only 15 minutes. En route, the only traffic we encountered was UN vehicles, military Jeeps, and army personnel carriers. It was odd that there were also a number of soldiers driving vans rented from Hertz. I wonder why they are doing this.

December 31st 1988

This is the last day of 1988, but in Gaza it is no different from a hundred others. It is a strike day, and we are at home. Last night at about 2:45 a.m. the soldiers came around with a loudspeaker to say they were putting the Sabbra district under curfew. This neighborhood begins only about 100 metres from our apartment, so there is not much happening in our area at the moment. Although, there was some activity early in the morning.

At about 6 a.m. there were two explosions outside, but I was too tired to get up and see what was happening. A little later, I was awakened by banging in the street. This time I got up and came upon the end of a burning tire incident. Two soldiers had taken a man in pajamas from his home and, presumably after getting him to extinguish the blaze, wanted him to throw the remains over a wall into his neighbor's garden. The tire was too heavy so the soldiers banged on a nearby door to get some help. There was no reply, so a soldier finally helped the Palestinian man throw the remains of the tire into the garden. The other soldier seemed angry that nobody had answered the door, so he took his stick and smashed in the intercom.

Yesterday we had nearly all of the students over for lunch. Rhona, Sabah, and the women cooked *fatta*, which tasted wonderful. The male students mostly sat around playing cards or watching television. But, they did help with the clean-up. Ahmed said it was the first time he had eaten meat for ten days. Overall, it was an enjoyable occasion and I think the students appreciated spending some time in a relaxed setting.

Unfortunately, Yasser, Aida, and Mohammed were unable to attend because their homes were under curfew and Fatima refused to come because she was not willing to risk her reputation by being seen at a social event with young men.

The Photography Studio

The photographs are deceptively commonplace in appearance. They look like any passport or visa snapshots: faces against a plain colored background. If they had been taken anywhere in the West they would look exactly like this. Looking at them you might visualize where and how they had been taken, imagining perhaps the small studio room at the back of your local camera shop; or a booth in a shopping mall or air terminal. You would envision the special lighting, the standard pale-colored background, reflectors and a camera on a tripod. Well, it didn't happen that way at all.

We were planning a badly-needed break of a few days in Egypt. Back home in Canada, a visit to our American neighbors was a simple matter of digging out the passports, throwing a few things in a bag, and heading for the border. Visiting neighboring countries in the Middle East doesn't work that way. It is a completely different ball game, based on mutual mistrust, suspicion, and an apparently inexhaustible penchant for red tape.

We were fortunate in having Hatem at the Centre to pull strings for us at the Egyptian Embassy in Tel Aviv. Travellers to Egypt must purchase the special visas sold at the embassy. Dozens of people line up in the street each day to stand and wait their turn to buy the visas from the small, heavily-guarded booth outside the embassy. There is no guarantee that your patience will be rewarded, for after hours of waiting, the window is likely to be slammed shut without explanation, and that is it for the day.

With Hatem's intervention we were able to obtain an appointment with one of the aides to the Egyptian Ambassador, and thus avoid the humiliation of the lineup at the booth and the risk of an abortive journey from Gaza to Tel Aviv.

A photograph was required to accompany the visa application, and so it was that we were taken by Abed, one of the drivers from the Centre, to the shop in Gaza that dealt with such matters.

An awning extended outwards over the sidewalk from what looked like a garage with its doors open. I was led to a chair inside the garage and told to wait. I looked around. In front of me was a huge old desk piled high with pictures cut out of magazines, pens, dust-covered file-folders, pieces of film, a battered old steam typewriter, and an adding machine. Behind this charade of busyness sat the grandfather in a white *galabiyya* and the *hatta* head-dress. He was obviously the receiver-general.

The walls were covered with what I took to be the Gazan equivalent of pin-ups; young women wearing makeup that looked alternately sluttish or horror-movie gross, leered unsexily from the pictures, their clothing very un-Palestinian and immodest by Islamic standards.

Abed explained to the owner the reason for our being brought to him, and then my visual inventory-taking was interrupted by a call to come outside. Meanwhile, Peter sat and tried some Arabic on the old man behind the desk.

I was seated on a wooden kitchen chair placed on the sand outside the shop. Being totally unfamiliar with the procedure, I presumed this must be the waiting area for women. But then the owner appeared with a motley set of equipment. Beneath his arm was a piece of cloth rolled around a stick, and in his hands he carried what must surely have been the first ever Polaroid camera. Abed was handed the roll of cloth and positioned himself behind my chair. I was informed that if I wished I could remove the scarf covering my hair. Then, with much rasping of rusted hinges (everything turns rusty in Gaza) and unfolding of mysterious doors, the camera was opened and held steady in the owner's hands as he adjusted the focus.

He signalled to Abed who seemed to know exactly his role in this scenario, for the blue cloth was unfurled behind my head and held very still while I tried to appear composed for the photograph that would belie the goats, camels, donkey-carts, and dust that were peripheral participants in this unusual scene.

The owner produced an ominous-looking long metal pin which was inserted into the appropriate cavity on the camera, and with some whirring and grinding the photograph was produced in a matter of a few minutes. Its ordinariness was amazing!

The procedure was repeated for Peter, and then, when it came time to pay, the money we tendered was refused because we were foreigners, had spoken Arabic, and had "honored" the family by visiting the shop. This was always a difficult moment, for the Palestinian people work hard for the little money they are allowed to earn. We appealed to Abed to rescue the situation which he accomplished in his inimitable brusque style by taking the money from Peter and slapping it firmly into the photographer's hand. The expression on Abed's face was a sufficient inhibitor to any further tomfoolery!

You would never guess all this from the remaining prints now stored away in a trunkful of memories. But they are some of my favorite souvenirs, for on the occasions when I browse through the trunk, the Gaza morning air seems to waft around me as I look at the spare photos. Once again I hear the sounds of the busy, sand-covered street as Abed stands holding the blue cloth behind Peter's head, and the camera wheezes itself into a frenzy of production.

Symbols

They appear unexpectedly, anywhere — the colors and symbols of Palestine. The more the Israelis strive to eradicate them, the more ingenious are the circumstances in which they resurface. People do not surrender their strong nationalistic ties willingly, and forced suppression of a nation's icons only serves to strengthen the forbidden allegiances to country and culture. It is sad and ironic that the Israelis, given their own tragic history, do not recognize the futility of the task they have set themselves in denying the Palestinian identity.

A Palestinian flag flutters on the power lines at the intersection near our home. It is only a matter of time before an army Jeep or foot patrol spots it and then forces someone on the street or in a nearby house to remove it. Sometimes the means employed are dangerous. I once saw a young man forced at gunpoint to remove such a flag by standing on the metal hood of a Jeep and trying to reach up to the power-lines with a long stick. The ensuing flash of electricity and explosion convinced me he must have been electrocuted, but fortunately he appeared safe. Others have not been so lucky, sustaining severe burns. It is all an exercise in futility, for another flag will appear hours or days later, and the game proceeds along its familiar, predictable path.

Just before Land Day, the Israelis announce that there will be severe punishments for anyone displaying the Palestinian flag. On Land Day itself I decide to do some laundry, and take the wet clothes up to the roof to hang on the clothes line. As I clip pegs onto the clothes I look around at the neighborhood. On the roofs below and across from where we live I can see other Palestinian laundry: a white sheet, red tablecloth, black trousers and green shirt — the colors of the Palestinian flag legally displayed!

In the street, I see two young women walking along together. One wears a black skirt and red blouse, the other wears a black skirt and green blouse, and both have their heads covered with white scarves. Either the soldiers miss the point or are non-plussed, for the women proceed without incident. They are a mobile Palestinian flag.

One day children are suddenly wearing fleece sweaters, the top half of which is made in the design of the *keffiya* (the Palestinian black and white checkered headdress viewed by most Israelis as the symbol of terrorism). Likewise, we are given a set of water glasses decorated with the *keffiya* pattern and the words *Allahu Akbar* around the top.

On another occasion, I am given two hair-slides made from lengths of ribbon the colors of the Palestinian flag. Often people will wear something that has all the national colors except for one. Gloves, for example, where a yellow finger has been substituted for the white, so that when stopped by the military the wearer can truthfully say these are not the colors of the Palestinian flag.

The supreme provocation is probably in the hands of the gentleman in the Tufah area of Gaza. He sits beneath the awning of his shopfront, facing the young Israeli soldiers who have occupied a building and set up a checkpoint directly opposite him on the narrow street. The awning comprises sheets of fabric colored black, white, pink and turquoise. It is so close to the forbidden symbol, and yet, after all, turquoise is not green, and pink is definitely not red. The soldiers look as if they could spit tacks, or worse.

I am invited to attend a party at the Canadian Embassy, and decide to wear a *keffiya* around my shoulders as a shawl. Four Israeli guests descend on me in a rage, shouting and telling me I am encouraging terrorism by wearing this item. I am confounded by their lack of consistency, for in the tourist shops throughout Israel, *keffiyas* are readily available to anyone and must make a considerable contribution to the souvenir industry. Those same shops sell t-shirts with slogans such as: "Visit Israel before Israel Visits You!," "America Don't Worry; Israel is Behind You," "Israel — Uzi Does It" and "Join the Army, See the World, Meet Interesting People — Kill Them."

Somebody has a sense of humor somewhere in this dour land, but they're sure not in Gaza or at the embassy party!

CHAPTER FIVE

January – February 1989

January 8th 1989

We have just returned from a couple of days' holiday in Jerusalem. It proved to be far from peaceful as we were tear-gassed near our hotel, and Rhona had her wallet stolen in the crowded market of the Old City. We were glad to get back to Gaza!

The tear gas incident occurred on Salah Ed-deen Street. Because it was the Orthodox Christmas on January 6th, the United Leadership of the Uprising had given permission for the stores to remain open during the afternoon. This miffed the Israelis who had previously been trying to get the stores to stay open, so they said the stores must close at noon. To enforce this directive, the police threw tear-gas bombs into the street. We left the area at the beginning of the incident and did not return again for an hour or so. However, when we entered the store of a moneychanger, our eyes became painful and irritated while tears poured down our cheeks. Obviously there was some tear-gas trapped inside the shop. This was a very mild encounter with tear-gas, but as the symptoms persisted for some hours, I cannot imagine what it would be like to experience the full effects of such a device.

We stayed at the National Palace Hotel which is now very different from the bustling tourist trap we experienced in the summer of 1980. It was less than half full and most of the people we saw there seemed to be either Palestinian intellectuals or foreign university students. Still, the staff was very good to us, and it was much cheaper than staying in an Israeli hotel in Tel Aviv.

We talked to many people in Arabic, and they were very kind. We did a good deal of shopping and visited Temple Mount with its famous mosques. I was very taken with the inscription on the

Moors' (Morroccan) Gate which said "This is the entrance to Paradise." I tried to imagine how it must feel to a Muslim to have Israeli soldiers guarding the entrance to the Mount and patrolling the holy areas inside. The Dome of the Rock is very spectacular in comparison with the Christian and Jewish buildings.

While inside the Old City, we saw soldiers guarding a house which is situated in the middle of the Arab quarter. It is owned by Ariel Sharon, the Israeli cabinet minister whom the Palestinians hold responsible for the massacres at the Sabbra and Shatilla refugee camps in Lebanon. His occupation of this building must be one of the most provocative acts of the Occupation. There is a rumor that for security reasons Sharon has never spent a night in this house.

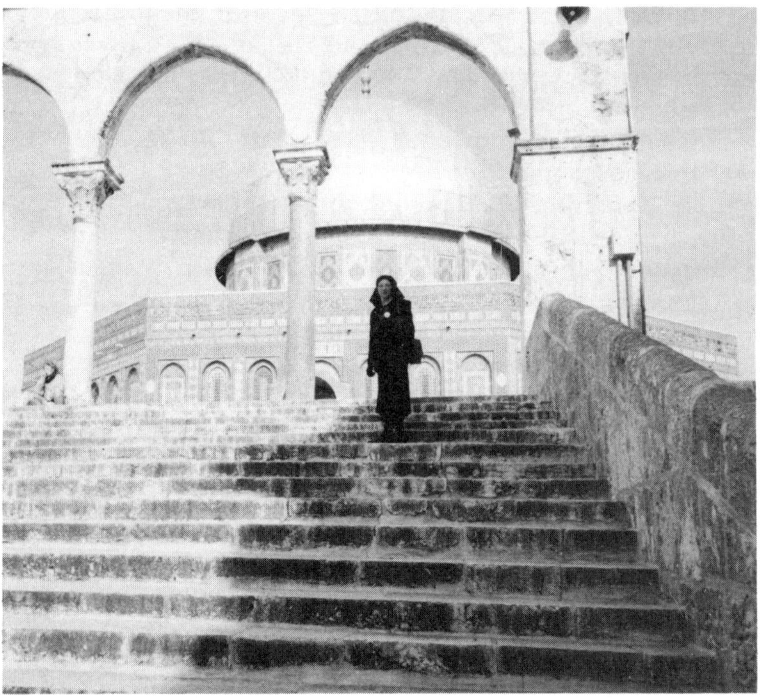

Rhona on the Temple Mount in front of the beautiful Dome of the Rock. This was the scene of a massacre in November, 1990.

Today I learned that the people from CBC's *Morningside* program have been trying to contact me via the Canadian Embassy in Tel Aviv. They want to do an interview and perhaps air some of my letters.

January 10th 1989

For some unknown reason the international telephone lines have been re-connected, so this evening I managed to call the CBC from Salah's office. Unfortunately, both Shelley Ambrose and Ken Wolf were out of the office so I will try again next week.

Today in Hatem's office, there was an interesting meeting with a visiting delegation from the United States. The group included two congressmen, Bart Gordon and Joe Kennedy II, and their entourages. While the group was visiting the Beach Camp School, their Palestinian driver was beaten up by the soldiers as he waited for them outside. There was a small uproar about this incident, but the visitors seemed unconcerned.

These Americans were incredibly uninformed of the situation in Gaza. Hatem did his best to enlighten them. I think they never recovered from the cognitive dissonance of discovering that Hatem is a Palestinian but not a terrorist. In their simplistic way, they saw Yasser Arafat and every member of the PLO as terrorists. They also believed that the Palestinian people were afraid of the PLO and, therefore, would not negotiate a separate peace with Israel. I don't think we were able to convince them that the PLO truly is the legitimate representative of the Palestinian people.

The Americans wanted to know when the Palestinians would stop the violence so peace negotiations could begin. When Rhona suggested that perhaps the Israelis should also make some concessions, her comments were quickly dismissed. The visitors didn't seem to realize that in Gaza, Palestinian teenagers and children die daily at the hands of the Israelis and not vice versa. I also wonder if they have been shown the hundreds of empty tear gas canisters, each bearing the words "Made in U.S.A."

January 15th 1989

This is yet another strike day, the 23rd since I arrived in Gaza on September 7th. I welcome this one as I have been extremely busy with the diploma program. We are into a new and hopefully final stage where I am lecturing five or six hours each day so the students can graduate by the beginning of March. Therefore I need a great deal of preparation time.

Two days ago, we had lunch at Ali's house in the Jabalia refugee camp. The poverty and overcrowding are unbelievable as are the large pools of sewage water which we saw in various parts of the camp. While we were there we visited the graves of the Jabalia martyrs — the young people who have been killed in the intifada. Seeing their names and pictures on the tombstones somehow made their deaths more real.

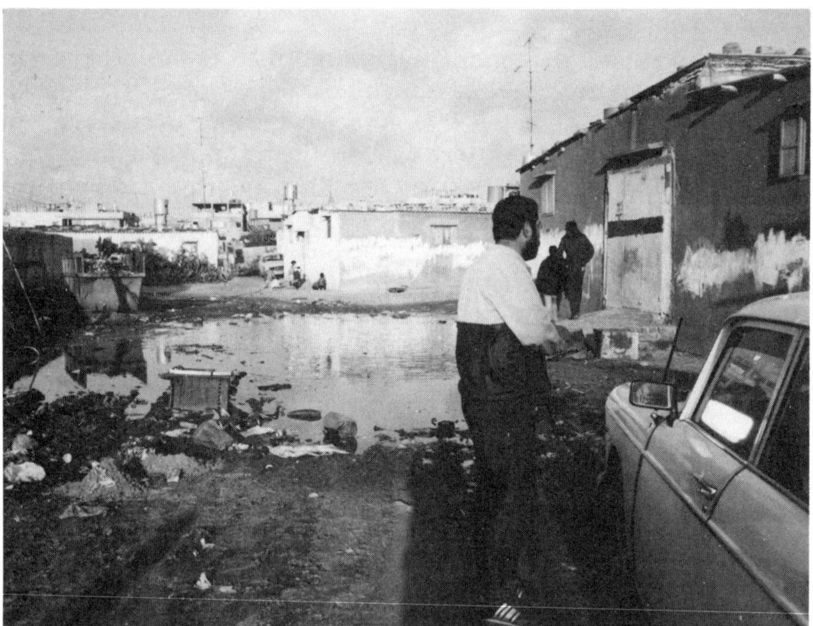

Jabalia Refugee Camp: Stagnant water, sewage and garbage adjacent to human dwellings

I had some rather perplexing news from the producers of CBC *Morningside*. Previously, they told me they liked my letters from Gaza and wanted to put them on the program. However, they first asked if I would be prepared to travel to Tel Aviv so they could interview me for the show. Of course, I agreed, but now find they do not wish either to broadcast the letters or do the interview. This leaves me wondering why they changed their minds.

Yesterday we visited Tewfik Abu Ghazaleh to assess the progress on the new college building. It is coming along very slowly. We were invited into Tewfik's house and served coffee in beautifully-ornate green and gold cups. His wife, Rebab, was very upset and described a recent incident where the soldiers had broken into their home and verbally abused her. This has happened several times, and she finds the incidents quite devastating.

January 28th 1989

This was a very sad day at the Sun Centre. Our friend Fahed Lababidi died suddenly. This kind, generous, and sensitive man who was only 37 years old leaves behind a wife and four children. I was with Fahed at the new college building the day before yesterday. At 5 p.m. he rushed off to a meeting with Hatem and that was the last time I saw him alive. Later that evening, he began to vomit and was taken to hospital. Soon he slipped into a coma and died within a day.

Five years ago it was discovered that Fahed was suffering from a brain tumor. Hatem arranged for him to travel to Switzerland where neurosurgery was performed. Although the doctors were not able to remove all of the tumor, Fahed made a good recovery and within a few months was able to return to his position as Director-General of the Society for the Care of the Handicapped.

A recent neurological examination showed that the tumor had continued to grow and was occupying about 40 percent of the space inside Fahed's skull. It is a miracle that he was able to function at all during the last few months.

At about 10:30 a.m. Rhona and I along with Sabah and the students went over to Fahed's house. It is the custom in Palestinian culture to visit the dead person's family for three days following the death to pay respects and support the bereaved persons. During the time we were there, we saw perhaps 100 people coming and going.

Because Fahed has no surviving male relatives save his small sons, we were greeted at the gate by the male members of his wife's family. The women were taken into the house while the men were shown to seats under an awning in the garden. Cigarettes were offered and small cups of the strong, bitter Arabic coffee were served. It was very quiet and peaceful in the garden — a gentle breeze shook the leaves of the trees, which cast moving shadows on the ground. There was little talking and a cassette recorder played taped selections from the Koran. People sat quietly and, I suppose, thought of Fahed. In some ways, the gathering was quite informal as a constant flow of visitors entered and exited via the gate into the street.

In one corner of the garden, a fire was burning in a metal fire pit. The embers were being used to brew coffee and to heat water to clean the cups. One of the young men kept putting hot embers right inside the coffee pots, seemingly to add flavor.

Fahed's two young sons, Mohammed and Nimir, were also present and sat among the men. I don't know what they were thinking, but they looked drawn and sad.

January 31st 1989

Since the beginning of the year, I have started to collect some current statistics related to the intifada. The sources of this information are either personal or conservative. In other words, they relate to things which I have personally experienced or heard on the Voice of Israel radio station or read in the *Jerusalem Post*.

This month 20 Palestinians were killed and 159 wounded, while no Israelis were killed and two were wounded. There were four strike days and we were under curfew for three days in addition to our regular nightly incarceration.

February 5th 1989

Yesterday there were many problems in the Khan Younis refugee camp near the home of Khaled El-Batrawy, the acting Director-General at the Centre. Two people were killed by the soldiers and 23 were wounded. One of the wounded is not expected to live.

There are several versions of what happened. A local one is that a group of soldiers told a teenager to take down a Palestinian flag. As he did so, another group of soldiers came along and thought he was raising it, so they shot him. From this point, the violence escalated.

The Middle East television station in Cyprus reported that the trouble started when the soldiers surrounded a secondary school early in the morning and questioned students as they entered. The clear implication was that there would have been no trouble if the army had stayed away. A similar report was later aired on the BBC World Service.

A fourth report from the Voice of Israel radio station said that a group of women and masked men had attacked an IDF station in Khan Younis and the soldiers were forced to fire because their lives were in danger.

All the reports mentioned that a Swiss Red Cross worker had been injured in the incident. The BBC reported he had been deliberately shot in the legs. There seems to be an increasing number of reports of Israeli soldiers behaving as if they were out of control.

Overall, the incident was very bad, but was typical of the way in which the Palestinians are dying daily, and I think willingly, in their struggle for freedom. The clashes have continued today with many camps under curfew and reports of ten people wounded in Jabalia Camp. These casualties include children aged three and ten years.

February 19th 1989

I am finding living under occupation becoming more and more difficult. It is not so much that any one day is very bad, but the accumulation of days in Gaza has its negative effect. For example, we cannot shop after midday, we are not allowed out after 9 p.m., we are in constant danger of being stoned by Palestinian teenagers or harassed by Israeli soldiers, and we don't have any recognizable pattern in the week due to curfews and strike days. We are living under chronically stressful conditions.

The intifada itself continues. I think we may be in a new phase as the Israelis presence is a little less obvious, and there are reports of much diplomatic shuffling on the international scene. This is the first day of a three-day strike called by the United Leadership and Hamas to protest the Israeli government's proposal to hold Palestinian elections which would exclude the PLO. It is difficult to believe this plan is to be taken seriously.

Last night the soldiers came round and announced the overnight curfew would be lifted for the first time in nine months. We are not sure why they are doing this, but the timing coincides with the beginning of the Islamic Holy Month of Ramadan. The United Leadership has said that due to the intifada there are to be no large celebrations this year and all cars must be off the street by 7 p.m. Perhaps the Israelis have lifted the curfew in an attempt to break the hold the United Leadership has on the people.

Recently, the Occupation has taken on a decidedly economic bent. The Palestinians are being forced out of their own businesses and into the Israeli labor market to work at unskilled jobs in very bad conditions for low pay. From an economic point of view, the Gaza Strip has become the Soweto of Israel.

February 28th 1989

Over the last few days, the weather has changed. It has become warmer, and there is a feeling of spring in the air. This has lifted our spirits. This morning we ate breakfast out on the balcony for the first time since November.

Today is a strike day, and all morning the smell of burning rubber has been borne on the wind. We have heard intermittent shooting for the last couple of hours and military vehicles are hurtling by at regular intervals. We don't know what is happening and when we listen to the news nothing is reported. Censorship of the media seems to have become more profound, and I sometimes feel that Gaza is not connected to the rest of the world.

Two days ago a person in the Sheikh Radwan district was killed in an argument with the Israeli income tax people. The economic pressure on the Palestinians is increasing daily. The latest punishment is that drivers of cars travelling through the Eretz checkpoint must now buy a license to go to Israel. As usual, people are not told how much they will have to pay, nor the period of validity of the ensuing license.

So far this year, three Israelis have been killed and three wounded in connection with the intifada. Comparatively, 36 Palestinians have died and 339 have been wounded. This month there were three strike days and no daytime curfews.

Children And Politics 2

Sitting cross-legged on a divan in the small central room of the house in Jabalia Camp, Umm Anwar is smothered by her young grandchildren who use her as a sort of jungle-gym, sprawling over her cushiony bosom and collapsing sleepily in her lap. She indulges them with smiles and verbal encouragement. They are her treasure and her pride.

Yewsif, barely two years old, is just starting to talk. Umm Anwar peels him off the back of her neck, bounces him on her lap, and prompts him to recite his political slogan. In his baby's voice he sings out cheerfully, "Israel no! PLO!" and gives the V sign with his tiny hand. Everyone applauds and tells Yewsif he is a clever boy.

"Shatir ya Yewsif!" they say, laughing.

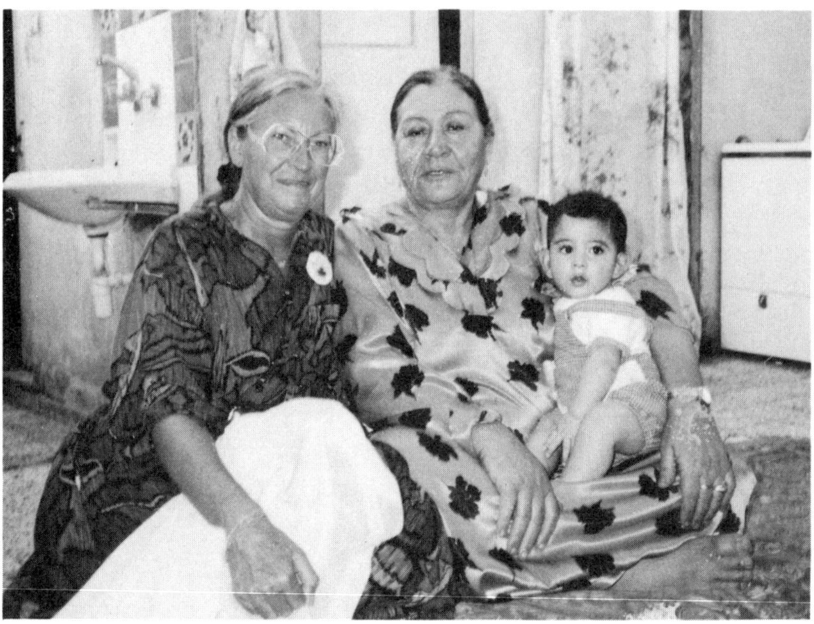

Jabalia Refugee Camp: Rhona sits with Umm Anwar and one of her many grandchildren.

I look at the baby and wonder what kind of human being evolves from a childhood that is rooted not in cultural fantasy rhymes of "Humpty Dumpty" or "Twinkle Twinkle Little Star," but in the continuation of an historic antagonism between two groups wanting to have, not share, the same piece of land.

An older, married brother arrives with his delicate-looking little daughter of six years. He wears the long white *galabiyya*, spotlessly laundered by an unseen wife next door. His daughter Nadia wears a clean, crisp, bright red dress, white ankle socks and neat patent leather shoes with ankle straps. Her skin is like porcelain. She sits quietly with her father, looking at the foreigners and responding to their questions politely. I ask if I may take her photograph and everyone responds enthusiastically. Her father takes her onto his knee, smiling. I squat down to focus the camera, and on cue Nadia smiles and gives the V sign.

The father disappears and returns after a few minutes with a studio photograph of Nadia. In the picture, she sits on a stool placed in front of a mural showing fields of tulips, her ankles demurely crossed, her outfit as immaculate as the one she wears today. There is the addition of a *keffiya* which is draped over Nadia's shoulders as she sits in her dainty pose in front of a picture of flowers she has never seen. A serious expression is on Nadia's child-face as she looks directly at the camera, her fingers raised in the V sign of defiance.

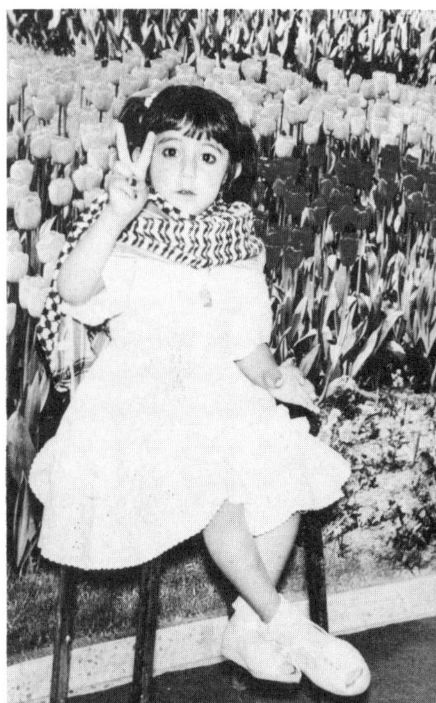

Six-year-old Nadia gives the V for Victory sign.

For an instant, juxtaposed in my mind, I see my own children when they were Nadia's age, teddy-bears clutched in their infant hands as they grin at the camera wondering what the heck is going on.

Nadia is only six years old, and politically she already knows what is going on.

A Home Visit

One morning, I hear that Beach Camp is under curfew again so I cannot, as planned, spend a few hours working at the Lababidi Centre. A little later, I see our student Sabah leaving on her home visit to work with Ali, a seven-year-old physically handicapped boy. She is doing her practicum in the Mothers' Home Education Program which is based on the well-known Portage system developed in the United States. She will demonstrate the teaching techniques to Ali's mother, who will then repeat the lessons and record his daily progress until the next weekly visit by the teacher.

Sabah invites me to join her, so I climb into the minibus with the other teachers and their driver. At first we follow a familiar route along El-Waehda Street, and down past the cement brick works where there is always a flood of water even in the height of summer when rain has not fallen for months. Then suddenly we are in a labyrinth of narrow, twisting back streets I do not recognize. There is some kind of problem ahead for we see army Jeeps in one of the streets, and soldiers, armed and helmetted, seem to be stopping people. For some reason, possibly because they see me in the front seat of the van, we are waved on by.

Now we wind past a large cemetery, the grass and weeds cropped low by wandering flocks of goats and sheep. Then into another maze until we stop by a narrow alleyway. I have no idea where we are, but think we're in the part of Gaza known as *Tufah* (Apple). Sabah tells me I must get out now because Ali's house is not far. We walk down a sand-covered path, with large tenements on either side; there is barely five feet of space between the buildings. Sabah stops at a doorway and rings the bell, telling me please to wait. From inside a woman's voice calls inquiringly, "*Eywa?*" Sabah says she is here with her foreign professor to give Ali his lesson and asks if we are welcome. Assured that we are, she leads me into a dingy hallway with cement walls and bare cement floor. Stairs lead up to other levels above us, but we remain on the ground floor. We enter another hallway off which are several small rooms with narrow windows placed high up in the wall. A teenage girl is sweeping out the sitting room where Ali is waiting.

The room is sparsely furnished. Along one wall are the divans, fabric-covered foam mattresses, on which we sit after removing our shoes at the door. A second wall is lined with the cane chairs the making of which comprise quite a large industry in Gaza. The cushions on them are covered with bright, attractive material. Along a third wall a television set covered with a decorative cloth occupies the major portion of a couch. On the walls are glass-framed writings from the Koran, photos of older male family members (I never saw photos of females displayed on walls or anywhere else), and an elaborate-looking clock framed by two minarets, its top edged with gilt-colored domes and flourishes. Ali has been placed on one of the foamies where we now join him. I am surprised at his small size compared to the healthy, thriving children I see back home in Canada. He seems very weak and weary and sits with his legs half-buckled beneath him. He cannot stand, and even moving his arms takes all his energy and concentration. However, his face lights up at the sight of Sabah, who introduces me. Ali offers to sing a song for me, and in a husky little voice he chants out one of the popular political songs of the intifada about a father giving his child a gun for his birthday so that he can fight for his country. It takes every bit of his energy, but he gets through it and sits breathing heavily. He asks Sabah if I will now sing a song for him, a fair enough exchange. I try out a little song Peter and I made up about a dog called Sami; it is a classroom creation in simple Arabic using only two or three notes and of course minimal vocabulary. Ali listens politely. "Was that Arabic?" he asks Sabah, reminding me of the time I had heard the tenor in the Peking Opera Company sing *Shenandoah* as a gesture to the English-speaking audience. It had sounded like Chinese.

The singing has attracted other family members and neighbors who now begin to fill up the small room. I am introduced to Ali's mother who looks old and exhausted. She comes in with two other children who have the same handicapping condition as Ali. Using their hands and arms, they drag themselves across the floor, stunted legs crumpled beneath them. When I question her about this, she explains through Sabah that the fault lies with the doctors who gave the children immunization shots when they were small. She says it is the injections which are to blame. The truth lies of course in the extremely high rate of endogamous marriage whereby first cousins marry and thus increase the risk of genetic handicaps. This can never be stated, however, as it would mean ostracizing the whole family, and so the health programs of both indigenous and foreign aid medical personnel serve as a convenient scapegoat.

The room has filled with women of all ages, and Sabah's lesson commences. It evolves into an audience-participatory event as Ali, sitting at the piece of wood nailed to a couple of blocks which serves him as a low table, recites by heart passages from the Koran, sings songs, tells time, and attempts some math equations prepared by Sabah. He is reinforced by much applause as each task is accomplished, and there is voluntary intervention, accompaniment, and advice in abundance.

I feel proud of Sabah in her handling of the situation. She is professional but kind and understands very well when to call a halt to the enthusiastic participation of the onlookers. She is wise enough to realize that it is not only Ali who is benefitting from her lesson, and she has taken our lectures on education-by-osmosis to heart. Her skillful handling of what could so easily develop into a session of happy bedlam, emphasizes for me why this work must be done by the people indigenous to the culture, not foreigners on some goodwill mission. I appreciate the insight of our program's mandate calling for eventual takeover by the local population.

The teaching hour comes to a close as a child runs in from the street to tell us that the bus is waiting, and we get up to leave. But the word has got out that the *ajnabiyya* has a camera with her and now everyone in the neighborhood wants their picture taken. Sabah tells them we must hurry. Adults hastily line up in rows, standing cramped close together in the small room; children are shoved to the front; babies are picked up and pointed proudly at the camera; mothers cram the doorway trying to squeeze their children in; people fall down in the crush but are picked up, dusted off and re-posed, and the handicapped kiddies pose in a little huddle at one side. *"Yalla! Yalla!"* I say, holding up my camera, "Come on, let's go!" The writhing mass immediately stands absolutely still, eyes on the camera, total silence. I press the shutter and the moment is captured. Everyone mills around as Sabah and I scramble for our shoes and walk to the street door surrounded by the throng. I am smothered in kisses and *ma'asalaama*'ed all the way to the minibus.

CHAPTER SIX

March 1989

March 3rd 1989

Yesterday I drove to the Egyptian Embassy in Tel Aviv to obtain visas for our upcoming trip to Egypt. It took me an hour at the Embassy but everything worked out in the end. The Egyptian officials kept telling me I couldn't have the visas because our applications lacked photographs and I didn't have the right change in shekels. I didn't argue, I just shrugged my shoulders and said "Okay." This resulted in a good deal of shouting and waving of arms, but the visas arrived in due course. Perhaps I'm learning something about how to deal with Arab officials.

When I returned from Tel Aviv I discovered that thieves had broken into the Sun Centre and stolen the staff's salaries. Everybody was very upset about the incident and Hatem must now travel again to bring in more money. The thieves knew the exact location of the money, and this suggests they had inside information. Usually, money is not left at the Centre overnight. This was the first time in years that the salaries were not distributed as soon as they arrived on site. Some people are saying that the thieves are Palestinians who don't care about their own people. Others are saying that the Israelis are involved and want to close down the program because Hatem keeps putting large amounts of outside money — his grant from USAID (United States Agency for International Development) — into the Gazan economy.

Of course, Hatem is in a difficult position because Palestinians do not want to deal with the Israeli police. Little will be done to recover the money. It's quite unbelievable that there is so little crime in Gaza when you consider there is no law enforcement agency which is recognized by the people.

Recently, an increasing number of homes in the Gaza Strip have been "sealed" or demolished. This abuse of human rights occurs when a Palestinian is *suspected* of involvement in the intifada. As usual, innocent people are punished — the uninvolved parents, siblings or children — while the suspect is seldom found guilty under due process of law.

March 12th 1989

Two days ago, we returned from a trip to Cairo. We stayed at the Marriott for four nights and had a wonderful time.

When we got back to Tel Aviv we heard that somebody was trying to contact us through the Canadian Embassy. I called Shelley Ambrose at *Morningside* because I thought she might have been trying to contact me regarding a piece of writing I had sent her. She explained that my last letter had been aired on the programs of March 7th and 8th under the title of "Gaza: The Twilight Zone." Shelley, as the editor, had decided to split the piece into two halves. The first was called "Twilight of the Dawn" and the second "Twilight of the Dusk."

The first part was well received but the second in which I wrote about the occupation and the intifada provoked a strong reaction from part of the Jewish community in Canada. In addition to individual calls, both the Israeli Consulate in Toronto and the Canadian Jewish Congress called the CBC to complain. I suspect they were angry because my stories did not reinforce their positive perception of the Israelis. Poor Shelley bore the brunt of the attack as she was available in Canada and had allowed the letter to be broadcast. She said she was dreading the negative and perhaps abusive comments she may receive in the mail which would not begin to arrive for several days.

Personally, while I don't enjoy being the target of anybody's anger, I am very pleased the material was aired. My intent was not to upset Jewish Canadians. I just wanted to reach as many people as possible to balance the media's distorted depiction of life in the Occupied Territories. Shelley was very brave and took quite a chance in airing this material, although I don't think she will do it again. This looks like the end of my contract with CBC.

March 14th 1989

The body of a Palestinian informer was found yesterday in Palestine Square. He had a sign around his neck which said he should be left lying there until his friends in Israeli intelligence came to bury their dead. It was claimed that the victim was a well-known local informer and drug dealer. People have accepted the "execution" with great equanimity, saying he had many warnings. I agree with Rhona's comment, "What about due process of law?"

This morning from my office in the Sun Centre I watched a demonstration at the neighboring preparatory school. About 50 boys, aged 12 to 14, blocked the street in two places just outside the school gates. They used derelict cars, pieces of scrap metal, and large rocks. They hid behind these barricades and threw stones — at nobody! They also whistled, and chanted slogans. The noise rose and fell in unison with a similar demonstration at a nearby high school which is just out of sight from my vantage point. Eventually, there was the sound of shots fired from that location.

A little later the soldiers approached the preparatory school. They entered the street from both ends in an attempt to trap the demonstrators. The boys were alert and disappeared before the Jeeps roared up to the gates of the school. The soldiers leaped out brandishing their clubs, but there were no children in sight. They looked very frustrated because the whole exercise had been a waste of time and energy. As the United States government donates several billion dollars a year to support Israel, I thought the episode should have been filmed and shown on American television under the title "Your Tax Dollars at Work!"

March 18th 1989

Two days ago we were awakened in the middle of the night by soldiers driving around the area with their loudspeakers. They were telling everybody that the IDF reserve soldiers were leaving and would be replaced by the Border Police. Apparently, the Border Police have a reputation for ruthlessness. Their title is a misnomer for they are a division of the regular army consisting mostly of Druse, members of a heretic Muslim faction.

Today the true effect of the replacement was felt in Gaza. As we drove to the Sun Centre this morning, there were burning tires in El-Waehda Street, and a little later, I saw two men in civilian clothes get out of an unmarked car carrying uzis. The Centre was being used by a group of about a dozen boys from the preparatory school who were hiding from the Border Police. When it was relatively safe these boys escaped by scrambling over the walls into the grounds of the adjoining orphanage and Near East Council of Churches.

Later, Rhona looked over the balcony outside our office and saw two men in uniform and one in civilian clothes chasing boys through the orphanage grounds. When the man in civilian clothes saw Rhona, he suddenly picked up a large rock and prepared to throw it at her. She remained quite still, and luckily he checked his action, hurling the rock against the building instead. Rhona was quite un-nerved by the violence.

All morning we saw signs of burning tires, roadblocks, and demonstrations. I counted four tear gas grenades fired in the vicinity of the Centre. Later, we learned there had been trouble in the Sheikh Radwan area — three people killed and at least 17 injured.

It seems to me that the numbers of casualties mentioned in the media are under-reported. The BBC World Service gave the best coverage of today's events saying it was like a return to the conditions at the beginning of the intifada. Both Egyptian and the Israeli television downplayed the incidents, each devoting one sentence to this news item.

This is in marked contrast to the Voice of Israel devoting at least five minutes of reporting on the death of an Israeli soldier in an ambush near the Jordanian border. While I regret equally the loss of an Israeli life, I am appalled by the systematic bias in the reporting of the media.

March 19th 1989

This morning it was very difficult for us to get to the Sun Centre due to widespread demonstrations by children and teenagers who were on their way to school. Many streets were blocked with rocks, garbage, burning tires, and chanting children. We eventually reached the Centre by a circuitous route winding through a combination of main and side streets.

At the school there was little activity, with no children and few teachers in attendance. We went into our office to work and when we emerged at about 10 a.m. the place was almost deserted. It was then we learned that a strike had been called, and we should go home. Rhona was nervous about driving during a strike, but we made it without incident.

Just after arriving home, I was discussing the general situation with Salah while standing in the street by our gate. As we were talking, a new maroon-colored van passed us slowly. We didn't take any notice, until I saw the door on the passenger side swing open and the end of a gun became visible. A few seconds later shots were fired from inside the van at two boys aged about 12 or 13 who were standing on the corner of a side street where it looked as though some garbage was burning. The boys were not hit and they ran into a nearby alley. This is the first time I have witnessed the well-known tactic of the Border Police — dressing in civilian clothes and driving confiscated vehicles in order to launch surprise attacks against Palestinians.

March 21st 1989

The troubles continue. We are now in our third day of a spontaneous strike which began in response to the problems in the Sheikh Radwan district. During the last few days, the tension has been exacerbated by the deaths of several other young people in Gaza.

This morning we decided to walk over to the Sun Centre just before 8 a.m. It was too dangerous to drive a car, and anyway, we needed the exercise. As we walked through our neighborhood, there was an unusual number of people standing at their gates, and the atmosphere was very tense. When we asked at a local secondary school on El-Waehda Street, we discovered this was an under-statement! Last evening, stones were thrown at a passing patrol, and an Israeli soldier was injured. In the general uproar somebody had stolen his gun which was probably an uzi.

I had heard about this incident on the radio yesterday but assumed it had happened in some hotbed of Palestinian dissent, not our quiet Rimal neighborhood. We were told that the soldiers rounded up all the 10- to 15-year-old boys last night and took them to the police station. I don't know what happened there, but the gun was not returned. The soldiers announced that at 8 a.m. today the area would be under curfew in order to conduct a house-to-house search for the missing weapon. At 7:45 a.m. we were walking through the streets wondering why everybody seemed so tense!

The area between Ittalatini Street and Omar El-Mukhtar Street is now under curfew. As we live on the former we are on the edge of the curfew zone and can leave the house quite easily whenever we wish. I doubt whether the soldiers will ever find the gun, as it is probably in Rafah by now!

Two points come to mind in considering this incident. The first is how often Rhona and I seem to walk through life blithely unaware that just behind us all hell is breaking loose. The second point is the Israeli's almost instinctive use of group punishment in response to opposition. It is ridiculous to be rounding up and detaining ten-year-old children.

March 23rd 1989

The curfew was lifted at 10 a.m. this morning. The gun was not recovered.

I need to remind myself that in writing this journal I am constantly taking a conservative viewpoint. The stories I hear are much worse than I report. This is because I only accept the validity of information from reliable media sources or my personal experiences. In taking this position, I may be doing a disservice to the Palestinians.

March 25th 1989

Today it was fairly quiet at the Sun Centre and in our neighborhood. There were visitors to the Centre from a Swiss organization which is concerned about the rights of children. Tewfik Abu Ghazaleh, Khaled El-Batrawy and I had an interesting conversation with them. Two of the visitors were Israeli volunteers, a psychologist and a child development worker who are members of the Peace Now movement in Israel. I admire them very much for taking the risk of coming to Gaza to get a first-hand look at the situation.

This evening Sara Roy came by as she is back from Jerusalem for a short time. It was very nice to see her again, and we drove her down to the Ahli Arab Hospital to meet Jay. This afforded us the opportunity to tour the hospital with him. Ahli is reputed to be the best hospital in the Gaza Strip, but by Western standards, it is a primitive nightmare.

The setting of this small hospital seemed incredibly beautiful by night. Its stained sandstone buildings were erected around small courtyards by the British in the early days of the Mandate, and the builders incorporated some pillars believed to date back to the pre-Christian era. With a warm breeze from the Mediterranean rustling the fronds of the mature palm trees under a midnight blue sky ablaze with stars, it seemed the perfect setting for a scene from a Hollywood movie.

The spectacle inside the buildings was in marked contrast to the romantic setting. The men's surgical ward contained ten people with bullet wounds. Eight or nine of these were in the abdomen and reflected Jay's concern that the soldiers are no longer attempting to aim for the legs. Most of the patients were young men but at least two were obviously in their early teens. One young man had been hit with a plastic bullet which entered his left chest area and passed through his diaphragm and stomach before lodging in his liver. Another young man had two bullet wounds, while three or four had lost several feet of their small intestines during surgery. Clearly, plastic bullets can be lethal.

The mood in the room was dissimilar to the chronic dysphoria to which one becomes accustomed on visiting surgical wards in the West. The young people were quite cheerful and didn't seem depressed. This is perhaps because they are now considered heroes by family and friends.

In a small sub-ward upstairs, we saw a 14-year-old girl who had a large hole in her forearm. It had been caused by a bullet fired from close range. We were told that the soldiers had entered her home and as she went to protect her little brother by putting her arm around him, she moved into the path of the bullet. It appears that she saved the boy's life. The young girl seemed bewildered by the attention she was receiving, so Rhona spoke to her in Arabic to try to make her feel more comfortable.

Later, we went to the children's ward to see a four-month-old baby who had been struck in the head by a bullet while she was being held in the arms of her mother. Jay said that fortunately there appeared to have been little brain damage because the bullet did not penetrate the skull. Instead, the child had cuts and a large bruise. When we arrived in the ward we learned that this baby had just been taken home by the family.

March 30th 1989

This is Land Day and we are again under curfew because the Israelis are expecting large demonstrations. These expectations are not unrealistic given that the latest bulletin issued by the United Leadership calls for violent clashes with the occupiers. So far, however, we have seen no trouble, only the usual military presence in our neighborhood.

This morning at about 10 a.m. we heard a commotion downstairs, and a few minutes later Mellika screamed for help. Her father, old Abu Kamal, had been working in the garden when he suddenly keeled over. I arrived in time to help Salah and two of the neighbors carry him into the bedroom. Abu Kamal felt like a deadweight and once we got him into the bedroom, I tried to find signs of a pulse. I was unsuccessful, and although he was still warm, I was convinced I was looking at a dead man. A few minutes later Dr. Wa'el Shawwa arrived and confirmed that Abu Kamal was indeed dead.

There was naturally a great outburst of emotion in the family, and Mellika in particular was distraught. We did what we could to help, but of course there is really little one can do. Basically, they found it comforting to have us with them.

Later, I changed into good clothes and stood by the gate with the men as the news slowly spread and the mourners arrived. Meanwhile, Hatem had been contacted and asked to intercede with the Military Governor of Gaza to obtain permission for the funeral to take place during the curfew. At first, he was told to call back tomorrow. Hatem was outraged but after several more calls was able to obtain approval.

The funeral then proceeded according to Islamic law. Water was heated so that the male relatives could wash Abu Kamal's body in preparation for burial. As the people gathered, palm fronds were displayed around the gate, and chairs were set out in the courtyard. The men sat in this area and were led in prayer by the sheikh.

Soon a wooden bier arrived to transport the body. Within an hour, accompanied by much wailing and keening from the women, the remains of the old man were placed on the bier and carried out of the house, down through the garden, and into the waiting municipal hearse which was to carry Abu Kamal to his last resting place. The women remained behind while the men followed in a slow procession of 10 or 11 cars.

I rode with Hatem in a car driven by Abed. Also with us was a cousin of the Sakkar family and Salah who was trying hard not to break down. He, more than anybody, must have been dazed by the speed of events.

The journey to the mosque was quite magical. First, the streets were completely empty and we had to stop at several points to remove barricades which had been erected by the *shabab* (young people). It was a strange sensation to drive through the deserted streets, and this feeling increased as we left the city and turned south on to the coast road. There in the bright spring sunshine lay the enormous expanse of the Mediterranean beach with its beautiful flat sand and ultramarine waves crashing on to the shore in a frothy spray of dazzling white. After a while, we turned inland and drove past the neatly cultivated fields which were just turning green and on past the sand dunes covered with blooming juniper and crowned with stands of date palms.

At last we reached the small mosque which Abu Kamal had built for the people who live on his land. As he had mentioned many times, this was to be the site of his grave. After a simple ceremony, this polite, dignified old gentleman was laid to rest in a newly-dug grave beneath a lemon tree in the beautiful, small garden behind the mosque. At this moment, a flock of palm doves in a nearby tree became startled and flew over the silent gathering, the sunlight catching the iridescent green and purple sheen on their wings and the white bands of their tail feathers. They swept round in a circle above us, climbing ever higher in the sky; a living symbol of the release of the soul from its body.

Even in this sanctuary the Occupation had made its mark. Some of Abu Kamal's land had been expropriated by the Israelis in order to build the settlement which now crowns a nearby bluff.

Within a few minutes, we were on our way home, and upon checking my watch I found it had been only three and a half hours since I had gone downstairs in response to Mellika's anguished call. There is something simple and honest about the Muslim way of death. The person must be buried the same day and there is no professional funereal service, just family and friends. They dig a grave in the sand, reinforce the sides with gray breeze blocks, cover the top with concrete slabs and fill the cracks with a simple sandy cement. They wash the body, carry it to the grave and bury it without a coffin. As I have long been concerned about the Western funeral industry and its potential for gouging grieving relatives, I admire Islam's forthright treatment of death.

March 31st 1989

This month two Israelis and 21 Palestinians were killed. Since the beginning of the year, five Israelis have died and ten have been wounded. In the same time period, 57 Palestinians have been killed and 635 wounded in clashes with the soldiers.

We were under curfew for one day this month and there were six strike days called by the Palestinian leadership.

Across The Sinai To Cairo

Taking the bus across the Sinai desert from Tel Aviv to Cairo seemed like the experience of a lifetime, the sort of thing one reads about in National Geographic or experiences vicariously by watching documentaries on television. We would have preferred to have done the journey by train, from Gaza to Cairo, but the station has been closed since the beginning of the military occupation.

The first stretch of the journey, from Tel Aviv to the Egyptian-Israeli border at Rafah, was completed in what I remember as deadly seriousness. My impression was that we all sat very straight in our seats and talked in whispers. I'm sure it wasn't really like that but only seems that way in contrast to the atmosphere on the Egyptian bus once we had maneuvered through customs at the border.

It took some time to complete the necessary formalities. The Israelis go through painstaking security checks. The Egyptians are relatively easy-going but employ ten people to do the job of two, and all of them want to fully-use their rubber-stamp authority.

It was interesting to see how the tourist bus followed a route that carefully avoided the occupied territory of Gaza, though it came so close to it. Not even the village of Beit Hanun was visible, and nobody seemed to notice the road sign pointing south to Gaza as we suddenly swung eastward and away from the Eretz checkpoint barely two kilometres in front of us. There were mostly foreigners on the bus, people from Sweden, Australia, South America, Mexico, Germany, and ourselves from Canada.

The town and refugee camp at the southern tip of the Gaza Strip were likewise invisible to the tourists. This is the town where Palestinian families have been separated from relatives by the massive barbed wire fences which, when the border was established, ran right through their land. Now they can only visit at the fence, where they shout news and show their new babies, but are unable to touch.

We emerged from the customs building on the Egyptian side of Rafah and were guided to a different and not-so-clean bus in charge of a guide claiming to be called George. The atmosphere changed immediately, and later it was difficult to recall which had been the most fun, the exotic scenes outside the bus or the pairings-off, flirting, and general party atmosphere inside the vehicle.

The best seats at the front were allotted, not surprisingly, to two rather jaded-looking women with bleached blonde hair, whom we assumed, from the shenanigans that followed with George, the driver, and some customs officers, to be a couple of hookers from Tel Aviv. The two women had all the Egyptian males eating out of their hands, feeding their egos, chucking them under the chin, and pinching their cheeks. From time to time, prices of rooms seemed to be discussed amidst gales of laughter, but I don't know if anything ever came of it all.

In the seat in front of us, a young man moved in on an older, very attractive South American woman, and they seemed to get along very well. However, two days later we saw her in Memphis looking at the antiquities with another gentleman. We wondered what had happened to the romance on the bus.

Early in the journey, we passed through the small resort town of Arish with its beautiful, palm-lined beaches. The holiday apartments, hotels, and small villas were as you would imagine an Arab town to be, set amid the palms with arched entrances and tiled pathways leading right onto the beach. However, there was no one on the beach. Perhaps it was not the time of year for beach holidays. We also wondered how comfortable it would be to visit such a place for, despite its holiday appearance, beach activities might be difficult for Western women due to the Muslim culture. Whenever we saw beaches in our travels in Arab countries, they were populated almost exclusively by men. Swimsuits and water sports for women seemed unheard of and considered inappropriate.

Onwards into the Sinai we passed many Bedouin encampments which caused us to marvel at the adaptability of human kind to the harshest of environments. Houses were made of cement breeze blocks or mud-brick and wattle, with wattle-fenced areas where donkeys, camels, and goats were retained. Other fenced areas contained small gardens where vegetables were cultivated.

A little girl dressed in bright red, and covered from head to toe with veils, tended a flock of goats out on the sand dunes, driving the animals with a stick and waving to the bus as we passed. Towns emerged like mirages wavering in the heat-haze, and then we would see the spires and domes of mosques, some of them tiled from base to apex in the most beautiful mosaic patterns. Often the towns were miles from any major centre, and we were unable to determine the economic base of these isolated communities. But all had a school, proudly flying the Egyptian flag, and although the living conditions must have been very poor, we saw children on their way to school dressed in neat uniforms and carrying satchels.

The desert became increasingly barren. Along some stretches of the highway were the remains of tanks and other army material left over from the Six-Day War, reminders of recurrent conflicts in this region where peace continues to be tentative.

After about four hours of non-stop driving, we reached the small town of Kantara close to the Suez Canal, and here the bus pulled into a not very inspiring roadside restaurant where we were able to buy refreshments — packets of poor quality chips, biscuits and juice. The surrounding small village seemed quite dreary and surprisingly dirtier than anything we had seen in Gaza.

A few kilometres out of the town, apparently in the middle of nowhere, a sign suddenly appeared in the sand-dunes. In large capital letters it simply said THE SHIP, preceded by an arrow indicating the appropriate direction — south. It looked ridiculous set amid the sand with no water in sight, but amazingly we were closer to the canal than we had imagined. This is the region where you suddenly see the top half of a ship apparently sailing through the desert, but in actual fact it is in the Suez Canal which of course lies well below the level of the surrounding sand.

As it transpired, THE SHIP was a rickety old ferry across the canal. There appeared to be no formal system of organization such as those we are used to in North America. No respect is accorded the token lanes painted on the road. You simply used your wits to get across in the least time possible given the ancient state of the available technology. If you were smart and well-off, you drove into the second lane at what passed for the terminal, handfuls of *baksheesh* at the ready. These bribes give you some priority in being selected to board the vessel. Lord only knows how long you waited if you didn't have a lot of cash on hand.

The canal was exactly as I expected it to be from pictures and newsreels, and although we were told it was forbidden to take photographs, nobody seemed to enforce the rule very seriously. I was reminded of the secret army base in Cairo, which all the tour guides take care to point out to visitors and which is easily reached by public buses which unabashedly announce their destination above the windscreen and at bus stops. Maybe this is the best way to treat all the trappings of war!

A couple more hours of driving along palm-fringed roads running parallel with irrigation channels that nourished the lush fields of crops eventually brought us to the insanity that is Cairo. Here in this filthiest of cities fifteen million people jostle, scrounge, beg, borrow, and hustle daily to eke out some kind of living. In the evening, the number drops to twelve million. The poverty is appalling, the issues overwhelming. We knew these things, but decided to put them on hold for the time being. We had come to escape the hardships of Gaza for a few days and hardly needed to replace them with those of Cairo. At least the people of Egypt had their own government, flag, and nationality, which put them way ahead of the Palestinians.

The bus dropped us off in Tahrir Square, and we set about finding a taxi to our hotel. We had switched into tourist mode for four days.

Abdullah's Briefcase

He is the model student; a bit overly-compulsive when it comes to his assignments where any mark less than one hundred percent transports him into a frenzy. Ninety-four percent produces endless arguments about what could possibly have been omitted from his essay, and how it must be the fault of Peter and I because he has studied and memorized absolutely everything we have said in our lectures. It takes him some time to come to terms with the kind of thinking processes we are demanding. His sole method of learning, like that of the rest of the students, has been to memorize what the teacher has taught and to regurgitate the information on a test. This has been the way of education for as long as anyone in Gaza can remember. Generating thoughts and opinions of their own is something new that the students are all having to come to terms with.

Abdullah has found it difficult enough just dealing with Peter's assignments along these lines for two months. Now he finds his frustration exacerbated by this new female professor who should be at home in the kitchen doing something that men will find really useful. So we have the added dimension of the threatened male ego. In the end, we tell him that it is his choice. If he wishes to rewrite the essay, he may do so, but he must understand that this in no way guarantees a higher mark. He will have to take a chance on the mark being reduced. He hasn't anticipated this and falls silent immediately. Next day he returns, subdued, to say that he will accept the ninety-four percent.

He dresses well, as all the students do. This took us by surprise when we first arrived in Gaza. Accustomed to seeing the rock-throwing youths on the news, we assumed that Gaza was poor and that it would be wise not to appear to be flaunting our Western affluence by wearing expensive clothes. As it turns out we are correct in the assessment of poverty in the Gaza Strip, but wrong in assuming that our dressed-down approach would be appreciated. It wasn't. Students and staff at the Centre were very polite at first, and merely scrutinized our casual garb without comment. Had we been more experienced we would have known that something was not right, for it is common for people to make positive remarks about appearance. If nothing is said, then something is wrong.

After several weeks of polite observation, Abdullah organizes a collection and Peter is presented with some nice trousers. Furthermore, I am taken aside by Aida, the Director of the Centre, and offered a beautiful assortment of clothes which are no longer the right size for her. I emerge, Cinderella-like, decked out in outfits from Paris, England, and Italy. Everyone smiles with approval and says, "Aah. Yes. This is very nice."

Later, when we are much more familiar with the people and culture, we understand what an insult it has been for us to dress down. The message we unintentionally conveyed seemed to be that the Palestinians were not worth dressing up for. This concerns them greatly for they are very sensitive to the fact that Arab people have tended to be portrayed in Western movies as rabble-rousers living in tents in the desert with flocks of goats and herds of camels. They also have preconceived ideas about the way professors should dress and are puzzled by our inexpensive outfits. They tell us they thought people in the West were more affluent, and they worry that perhaps we have spent all our money in travelling to Palestine and now are poor. Abdullah, with his dark suit, polished shoes and white, high-necked shirt, must have been very aware of all this.

A smart, black briefcase completes his image of the serious student; and he is not alone in carrying this token symbol of upward mobility. Iyad also has one. Another sharp dresser, he has been given the title of Minister of Education by the rest of the class. It is a joke made in affection, for unlike Abdullah, Iyad only responds with quality work when threatened with dire consequences. He has an easy-going nature, is extremely kind to others, and is not driven in the same manner as Abdullah. But in appearance, the two of them would pass anywhere for businessmen engaged in a serious enterprise.

The illusion is completely successful as far as Peter and I are concerned, until the day when I am sitting in the lecture room during the fifteen-minute break. Abdullah is hovering nearby, and I hope we are not in for another wrestling match over marks. As I sort out my notes and overhead transparencies, he approaches politely and pushes a green pepper across my desk, saying, "Miss

Rhona, you like this?" I answer that I certainly use them from time to time in cooking and salads. "Aah," he smiles, placing his briefcase on the table. Snapping the catches, he opens it to proudly display what is in essence a miniature vegetable market! Onions, peppers, cucumbers, and tomatoes spill out of what I had assumed to be the safe haven for his essays and textbooks.

My astonishment amuses him in the extreme. "*Faddali!*" he says, "Help yourself!" I inquire where he keeps his papers if his briefcase is a veritable *suk*.

"Do not worry, Miss Rhona. They are safe," he replies with a quiet smile. "But we cannot carry those things with us all the time, because if the soldiers stop us there may be a problem." I know he is right in this respect.

My vegetable larder duly replenished, I assume this is just an isolated incident and that the briefcase has returned to its usual Western role. However, some weeks later Abdullah overhears Peter mention that he needs a hair-cut and beard-trim. Next day, as Peter's lecture comes to an end, Abdullah approaches with the mysterious briefcase which is opened to reveal what is no longer a vegetable *suk* but a barber's shop! With great respect and seriousness Peter is duly coiffed and shorn.

We now begin to speculate on what the other briefcase carriers are toting around. We are quite sure their contents would be a surprise to Westerners. The contents are more likely to be those items being currently traded in the Gaza community, probably t-shirts with a forbidden political slogan, or some new kind of candy, or *falafel*, or in-season fruits to share with friends and colleagues.

My last encounter with the briefcase is on the staircase as I am going up to the lecture room. On the landing, I bump into Abdullah, briefcase in hand, a conspiratorial look on his face.

"So what's in the briefcase today, Abdullah?" I ask jokingly. Today he is being very mysterious and loving every dramatic moment.

"Miss Rhona, do not ask," he replies quietly, eyes downcast. I know the game. He can't wait to tell me but must go through the motions of being involved in intrigue. He would love me to beg him to tell me, but I'm not playing.

"Aah," I reply, blank-faced, "I understand," and move as though to continue up the stairs. He cannot stand it. With a bound he gets ahead of me and blocks my way, his face close to mine as he asks in a hoarse whisper, "Miss Rhona, you want a Palestinian flag or picture of Mr. Arafat for your apartment?"

"Ya Salaam Abdullah!" I cry out in consternation, apprehensive about his safety in carrying around these forbidden items. If he is caught by the soldiers, it will be prison for sure!

I have given him the reaction he wanted. He is completely happy with the net result of his dramatic performance as I continue to reprimand him. Eyes cast down, he listens respectfully, a satisfied smile playing around his mouth for he sees that I care about him. All the students are gluttons for this. They say we are their Canadian parents.

"Inta majnun!" I admonish him. "You are crazy!"

"Do not worry, Miss Rhona. I will not get caught," he says as he takes the stairs two at a time up to the lecture room. I have made his day.

CHAPTER SEVEN

April 1989

April 3rd 1989

Today we planned to receive three sets of visitors at the Sun Centre. However, I had a telephone call from John McNee, the First Secretary, saying that he was cancelling the visit of the Canadian Ambassador. In the uproar following Canada's decision to hold talks with the PLO, all Canadian ambassadors in the region have been recalled to Ottawa for consultation. A few days ago the *Jerusalem Post* said that the Canadian ambassador had been summoned to the Israeli Foreign Office in Jerusalem for consultation. Obviously, a few feathers have been ruffled in the diplomatic world.

The first visitors to arrive at the Centre were much more ominous than the Canadian Ambassador and his entourage. In a cavalcade of Jeeps, a man whom Hatem calls "The Chief Occupier" stopped at the main gate. His name is Shmuel Goran, and he is the Israeli Governor of the Occupied Territories. We were in the library when he arrived and was introduced by Hatem. This man wore civilian clothes, but he was accompanied by four or five other men in army uniforms. We were told they were generals and other high-ranking officers.

Due to our experiences of living in Gaza, we found it difficult to be polite with them but were so for Hatem's sake. One particularly offensive man came into the library smoking and carrying an uzi over his shoulder. I found his sullen expression and other non-verbal behavior to be quite threatening. Rhona told the man he was in a non-smoking area, and he very reluctantly went outside to extinguish his cigarette. We later learned that this man is the Chief Intelligence Officer for the Gaza Strip.

Mr. Goren inquired about our program and then went on to ask about our lives in Gaza. When he asked if we faced any difficulties in living here, I told him I was surprised that the answer was not obvious to him. Rhona added that problems with the soldiers were unavoidable since we lived in an Arab house. Mr. Goren then offered to supply us with special papers which would ensure we would not be hassled by the soldiers if we were stopped. We refused on the grounds that we should not need special papers if the soldiers are fair and disciplined. Our position was also an expression of solidarity in sharing the lives of our Palestinian friends.

Overall, I found this to be a very disturbing session.

We had a happier time at lunch when we went to Hatem's to meet the Charge D'Affaires from the American Embassy. Today he was accompanied by John Chamberlin, a Political Officer at the Embassy.

Initially things went well, and I found them to be very friendly. However, when I challenged John for saying that a high-ranking Israeli officer was "not a bad guy," the atmosphere became a little tense. Calmly, I said, "Many people in Gaza would consider this man to be an accessory to murder." At this point, the Charge d'Affaires became very withdrawn and let us know non-verbally that we had crossed the line of diplomacy. He then made some innocuous remarks about there being tension on both sides. However, I am not deterred. If these so-called liberal people lived in Beach Camp for a month, I doubt they could remain so detached. When people from the outside come to Gaza and criticize our opinions I am reminded of a line from the movie *Desert Hearts*: "You're only visiting the way I live."

John Chamberlin was more open and challenging. I enjoyed our discussion as I am not irrational about these issues. I hope we will meet again in the future.

April 4th 1989

I observed a small but significant incident through the window of my office at the Sun Centre. The window overlooks the neighboring preparatory school. It was about noon when the children were returning home. They were fairly noisy with much chanting and whistling, but nobody was throwing stones. Suddenly the soldiers appeared, as if drawn by the sound, and fired two teargas grenades. One fell at the feet of an old man who was selling *falafel* at the entrance to the school. Children fled in all directions. Within minutes the Palestinians had been vanquished and the victorious soldiers were in possession of the street.

What did the soldiers achieve? What would have happened if they had not appeared? I suspect that the answer to both questions is "nothing."

April 13th 1989

It is 9 p.m., and I am sitting in almost-total darkness writing this. The electricity was cut off at noon and has not yet been restored, so I am writing with the aid of a dim, battery-powered lamp. We are not sure why there is no electricity.

From the Voice of Israel radio station we learned of a very serious incident in the village of Nahaleen near Bethlehem. Although details are still sketchy, it appears that soldiers broke into homes there at 2 a.m. and started to beat young people. Not surprisingly, there was a reaction and in the resulting melee five people, including two brothers, were killed. Many others were reported wounded. Two other people were killed in demonstrations which started as news of the original incident spread through the West Bank.

We heard about Nahaleen this evening while we were visiting the home of Mohammed Abu Hamda for a Ramadan supper. Mohammed, who is the principal of the UNRWA School for Blind Students, has a delightful family, and we spent a very happy evening with them.

On our way home we encountered the ugly side of the intifada. As we were driving past the Islamic University, two young men stepped from their hiding place in the bushes and from short range pelted our car with rocks. There was no serious damage either to ourselves or the car, but, we were badly shaken by the sudden violence, while the car sustained some small dents and scratches. Later, we learned that the United Leadership is enforcing their rule that no cars should be out on the street after 7 p.m. Unfortunately, our students had forgotten to warn us about this latest change in the local situation.

April 14th 1989

All the refugee camps in the Gaza Strip have been put under curfew to prevent disturbances resulting from the incident in Nahaleen.

This evening we were invited to Ramadan supper with Hatem and Aida. As usual, the meal was delicious and the company friendly and relaxing, but after last night's experience, we decided not to drive. As we were walking home along Omar El-Mukhtar Street, we saw a group of boys throwing stones at the passing cars. They seemed to be out of control and when a stone was hurled in our direction we confronted them. After shouting at them in Arabic, they calmed down somewhat, but the effect was only temporary. By the time we turned the corner by the prison, they were out on the street again yelling and slinging stones.

April 15th 1989

This afternoon we went to visit Sara and Jay at Marna House. While we were there, we met two Israeli media people who were working as a camera crew for ABC. David, the cameraman, spoke very good English and apparently passable Arabic as well. It was interesting to talk to him because he claimed to have good connections with the underground leadership in Gaza. Perhaps he does, because I would not like to be in the shoes of any Israeli roaming around Gaza with a video camera.

David believes Gaza is a very different place from the West Bank with regard to its political make-up. For example, the Communists and the PFLP (Popular Front for the Liberation of Palestine) are more powerful in the West Bank, while Hamas is stronger in the Gaza Strip. Evidently, there is much criticism of Chairman Arafat for his former corruption. People feel that while he was in Lebanon he was given a good deal of money which was not passed along to the refugees. It seems that Hamas has been more honest in using its funds in support of the ordinary people in Gaza and thus is widely respected, especially in the south of the Strip.

The situation here remains very tense. Much of Gaza is under curfew today. Last night the soldiers came round and announced that all schools would be closed for two days. Only eight children arrived at the Sun Centre today, and they were sent home. Tomorrow marks the anniversary of the assassination of Abu Jihad, and there have been many calls for a "Day of Rage." Not surprisingly therefore, there have been many rumors that we will be put under curfew.

April 17th 1989

Yesterday we were under curfew and three people were killed in demonstrations. Today the curfew was lifted, and this morning we decided to go to the Egyptian Embassy in Tel Aviv to obtain visas for our planned trip to Cairo. It was very difficult to get out of Gaza because there were many demonstrations and burning tires. We couldn't go to our usual gas station because soldiers were blocking the road. Many streets were also barricaded. We managed to drive out through the main streets of the Tufah district, but it looked like a battle zone. There was rubble all over the street with the remains of about six barricades in the space of a few hundred metres. I doubt if the army was in control of this area yesterday and believe it was "liberated" for a period of time. Because the media are not allowed into Gaza on curfew days, outsiders are never aware of the extent and success of demonstrations against the occupation.

(My "liberation" theory was later confirmed by the establishment of an Israeli soldier station in the centre of Tufah and the eventual closing of the street to through traffic. It is Israeli policy to set up a permanent presence in any place where they have suffered a defeat.)

On a more pleasant note, we were greeted again at the Egyptian Embassy by Mr. Abdel Ghaffar El-Deeb who, by presidential decree, had just been promoted to First Secretary. He was very helpful in obtaining the necessary visas and wanted to discuss the Palestinian situation with us. He asked a series of questions about Hamas. I think the Egyptians are very concerned about the fundamentalists as they are also a de-stabilizing influence in their country. Mr. El-Deeb seems to think that if elections were held now, the PLO would win far more seats than Hamas. He thinks that Hamas holds many of its adherents by fear, but would not receive many votes in a secret ballot.

From the Egyptian Embassy, we walked over to that of our own country. As usual, we were made to feel at home by John McNee and Michael Mace who is the Charge D'Affaires while the Ambassador is back in Ottawa for consultation. Mostly we discussed the deterioration of the situation in Gaza. They were a little worried about our safety and are going to re-activate the emergency evacuation plan. I don't think this is necessary at the moment but expect their concern is triggered by information on the current situation which they have received from their international contacts at UNRWA headquarters in Gaza.

John McNee is leaving Israel in July as his tour of duty will terminate. He will be replaced by Michel Desalaberry who is an expert on the Palestinian situation. We will miss John who is always reliable, friendly, and concerned for our safety.

April 18th 1989

Yesterday three Palestinians died in the Occupied Territories. A man who sustained head injuries more than two weeks ago died from his wounds. And a 12-year-old girl and a 13-year-old boy were killed by army gunfire. So far this month, the total number of dead is 24. It is the worst month for casualties since we arrived in Gaza.

April 19th 1989

Tonight we were again invited to the home of Hatem and Aida for Ramadan breakfast, what we consider supper. However, Rhona was very apprehensive because we were stoned the last time we drove home after dark. Hatem attempted to reassure her by saying this was just a fact of life in Gaza, and we must learn to live with it. We left at 7 p.m. and arrived home safely a few minutes later.

At about 7:15 p.m. we heard loud noises from the street outside. When we looked out we realized we had returned home in the nick of time. A gang of youths had taken over our block and were stoning all the cars which passed. They hid among the bushes in the middle of the street so that passing vehicles had to run a gauntlet of ambushers. Many hits were scored on the cars, and the night rang with the sound of shattering glass and bending metal. We don't know if anyone was injured.

April 21st 1989

The ambush of two nights ago seems to have had the desired effect. The United Leadership demonstrated they were serious about cars not being allowed to travel the streets after 7 p.m. Since the ambushes, the streets have been deserted by early evening. Our students told us that the Leadership has adopted this policy because it wants people to refrain from celebrating during Ramadan as a mark of respect for the thousands of their compatriots who are languishing in jail.

April 22nd 1989

There were many troubles in the centre of Gaza today. This meant we had to take the coast road in order to make a house call near Khan Younis. This visit was to a home between the villages of Qaraira and Abasan in the south-eastern corner of the Gaza Strip.

The child we went to see is three weeks old and is being screened for entry into the Mothers' Program. He was born without arms, and in fact, looked very much like the thalidomide children who were born in Britain and North America about 35 years ago. Although he has no arms, there is what appears to be a small vestigial digit protruding directly from each shoulder. There may also be other skeletal deformities in the area of the collar-bone because the child cries when touched there.

We talked with the parents and extended family about a possible genetic cause for the condition. While the parents are both from the same extended family, they are not first cousins and also have six normal children. Furthermore, there are no other children with similar handicaps in the extended family. This makes genetic transmission quite unlikely.

We next discussed the possibility of environmental causes and asked the mother if she had taken any drugs during the pregnancy. This uneducated woman told us that during the fourth month she visited the local health clinic and was given oral polio vaccine. The mother went on to say that she spit out the vaccine when she remembered her pregnancy. My guess is she did in fact take the medication and believes this is the cause of her child's handicap. However, when I checked with Jay he said there is no evidence linking maternal ingestion of polio vaccine with congenital defects in the fetus.

The only other unusual piece of information we could uncover was the mother having been severely tear-gassed while visiting Khan Younis early in her pregnancy. The earlier in the pregnancy the tear-gassing happened, the greater the potential damage to the fetus. The mother was tear-gassed again in the seventh month but it is extremely unlikely that this assault caused the child's handicap.

From our brief investigation, tear-gas is the prime suspect in causing this devastating handicap. But, as with the thousands of alleged spontaneous abortions in the Occupied Territories, it is almost impossible to scientifically show a causal relationship between exposure to tear-gas and damage to the fetus. This is especially true in an area like Gaza where there are few epidemiological records at the best of times.

If tear-gas is causing this kind of damage, its use has tremendous moral and ethical implications for the government of Israel.

April 27th 1989

Life in the Gaza Strip has been particularly difficult for the last two days. The situation continues to deteriorate. Yesterday a teenage boy was killed in Sabbra which is very close to where we live. In addition, an eight-year-old was killed in the West Bank and many people have been wounded. There have been burning tires and demonstrations in many neighborhoods including our own.

Today trouble started at about 2 p.m. when a burning tire appeared in a nearby intersection. Sara Roy was visiting us, and we went up on the roof for a better view of the incident. We could hear the *shabab* chanting Palestinian slogans from the relative safety of a side street as the soldiers arrived to deal with the burning tire and the barricade which had been erected to block the street.

Four or five vehicles appeared and stopped outside our house. Soldiers jumped out and ran down toward the tire, brandishing their weapons. One who remained with the vehicles was posted to watch our position on the roof. Next, a man emerged from a civilian car waving a revolver. He was in civilian clothes, and Sara thought he was from the secret police. It is also possible that he was a settler.

Three soldiers took up position in the intersection and spent about 15 minutes trying to shoot the young people who had disappeared down the side street and were now taunting the soldiers verbally. The soldiers were kneeling down and had raised their guns to their shoulders. From time to time, presumably when somebody appeared in view, they fired their guns. We saw and heard the firing of about five bullets as well as one tear-gas grenade. As far as I could tell, nobody was injured.

I'm not sure why the soldiers took this action. We are constantly told that the soldiers are ordered not to fire unless they are in danger. In this situation, we did not see a single stone being thrown. Furthermore, their slow and methodical approach to firing down the sidestreet suggested they were feeling almost relaxed about the whole affair. I don't believe they felt the least bit threatened.

April 30th 1989

In April, 37 Palestinians were killed, making it the worst month for civilian deaths since the beginning of the intifada. In the same period, there were no Israeli deaths.

During this month, there were five strike days and the entire Gaza Strip was under curfew for one day.

Children And Politics 3

One evening in Ramadan, we walked over to the home of Hatem and Aida for "breakfast," the meal eaten at sundown during the month of what we called "fixed interval fasting." Ramadan is the festival during which Muslim people neither eat nor drink during the daylight hours, for the Prophet decreed that this was the time when everyone should experience what it is like to be poor and hungry. We found it rather strange, for once the muezzin gave the equivalent of the All-Clear at sunset, it was open season with enormous amounts of food consumed in a party-like atmosphere. The more honest people admitted that they actually gained weight in Ramadan, which did not surprise us.

During the usual sumptuous meal with our hosts, Hatem and Peter had persuaded me that there was nothing to fear from rock-throwing children this evening. Two evenings ago we had run into a stone-throwing ambush on our way home in the car after visiting other Palestinian friends with whom we had dined. I had been badly shaken by the episode. Our normally informative students had forgotten to tell us that the latest political leaflet from the United Leadership decreed no cars on the streets after 7 p.m. Those that were would be presumed to have been commandeered by Israeli forces and therefore subjected to stoning.

Although we had walked over to Hatem and Aida's house, I was nonetheless in a state of agitation to get back home before 7 o'clock to avoid any further horrors. Hatem had other ideas and insisted that I was to be desensitized by facing reality which, he believed, was that the intifada rules were clear and nobody would bother us if we were dressed appropriately and on foot. Nothing could go wrong, Hatem insisted. We were not driving a car, I was wearing a Palestinian scarf on my head, I was covered from head to toe, and Peter was wearing his CANADA jacket.

And so it was that we found ourselves on Omar El-Mukhtar Street, walking along in the darkness beneath the remaining street lights. With much begging and pleading on my part, we had managed to leave before seven, but there were only a few cars and people still around.

As we neared a dark intersection, we saw a group of small children run out from a narrow street and hurl rocks at a passing car that was obeying all the rules. It was not yet seven, the car had a Gaza licence plate and even had its interior lights on so that the scarf-covered female Palestinian passengers were clearly visible. None of this hindered the small army of children, and it was with some resignation that we saw them turn, spot us and then throw rocks in our direction.

I think this was the first time we were confident enough in Arabic to allow our anger to take over. It worked well on this and future occasions where we felt very strongly that what had originated as political protest had now become the vehicle for vandalism and delinquency among the children and youth. (To be fair, one has only to imagine the scenario in Canada if vandalism by teenagers were legitimized on political grounds!)

Peter ran shouting toward the children who retreated into the narrow street. We continued running to the intersection and came upon them standing in a disorganized group. Many of them were so tiny I couldn't believe it. Their commander was a boy of about nine or ten. We both shouted at them that they were not clever to throw rocks at Canadians who were trying to help Palestine, and they must stop. The boy understood. "Stop!" he called to what were literally his "infantry." "They are Canadians. Let them go by."

As we walked on, I could see adults standing hidden in doorways or leaning out of windows, watching what had transpired and yet doing nothing to intervene.

Back in the safety of our apartment we sat on our balcony in the dark and watched as cars were ambushed by rock-throwing teenagers hiding in the trees and shrubs on the median. The sound of shattering glass filled the street as headlights and windshields were smashed to smithereens, while stunned drivers either beat a hasty retreat or tried to run the gauntlet of organized groups at full speed.

After this night, there was no further mention of my desensitization program, which was just as well since, once I had managed to get home from work I refused to leave the house after dark.

The Selling Of Samira

I suppose it was inevitable in this extremely male-dominated society, but I am not happy about the engagement. The women tell me that they have the right to refuse to become engaged (which here means as good as being married; the actual wedding party is just a final formality). However, if the family wants the union for reasons of enhanced wealth, status, or protection, pressures are brought to bear upon the young woman and her refusals are ultimately overcome in one way or another.

Samira is probably the best female teacher in Victory School. At one all-female social gathering she had talked of wanting to become a doctor, but families will not allow their daughters to study in towns or countries where there are no relatives to chaperone their behavior. So Samira is stuck in Gaza and is lucky to have been permitted by her family to train as a teacher.

Mansour has pursued her for months, being charming, bullying, and lovelorn in an unending cycle of strategies aimed at wearing down her resistance. Recently, he has taken to visiting her sick mother, trying to enlist her support in his campaign for Samira. Sometimes at morning breaks I have seen this young woman cover her face as she tries to cope with her tears and confusion. She has consistently refused his proposals, and once, talking to me privately, confided that she does not want to marry anyone. Instead, she prefers to continue her work as a teacher. Samira says that she doesn't love anyone right now, as everyone in the school feels like her brother or sister. I try to understand and be supportive. She again emphasizes that the Koran says a woman must not be forced to marry.

However, in Gaza this is a dangerous situation for women as cultural factors can outweigh the wisdom of Islam. Males are used to having things their own way from birth (I only once saw a male child reprimanded for misbehavior, whereas girls were regularly slapped, kicked, and verbally abused), and if they encounter an obstacle, they behave like truculent children who cannot have a coveted toy. When the craved item is a young woman who refuses their offer of marriage, hurt can quickly turn to spite, resulting in spreading rumors of loose behavior that will ruin the young woman's reputation and possibly bring dishonor on her whole family. It is rumored that some situations like this still result in the murder of the young woman by her male relatives.

Samira's situation is not unique. I have witnessed situations where other females became so distressed by gossip that they were on the point of withdrawing from their jobs lest their father thought that they were trying to have relationships with male colleagues. These situations required careful handling, for in Gaza there are still very few females willing to risk their reputations by working in co-educational settings. In any case, as soon as a husband is found, the young woman's career is terminated, and she is relegated to a life of child-bearing and household drudgery on a scale far beyond what we know and tolerate in the West.

I listen to Samira and give my opinion when asked. However, I'm not sure if we even perceive these situations in a similar manner. Mostly, I try to stay out of it, though there are times when I want to strangle Mansour for bullying her in his sulky, aggressive way.

The two families have had the preparatory meetings. Samira keeps stalling, but Mansour secretly tells Peter that her older brothers have told him not to worry. If Samira will not agree they will lock her up in the house until she comes to her senses. So much for the Koran.

One day, Mansour is all smiles and charm, and the engagement is announced. We are invited to the celebrations after work the next day. At the appointed time, we drive to Mansour's home. Many relatives have arrived, some from as far away as Yemen. The women who will be going later to Samira's home are dressed in their best Palestinian finery: black gowns with the intricately-executed cross-stitch embroidery. I notice an older gentleman also dressed traditionally. The *keffiya* frames his white-bearded inscrutable face; a woven shawl is arranged over one shoulder. His long white *galabiyya*, sandals, and walking-stick all add up to an image reminiscent of scenes from the movie *Lawrence of Arabia*.

We sit on divans around the room and are served a hearty "lunch" of *fatta* which we eat with our fingers, Arab style. Relatives tear off large chunks of chicken and either hand them to us or put them on our plates. This is their way of making us feel honored and welcome.

The guests duly fed, it is time to leave for Samira's house which is in a village near Khan Younis. The guests total 20 or more; there are three cars one of which is our worn and weary little Renault. Breaking what must surely be Guinness World Records, the guests pile into the cars, and we are on our way.

At Samira's house we ascend a flight of stairs at the top of which the women are ushered into a room off to the left while the men are directed into the one straight ahead. Divans and raffia mats are on the floor and already quite a large number of older women is assembled. I notice that everyone is in traditional dress and that on this occasion no one removes her scarf. The room is sparsely furnished, the sole item of furniture being a cheap-looking cupboard containing china and glassware.

I am subjected to the usual scrutiny, especially from the older women. They do not expect foreigners to know Arabic and are therefore surprised when I pick them up on something they're saying about me. They question me about my work and ethnicity. Canada is in everyone's good books because it backs the Palestinians on human rights. Still, they ask if I am not afraid to live with Palestinians. I tell them no, why should I be? They tell me everyone outside of Palestine thinks they are terrorists and are afraid of them. I explain that I live with a Palestinian family in Gaza Town and am not afraid. I have the feeling they're disappointed.

Then someone asks me the question that was to arise time and time again in this kind of setting. Which country do I prefer, Canada or Palestine? I reply that every person loves their own country, but that I have chosen to live in Palestine for two years and think it is very beautiful. An old *Haja* enters the room and asks about the foreigner. They tell her, "She doesn't like Palestine. She says Canada is better." I tell them they do not speak the truth; that is not what I said. This was something I was to encounter on many subsequent occasions, and in the end, I either asked them what they thought should be the answer or said this was not a nice question to ask a foreigner. The older women were usually mistresses in the art of trouble-making, and I learned to deal with them cautiously. They make the lives of many younger women an absolute hell.

Fortunately, at this point, Samira enters the room and comes to kiss me. She looks pretty and happy. I meet her mother who is dangling a young boy on her lap. He is about two and a half years old. Samira takes the child from her mother and gives him a glass to play with. When he looks as if he is going to smash it, she tries to take it from him. He throws a terrible tantrum, and she immediately gives him back the glass, asking me what she can do to keep him happy. I am confounded by this ineptness in Samira who, in her teaching has worked with many young children in very deprived environments and who seems to understand the stages of development and need for toys and books and safe things to play with. I suggest substituting some plastic dishes for the glassware, since toys of any kind are not in evidence. She says this will just cause a problem because he doesn't like the plastic dishes, he wants the glassware. The child is in complete control of the situation.

Knaffa is served, in cake form. It is very sweet, soaking in honey. Then a short time later Samira comes around with a tin of chocolates. She asks me if I understand what this signifies, and I tell her I think it is to celebrate the engagement. She says yes, it means that everything is now agreed.

I learn later from Peter what has actually been agreed. His experience with the men had been entirely different. After much arguing, some of it very heated, Mansour's father had pulled out a plastic wallet and counted out the equivalent of five thousand dollars in Jordanian dinars. Samira had been bought and sold.

She tells me she is happy now, and explains how she could never admit this before because no Muslim woman can fall in love or express affection until she is engaged or married. So I guess our previous conversation about her not loving anyone was all part of her strategy to appear modest and chaste. I understand, for she is a very conservative Muslim. Samira went on to say they will not get married for a year because she and Mansour both want to work and save some money. This will give them time to make plans for the future and to get to know each other. I no longer know what to believe; the longer I remain in the Palestinian culture the less I understand.

Mansour is beside himself with happiness, full of dreams and plans. They will save and go to Saudia where they will work as a couple and live an idyllic life, he says.

Later at home, I cannot shake off a feeling of uneasiness. How can Mansour's family afford such a huge sum? How does this affect Samira's status when she marries Mansour and moves into his family home? Just how overjoyed does Mansour's mother really feel given that there is hardly a stick of furniture in the house and all this money has just exchanged hands? Does she even know? People tell us that the money is for the bride to buy clothes and jewellery. However, since the bride is not present at the business transaction, how does she know what is her due? And since the men in the family control all such money, how much does she actually get? To me it seems like a devious way of evading the ugly truth that is in fact a trade in female human beings. Like Samira's newfound happiness, I wonder how much is real and how much illusion? As always, who will ever know the truth?

Epilogue: Mansour and Samira were married six months later. Attempts to reach Saudia failed. Mansour now teaches in a school for deaf children. Samira remains at home, reportedly pregnant.

CHAPTER EIGHT

May 1989

May 9th 1989

I am writing this in our room at the Jerusalem Hotel in Amman, Jordan. We are having a rather frustrating time trying to get a visa to travel across the King Hussein Bridge on the way back to Gaza. Presently, we are waiting to hear from the Canadian Embassy, having spoken this morning with the First Secretary, Michael Chison.

So far, our holiday has been a little disappointing as we have had difficulty achieving our goals. Still, I think it is very good for us to be out of Gaza with its daily stress and tension. While travelling, we have read in the papers that the situation in Gaza has deteriorated still further, with hundreds of people wounded over the weekend.

Looking on the positive side, we have done some very interesting things. On the last night of Ramadan, we visited friends in Cairo for dinner. Our host, Tareq Ismael, who is from Iraq, teaches political science at the University of Calgary. His wife, Jackie, is a professor in the Faculty of Social Welfare. The other dinner guests were Dr. Abbas Hamdani, a professor of Middle Eastern history at the University of Wisconsin, and his wife, Zubeida, a teacher. It seems rather incongruous that Abbas, who was born in India and is an expert on Islamic Studies, should be teaching in Wisconsin.

Both Tareq and Abbas are lecturing at the American University in Cairo for the spring semester. Their wives are visiting Egypt for a short time as is a daughter from each family.

The two young women are pursuing academic careers. The daughter of Abbas and Zubeida is doing graduate work in history at Princeton, while Jenann Ismael is completing her baccalaureate in philosophy and will probably go on to do a Ph.D. at Berkley. Jenann is planning to come to Gaza for the summer to teach English to our students.

After supper we were taken to the Khan El-Khalili bazaar which was open until very late. For Rhona and I, it was a great novelty to be out after dark, and I felt quite nervous, expecting the soldiers to stop us or the local people to throw stones. Abbas, who had once lived in Cairo for six years, showed us the old buildings, including the Husseini Mosque. He knew the exact dates and histories of these places. Later, we strolled through the densely packed market and bargained for a brass bracelet. In fact, we were very restrained because there were many things we would have liked to buy, but how could we transport them back to Canada?

Tareq also took us to a small, crowded coffee house where we sat and listened to a genuine Egyptian folk band. The music, the instruments, and the musicians themselves were fascinating. A tall man in a red *fez* played a flute and smoked a cigarette at the same time, while his companion joyfully played the finger cymbals, obviously stoned out of his mind. There were very few tourists in this place so we were fortunate to have this kind of experience.

After coming to Jordan, we managed to take a trip to the hidden city of Petra. It was exciting to ride on horseback through the narrow gully in the mountains and into the hidden city itself. Since then, Rhona and I have been venturing out alone. Yesterday, using local buses, we went to the Roman amphitheatre in Amman. Today we used the same method to reach the beautiful ruins at Jerash, a site we last saw in 1980.

May 15th 1989

We are now back in Gaza, having returned from our ten-day vacation in Egypt and Jordan. The change was needed, and we feel all the better for a few days of freedom.

The situation in Gaza was very bad while we were away. From what we understand, there was a violent outburst when the body of a missing Israeli soldier was discovered near Ashqelon. Perhaps in retaliation, the IDF shot many Palestinians in the Occupied Territories. On the first day of the feast which marks the end of the Holy Month of Ramadan, there seems to have been a particularly nasty incident in Nusseirat Camp. The trouble started as people were leaving the mosque after prayers. Several were killed and perhaps as many as 200 were wounded. In addition, there were further shootings in other parts of the Territories.

Also, there has been something of an Israeli civilian backlash to the murder of the young soldier. Palestinian cars have been stoned, and individual Arabs have been attacked in the cities of Israel. For some days, all Palestinian workers were forbidden to enter Israel, but now they are gradually returning to work. The *Jerusalem Post* reported large demonstrations in Ashqelon with crowds of people chanting "Death to the Arabs." It appears that Palestinians are now forbidden to enter that town.

We arrived back in Jerusalem on May 5th, only to discover that there was a general strike in the West Bank, and the entire Gaza Strip was under curfew. Consequently, we had to hole up in the National Palace Hotel until the curfew in Gaza was lifted. The next day was Friday and Arabs were prevented from entering the Old City to pray at the Dome of the Rock. On May 7th the curfew was lifted and two drivers from the Sun Centre came to take us back to Gaza via Tel Aviv. We could not go by our usual route through the countryside because the IDF was searching for the body of another missing soldier and feeling against the Palestinians was running high.

May 16th 1989

This has been a very strange day. Really it began at about 10 p.m. last night when the soldiers drove by announcing that we were under curfew until further notice. This was an unexpected announcement which we could not link to any special event.

This morning we were awakened by a donkey cart going by. As the morning wore on there were a number of cars on the street, and partially due to the lovely spring weather, there seemed to be something of a holiday atmosphere. Then we heard we were to be let out for an hour to shop, and suddenly the streets were full of people. The bakery across from our apartment did a brisk trade, and at one point there was a minor riot because it seemed as though they were running out of bread. People were very anxious to get food supplies in case this is a long curfew.

Suddenly, about noon, another announcement was made saying the curfew was to resume immediately. The announcement was accompanied by an increased military presence. They stopped cars and ordered people to return to their homes immediately. Soon the streets were deserted.

A few minutes later a truck full of soldiers stopped at the bakery and started to hassle the workers who were in the process of closing the shop. Just then a taxi came by, perhaps trying to race home due to the sudden re-imposition of the curfew. Two soldiers stopped it and searched both the car and its young driver. After this, they started to beat him. First, they forced his head in the trunk of the car and slammed the top down hard on his neck. After a minute or so, they let him out and proceeded to slap his face. At this point, another soldier left the truck and came to join in the beating. They eventually allowed the young man to leave, and he staggered to his car and drove away slowly.

This evening there has been a burning tire at a nearby intersection. Many people were out on their balconies watching the fire. From time to time, the young people poured gasoline on it to make explosions. It was a long time before any soldiers appeared on the scene. Actually, several Jeeps drove past the spot without stopping.

Eventually, two army vehicles stopped, and the soldiers got out. They went to many houses to bring people out to extinguish the tire, but the residents seemed to have vanished, and the soldiers were left to throw rocks at the windows in frustration. When the young people saw this they began to verbally taunt the soldiers from a nearby sidestreet, and this provoked a rather strong reaction. There was the sound of gunfire, perhaps five or six shots. Then tear-gas was thrown. I don't know if anybody was injured.

We still do not know why we are under curfew, and even the Voice of Israel seems confused on this point. They said workers were being prevented from entering Israel and those already there are being sent back to Gaza. Perhaps this is part of some new crackdown on the already-beleaguered Palestinians.

A little later in the afternoon a large number of army vehicles pulled up to the house next door. This house has a beautiful, walled garden where a group of small children often play contentedly in peaceful security. The Israelis went into the house with a long electrical cord to plug in some kind of machine. Then, back out on the street, they proceeded to drill holes in the wall in preparation for blowing it up with dynamite. The officers then had a long discussion, pointing and gesticulating toward Rhona and I who were observing the scene from the safety of our balcony. It seemed that a decision had been made not to demolish the wall, so instead the soldiers painted happy faces on it with black tar. I think they were punishing our neighbors for the political slogans which had appeared on their wall. Needless to say, they were not written by the residents of the home.

We don't know why the soldiers decided not to demolish the wall. Our neighbors thought it was because we were watching and the officers were concerned about Israel's image in the West. Salah said we had been brave and thanked us. In my opinion, neither were we brave nor did we have any influence on the decision about the garden wall. The real reason for their decision remains a mystery.

May 17th 1989

Last Saturday, the evening curfew was again enforced. This means we are not allowed out of the house from 8 p.m. until 4 a.m. The break in the evening curfew lasted for about two months.

On Monday evening, we were informed that we are now under 24-hour curfew. This is the second day of this bout of punishment. At about 3 a.m., we were awakened by the soldiers and their loudspeaker telling us that the curfew is still in effect.

Israel continues to win the media war. No journalists are allowed into Gaza, and Palestine has not even been mentioned in the last two days on the BBC World Service. The Voice of Israel regularly speaks of "riots" in Judaea and Samaria, and of Palestinian corpses being "snatched" from the hospitals by their families before the cause of death can be determined. The implications of the first statement is that some violent Palestinian demonstrators are breaking the civil law in parts of Israel. The second suggests that victims of the military occupation have been killed *not* by the soldiers but by other Palestinians. It would be more accurate to report "violent clashes" between the IDF and Palestinians in "the West Bank," and that the dead bodies had been "taken" from the hospitals by the families for early burial according to Islamic law.

While the Voice of Israel did not mention the present curfew in the Gaza Strip, it did report that three Palestinians had been killed. One of them was a 15-year-old boy from Jabalia Camp. It was reported that he was the instigator of an outbreak of stone-throwing against the soldiers.

We are convinced that the situation has been steadily deteriorating since the beginning of April. As evidence, we cite the fact that there were more casualties in April than in any other month since the beginning of the intifada. Unfortunately, the Canadian government seems to have little idea of what is happening. A few weeks ago we spoke to the people at the Canadian Embassy and they said UNRWA was reporting no change in the situation. This is most unusual as we heard the young people had recently invaded the UNRWA head office and stoned the UN Beach Club.

May 18th 1989

Today we awoke to find the daytime curfew had been lifted in our neighborhood. But, people in many places are still under house arrest and nobody is allowed to travel to Israel to work. This is not only a cause of hardship for the Palestinians but also for the Israelis. Many businessmen in the manufacturing and construction industries are complaining because their pool of cheap labor has disappeared.

Although there is high unemployment in Israel, many people refuse to do menial jobs which are almost exclusively the domain of the Palestinian worker. The relatively few Israelis who are employed as unskilled laborers generally earn a wage which is two or three times higher than that of Palestinians doing similar work. To add insult to injury, the Palestinians who are employed in Israel must pay union dues and contribute to the health fund even though they are not allowed to join the union or receive health benefits.

The Israeli government has announced that Gaza Strip residents will now be required to obtain a permit before they are allowed to enter Israel. They have also said that the 28,000 people they consider to be security risks will not be permitted to enter Israel at all. This means that many more Palestinians will be out of work and deprived of even a meagre income. My guess is that the long-term effect will cause even more unrest in Gaza.

There was some confusion this morning because although Hamas has called a strike, there were many cars on the street. Since Hamas was evidently allowing people a few hours' grace, we drove to the Sun Centre. But we soon heard a rumor that two people had been killed in the Shezjiyya district and the strike would begin at noon.

On hearing this news we drove home, only to be stopped by the *shabab* close to our house. We told them we were returning home, and they let us pass. When we were inside I went upstairs to ask Salah if he wanted us to put our cars in the garage early due to the strike. Just then, we looked out the window, and across the street two masked youths were spraying the strike announcement on a garden wall. Suddenly, some other youths shouted a warning and a van containing two soldiers screeched to a halt. The young men fled as the soldiers jumped from their vehicle firing into the air. After the escape of the fugitives, the soldiers could not get their van re-started and had to face the ignominy of pushing it down the street.

When the soldiers left, the young men soon re-appeared and proceeded to stone any Palestinian cars which were breaking the strike. They worked for a long time in trying to enforce their position, and this time we felt some sympathy for them. Sometimes it seems that this is an uprising of only the young as many older people seem to want to take the easy way out.

May 19th 1989

Today we are under curfew once more — perhaps this is a punishment for supporting yesterday's strike.

May 20th 1989

Another day under curfew. We suspect that the Israelis will let us out again tomorrow to try to break the scheduled strike which has been called by the United Leadership.

Today on the BBC World Service we heard that the soldiers prevented a truck loaded with flour from entering Rafah Camp. In the ensuing clash, it was reported that five Palestinians were killed and more than 20 wounded. The Voice of Israel said that four were killed and four wounded in "riots."

May 24th 1989

We learned today that during the curfew and strike days, one of our students, Iyad, was arrested by the soldiers. His family says that the soldiers were chasing some stone throwers who took refuge in their home. The soldiers followed them in and arrested Iyad who, it is claimed, was an innocent bystander. He is now in the infamous Ansar Two where he will be interrogated. Iyad will either be held in custody until his trial or he will be in administrative detention for a period of six months. No trial is necessary for periods of imprisonment of up to six months.

Iyad is the most kind-hearted of young men, and it is difficult to imagine him being a threat to the state of Israel. His role at social gatherings is to look after everybody and make sure they have enough food and a comfortable place to sit. Iyad calls everybody *habibi* which translates as "my love." His older brother was killed in the first days of the intifada.

May 25th 1989

Today I visited the Arab Affairs Department in Gaza to sort out a difficulty with our visas. I was accompanied by Susu Abu Ghazaleh who also had some business there. Fortunately for me, my concerns were dealt with fairly quickly, no doubt due to my being a citizen of a free country.

Susu's business was much more difficult to resolve. She was trying to retrieve the identity card of Ratib who is one of the drivers at the Sun Centre. Yesterday when he tried to leave the Gaza Strip on business for the Society, he was detained by the soldiers who confiscated his identity card. Without his identity card he can be arrested by any soldier who stops him and consequently cannot work.

We started in the office of the Military Governor and were then directed to the tax department. Here, the staff have the full backing of the army and are armed at all times. In this office, we discovered that the reason Ratib's identity card was confiscated was the tax department's claim that Hatem owed them some money. It was unbelievable that they could see nothing wrong with victimizing an innocent man who is totally uninvolved with Hatem's taxes, to say nothing of the indirect effect of their behavior on the lives of the handicapped children who rely on Ratib to transport them to and from school.

I tried to point out to the tax people the injustice of the situation. They said they understood my position but could do nothing as they were "just following orders." Where have we heard that before?

After much protest, the tax people came up with a compromise. They said they would return Ratib's ID card if Hatem gave his car to the authorities in lieu of the taxes. Of course this was no solution, and we left pending Hatem's early return from the United States.

May 27th 1989

Yesterday, for the first time in about two months, I felt that the situation in our neighborhood was quite calm. The same feeling has persisted today. I do not know the reason for this and am at a loss to explain the waxing and waning of the intifada. Perhaps, with so many of the leadership arrested, there is confusion and inertia among the ranks. However, I see this as a lull rather than an end to the troubles in Gaza.

Today we went to the headquarters of UNRWA to make a presentation to a group of Canadian military people from the National Defence College who were accompanied by a few of the diplomatic corps. The group was headed by Ambassador Jim Bartleman and the Chief of Staff from the Canadian Forces. We only had about 20 minutes with the group, but we were well-prepared and made excellent use of the time.

It was very nice to be with a group of Canadians who received us very warmly simply because we are citizens of their country. The experience brought on a severe attack of patriotism. Despite our self-criticism, Canada is surely one of the most hospitable countries in the world.

May 31st 1989

This is written at 7:45 a.m. on a strike day. In the street outside, black-hooded youths from the Hamas organization are hiding behind a wall and stoning passing vehicles. They have even stoned at least one UN vehicle. Hamas is giving a clear message that nobody is to break the strike.

Events in Palestine seem to be heating up a little. Last night, at least six people were injured by gunfire. Among them is an eight-month-old baby who is reported to be in critical condition. After the troubles of some weeks ago, Nusseirat Camp was put under curfew for 23 days. Although the curfew was lifted two days ago, it was re-imposed last night after a person was severely injured in a clash with the soldiers.

This month three Israelis and 33 Palestinians were killed. Twenty and 310 were the respective numbers of wounded. There were four strike days, and we were under curfew for eight days.

The Car Repair

I need cushions for chairs in the apartment. By now, I know where to get bread, meat, and vegetables, but I'm not sure where to find foamy innards for the hand-embroidered cushion covers I have been given. I go downstairs to visit Mellika and her mother, Umm Kamal, and the old *Haja*. They will know, but it will require the best part of an hour's visit, for unlike in the West, I cannot just go down and say, "Hey, anybody know where to get cushions in this place?" The courtesies must be observed.

I am invited in for coffee and gossip, the standard fare of Gaza. It's a good workout for my Arabic, and I pick up a lot of the local phrases on these visits. This evening I notice the huge iron bar placed across the formal entrance to their apartment and ask what it is for.

"To stop the thieves," they reply.

I feel this needs some checking out because we tend to be a bit cavalier about locking and bolting all our doors and windows. However, we are located on the second floor which I had figured might be more daunting to would-be trespassers with questionable intentions.

I inquire if there are many break-ins round the neighborhood, and if anybody has ever broken into our building.

"It's not so bad now that we have a nightly curfew," they say, "but we have heard that yesterday thieves broke into the locksmith's shop and stole nearly one million keys, so now we are afraid!"

In my mind's eye I see what must be the most patient, dedicated criminals in the world, their pockets bulging with a million keys as they work up to a B and E trying one after another..."732, 733..." until the right key turns in the lock, *hamdulilla!* But I make no comment other than "Aah," nodding my head slowly. I know better than to start getting logical.

I bring up the subject of cushions. Mellika knows the right shop and will take me there tomorrow at noon when she finishes teaching in the school near the Centre where I work. It will be a tight schedule for I have to be back by 1 p.m. to give a lecture, but Mellika says an hour will give us lots of time. I'm not so sure. Time does not have the same meaning for the Palestinians, whereas in contrast we Westerners are pretty well enslaved by it. Reaching a compromise can be tricky.

The next day I am at Mellika's school precisely at noon. She is ready for me, and we get into her car. She turns on the ignition and presses the gas pedal to the floor with the car in neutral, producing a sound like a NASA lift-off. The car seems to go into shock from this abusive assault, and stalls. We go through the procedure several times until the car is willing to move, and then we drive down past the main *suk* on Omar El-Mukhtar street, then beyond and into the back streets of the old town. It is an exotic sight reminiscent of the bazaars of Jerusalem and Cairo, with bustling shops and stalls, all apparently run by men. Tailors sit at sewing machines out in the street, sheltered from the sun by beach umbrellas that advertise Coca Cola or Marlborough cigarettes. They are wizards at repairing almost anything that is handed to them: bags, shoes, clothing. Mellika somehow finds a parking spot, and we get out of the car.

I would like to stay and just take in the sights and sounds but am aware of my time constraints and so try to keep up with Mellika who has disappeared into a shop doorway. I find her in a large warehouse room filled with foam pieces of all shapes and sizes, bolts of material and knitting accessories ad infinitum. We both realize from the look on the face of the boy who is in charge, that we will not get a bargain today. He has immediately identified me as a foreigner and so quotes a high price for two small cushions. Mellika protests, but he is not pleasant and walks away. I am tempted to do the same except that I don't know when I'll have another chance to find another cushion shop. In any case, we are running out of time. I hand him the money, and we hurry back to the car which is still quite warm and does not need to be traumatized into momentum again.

Mellika starts back but instead of following a direct route suddenly turns down what always seemed to be the busiest sidestreet in the city. Here the vendors' carts and trolleys spill out into the road, and as the human mass parts in front of us we find ourselves almost eyeball to eyeball with a startled donkey which is staring at us through the windshield. Mellika squeezes the car through spaces I would believe impossible, her horn joining the cacophony of voices, bicycle bells, donkey-braying, and traffic. Then she stops abruptly, gets out and tells me to wait just one minute; she has seen something she needs in a store. She reappears after a few minutes and we continue through the crush of traffic and humanity.

Just as we reach Palestine Square at the busiest intersection in the town, the car gives up the ghost and sits in the midst of the melee, smoke pouring from beneath the hood. We are surrounded by drivers shouting and honking while Mellika just shrugs at them and raises her hands in despair.

From nowhere, a group of young men push their way through and lift the hood, peering inside. They tell Mellika the car must have water. She gets out and opens the trunk, handing them a large plastic bottle filled with water which she carries at all times for what is obviously a common emergency. There must be six of them unscrewing caps and digging deep within the innards of the poor car. Fuses are needed. Maleka doesn't have any. *Maelish*, never mind. One of them is dispatched to find some. While he is gone, another of the young men hands Mellika a handful of wires he has just removed from the engine. He tells her to keep them in case she needs them later! Then the spare fuses appear. The repair work moves into high gear as they all "fix" whatever is wrong, giving the car what looks to me like a complete servicing! I abandon all hope of getting back to my students in time for the lecture. There is nothing I can do. To get out and offer to give a hand would be an insult to Palestinian manhood, so I sit scarved and silent, apart from telling Mellika not to worry. Peter will hopefully be on hand to stand in for me.

Suddenly the hood is slammed down, and they wave us away. They will accept no reward; Mellika calls out *Tislam iddaeku*, "Bless your hands," and ploughs into the maelstrom of traffic once more. The whole incident has taken maybe 20 minutes. I keep thinking about the bunch of wires now lying on the back seat like a microwaved bouquet, and I wonder how far we will get before the next crisis. But Mellika is cheerfully rattling on.

"You see how kind people are? They do all that for nothing. Always somebody will help you. Why does the world think we are terrorists?" And then, looking at her watch, "There! I told you we had plenty of time. You still have five minutes left before you must teach your class!" She laughs in happy relief. "Allah will always find a solution to the problems."

I am trying to compose myself for the lecture I had thought would have to be abandoned and so refrain from commenting that, from my perspective, Allah cuts it awfully fine and seems to be batting a straight zero in the larger arena of Palestinian problems. We kiss on both cheeks and I promise to visit downstairs tonight so that we can recount our adventure in detail to Umm Kamal and the *Haja*.

Omar's Garden

We are waiting at the checkout in the euphemistically-named Central Supermarket. Mellika had told me that here I would find everything; the supermarket was very big, she had said, and they sold everything you could imagine. Being accustomed to doing our weekly foraging through the miles of shelving and displays of a giant Western supermarket, we find this one to be the size of a largish living-room, offering perhaps a hundred items in all. But surprisingly we find Cornflakes, Western coffee, HP Sauce, and Kraft salad dressing which is two years old.

I pass the time in the short line-up looking at the shop signs across the street, putting my Arabic reading to the test, seeing how many words I can decode. I am as pleased as a pre-schooler at recognizing *Mataam*; the shop directly opposite the supermarket is a restaurant.

Outside the restaurant is a vertical cooking grill made of metal. A revolving spit slowly roasts a cone-shaped hank of meat which I never was able to identify. I was told variously that it was beef, lamb, or goat. The meat seemed to have been mounted on the spit in layers, each of which was rubbed with delicious spices, and the entire roast was crowned with whole onions and sometimes tomatoes so that as the spit turned, the juice from these vegetables trickled down adding even more mouth-watering aromas. This is *shawirma*, the Big Mac of Gaza. Slices and small pieces are trimmed from the roast and put into a pocket bread sandwich and filled with pickled vegetables and salad items set out on display and from which you can pick and choose.

The proprietor of the restaurant is named Omar. He is a flamboyant-looking character with a turban wound elaborately round his head, Iraqi style, for he hails from that country. The turban and Omar's white overall jacket at first give him the appearance of an exotic chef at a barbecue. Dark locks of hair lie round the nape of his neck and a black moustache curls across his lip, arching down at the corners of his mouth the way one used to see in childhood fairytale books about the Arabian Nights. Although he speaks Arabic, it is with such a thick accent that we rarely understand most of what he says; but what is lacking in verbal comprehension is more than compensated for in his warm, friendly gestures.

Our comfort in talking with him would gradually increase, but on this first encounter he fits every stereotype we saw in the old movies which were probably inadvertently racist in their depictions of sinister-looking Arab gentlemen. We ask about the *shawirma*, and he gives us a sample to try. It tastes fantastic and so we go for two sandwiches. He gives us generous helpings of everything, and includes extra bread. We talk to him about the sign on his shop, and he explains that the restaurant is not open anymore except by special request, and even then everything must be closed up by noon because of the intifada rules.

As we are walking back to the car, he suddenly calls out to us and beckons us to return, pointing to the interior of the shop. We are not sure what this is all about and hesitate briefly as we have to get back to give our lectures. But curiosity gets the better of us, and we go to investigate. Omar is inside the store.

"Welcome, welcome," he says.

The place seems to be in darkness, but we can tell that it is big. Tables and chairs are pushed against the walls, everything covered in dust. Omar walks toward a high, dark staircase at one side of the room and beckons us to follow. Eight years ago, as naive tourists in the Middle East, we would never have done this, having been conditioned to see Arab people as potential dagger-wielding thieves with bad intentions toward foreigners. Now we know better, for whenever we have been taken somewhere by Arabs, it has invariably turned out to be an interesting experience.

We have no idea where we are being led and the top of the stairs looks like a black hole. We grope our way to the top step and find ourselves on some kind of balcony, looking down on the counter and the room that we have just traversed. Omar seems to be grappling with something in the wall. A bolt slides back and he lifts a latch. "*Ta'al*," he says, "Come!" and a door swings open.

We find ourselves blinking in the daylight, wondering if we have just followed Alice down the rabbit hole, for we are in a beautiful garden full of roses and other flowers. A trellis-covered walkway cascading in vines and climbing roses, leads directly ahead to an octagonal-shaped gazebo made mostly of glass.

"Come! Look! Help yourselves; welcome," Omar says, watching our amazement with pride and pleasure. "Take your time," he adds and disappears.

We stroll down to the glass gazebo, rub the accumulated Gaza dust from one of the small panes, and peer through. Within are dust-covered chairs and tables, looking like an old, long-abandoned movie set. We can almost hear the ghostly echo of past, happier times, with families laughing and eating.

"Before the uprising we had many parties here; many people came every day." Omar has returned with a pair of secateurs. He guides us through the garden. One area used to be where the children were allowed to play on swings; the other side was for adults to sit or stroll through. Compared to what we have seen in Gaza so far, it is like something on another planet. We meander through the garden smelling the flowers. Omar selects the best rose blooms and snips off the long stems. As he leads us back through the magic door he hands the bouquet to me with a flourish of Arabic about roses and beauty, and tells us we can return to the garden any time.

After that first encounter with Omar, we returned fairly regularly to buy his delicious shawirma. He was always courteous, kind, and friendly. Occasionally, if I had a break between lecturing and visiting the school in Beach Camp, I would go just to walk round the garden for fifteen minutes. It was such a haven of peace in contrast to what was happening down below in the streets where the people fought daily, personal battles against the military occupation. Omar would nod his permission, walk over to a desk, open the drawer and hand me the secateurs. I would close the door behind me at the top of the stairs, and stroll around cutting roses.

Later, as I set them in a vase back at the apartment, I would sometimes be interrupted by the sound of gunfire out in the street and the explosions of tear-gas canisters. Closing the windows against the gas, I would look down and watch the soldiers, bullying and beating the people they perceive only as a terrorist nation, sometimes smashing windows with rocks hurled in violent frustration.

And I would wish that, just for one moment, they would put down their weapons and go and smell the flowers in Omar's garden.

CHAPTER NINE

June 1989

June 5th 1989

This is the second day of a curfew which has been imposed on the entire Gaza Strip. The official reason is to allow the IDF to carry out "special operations." However, the reason is more likely to be that June 4th and 5th mark the 22nd anniversary of the Israeli invasion of Gaza.

Yesterday it was pretty quiet until the late afternoon when we saw the usual burning tire in the closest intersection to our apartment. A few minutes later we heard two or three shots fired. Then an Israeli truck with two people in the cab left from the location of the burning tire.

We thought little more of this fairly typical incident until I listened to this morning's news on the Voice of Israel. It was then I learned that a teenager had been killed in the Sabbra district of the Gaza Strip, and the IDF were investigating. A little later, three Jeeps of military police appeared and seemed to be searching for empty cartridge shells in the intersection nearest our apartment.

When we asked our neighbors, they confirmed that a young man had been shot and killed near the house in the early evening of yesterday. This is the day of the funeral, and the area is tense. Young people are lurking in doorways, and we can hear the funereal chanting of many voices. Meanwhile, the Israelis have maintained a large military presence in the area, and at irregular intervals a phantom jet streaks over the rooftops with deafening noise.

I am especially shocked by this death because it took place so close to the house. It seems that the worst thing the teenager could have done was burn a tire in a main street and shout anti-Israeli slogans. For these "crimes" the punishment of death without a trial is totally unacceptable.

June 6th 1989

We are still under curfew.

By scrambling over walls and through the adjoining gardens, Salah had managed to get over to our neighbors' house to pay his last respects to the young man who was killed. When he arrived he found a party in progress. A large number of young people had also broken the curfew and assembled in the home where they sang Palestinian songs and danced the *dibka*. Salah said the young man's father was both happy and proud.

The party was to celebrate a new Islamic martyr. The faithful believe the young man has gone straight to Paradise because he fell fighting for Islam. This belief is so strong that fallen martyrs are not even prepared for burial; they are put straight in the ground. From all the chanting and singing, it seems that the spirits of the young Palestinians have not been dampened by this death.

June 7th 1989

Our fourth consecutive day under curfew. At 5:10 a.m., the soldiers announced the curfew over their loudspeaker. Because neither my Arabic nor theirs is fluent and the sound is distorted by the amplifier, I wasn't sure whether they were announcing the continuation or termination of the curfew. I got up shortly afterwards to see what was happening. The first clue was that the bakery across the street was closed. Then I saw a taxi which I took as a hopeful sign. But by 7 a.m., only the occasional UN or army vehicle was moving on the street.

I went back to bed for an hour, and then we got up and exercised for a while. "Exercise" consists of calisthenics with weights and jogging around the apartment. Rhona has an aerobics tape, but by now we are heartily sick of the music, so it is difficult for us to drum up much enthusiasm for this kind of activity.

The days have assumed a timeless quality. The weather is wonderful, and the sunlit streets, surreal in their emptiness. There are visits back and forth with the neighbors and gifts of food such as oranges, eggs, and stuffed olive leaves. We listen to the news on the radio and generally find the world has forgotten us. We are waiting to be recalled to life.

June 8th 1989

Our fifth day of curfew began slowly. As usual, I was up at 6 a.m. to check the street. Ittalatini Street was still and empty in the pale dawn light. We are facing another day of house arrest!

Just before 6 p.m. this evening, Susu phoned to say she had heard the curfew would be lifted for two hours, so people could shop for food and other necessities. Sure enough, a few minutes later people appeared on the streets, and the soldiers came around to make the expected announcement. I went with Rhona to the little grocery store down the street and we bought a few essentials: chocolate bars!

Pretty soon a holiday atmosphere prevailed. People poured out of their houses, pleased to be released after five days of confinement. Cars appeared on the street, and the whole area became a hive of activity. People stopped us to shake hands and ask how we were. They were smiling with happiness, and nobody spoke harsh words about the soldiers. It seems that our Palestinian neighbors are completely beaten down by the occupying forces.

June 9th 1989

In the late afternoon, a foot patrol was walking up the street. As usual, they rang our doorbell. We did not respond as we are used to this mild form of intimidation. As long as they try to play mind games with us, we will win. They are more bothered by the presence of foreigners in the area, than we are by the sight of soldiers.

I watched as this unit continued down the street and reached the place where a large palm leaf was attached to a lamp post. This is a symbol of the recent death of our teenage neighbor. As one soldier drew abreast of the palm leaf, he raised his uzi above his head and began to sing and dance. Evidently, he was celebrating.

June 10th 1989

This is the seventh day of the current curfew, but we have heard it will be lifted tomorrow, and we can return to work.

In the early hours of this morning, Aida and Susu were able to leave Gaza with a group of teachers and children from the Sun Centre. They are going to Washington D.C. to perform in an international arts festival for handicapped people. Hatem's negotiations with the Israeli authorities allowed everybody to get the requisite travel documents. I hope they do well. But even if they only make an appearance, it will be a great diplomatic victory for the Palestinians. Understandably, the teachers who have never been outside Gaza and the West Bank are beside themselves at the prospect of travelling to the United States.

This afternoon we were invited upstairs to Salah and Wasfia's apartment to meet some people from the Save the Children Fund. One of them is the Director of the agency in Gaza and West Bank, and a well-known member of the UN Beach Club. We also met a young American couple who are being interviewed for positions in Gaza, as the present Director and her husband will soon be leaving for Costa Rica. We had never met these people before as most of the foreign community are only vaguely aware of our existence. Their lives and social contacts tend to be more sheltered and centre on the UN Beach Club, an organization to which Palestinians are not allowed to belong.

Afterwards, both Rhona and I commented on the colonial attitude of these charity organizations. Generally, they do not identify with the local people as exemplified by them using special passes and driving around Gaza on curfew days. After the guests had left, I raised this issue with Salah, and he agreed that many foreign aid workers don't really trust the Palestinians or respect their aspirations.

Salah was quite forthcoming today and spoke of the political situation in Gaza. He said that all the professional associations and benevolent societies support the PLO and will form the infrastructure of local government when the Palestinians get their own country. He also thinks that the current young activists will have no problems in taking direction from these groups after a new state comes into being. I think Salah may be wrong on this point for the *shabab* are the true leaders of the intifada and will want to retain their power.

This evening we heard on the Voice of Israel that a 12-year-old boy from Jabalia Camp had been killed by the soldiers.

June 12th 1989

Today I drove to Ben Gurion Airport near Tel Aviv with Emad, one of the drivers from the Sun Centre. We went to meet Jenann Ismael who has come for three months as a volunteer to teach English to our diploma students. She will live with us during her stay in Gaza. A couple of weeks ago she tried to enter from Egypt via the Rafah border crossing but was turned back by the Israelis. Today she flew from Canada and had no problems in gaining entry to the country.

June 15th 1989

It has now been five days since the curfew ended, and the situation in Gaza is surprisingly quiet. I'm not sure of the reason, but it may be due to the schools having re-opened for the end-of-year exams. However, today the preparatory schools finished, so perhaps Gaza will heat up again.

Although there have been no real events, the rumor mill has been working overtime. There are dire threats of curfews which will last from 8 to 14 days and could start at any moment. When I have asked why there will be a curfew I have been told:

–Israel has decided to impose a two-day curfew for every strike day, and Syria has called for a four-day strike in Gaza.

–The Egyptians have told the Israelis to do this to prevent cheating on the school exams.

–The curfew will be imposed to stop Hamas from encouraging the students to cheat on the final exams.

I think none of this will happen and that the rumors are due to the stress of being under curfew for a week.

Today the Voice of Israel announced that four Israeli soldiers had been found guilty of beating a Palestinian prisoner to death. They were each sentenced to between six and nine months imprisonment. The judge commented that he gave light sentences because he couldn't tell which of the four soldiers actually struck the blow which killed the man. I wonder what the sentence would have been if four Palestinians had beaten an Israeli to death?

June 23rd 1989

The last 24 hours have been interesting and somewhat tense. Yesterday Chris George, the Director of the Save the Children Foundation was kidnapped in Gaza. This of course put all foreign personnel in danger as we thought it might be the beginning of the mindless trend which is still prevalent in Lebanon. We decided to adopt a "wait and see" attitude, but felt quite tense, and as the obvious target in the group — the male leader — it was decided I should not go out unaccompanied.

Today we were invited to the farm of our neighbors, the Sakkar family. We travelled to the beautiful countryside of the central Gaza Strip and spent a few relaxing hours amid bucolic splendor in the company of very friendly Palestinian people.

When we returned home all hell was breaking loose. The Canadian Embassy had been desperately trying to reach us. The message was we were to remain at home until we received further instructions from John McNee. Because nobody knew of our whereabouts when the Embassy first tried to contact us, people had begun to speculate that we might already have been kidnapped.

When I finally contacted John, he suggested a couple of options which I rejected. He thought that we should move to a safer location such as our old apartment at the Sun Centre or a room at the UN Beach Club. Eventually, it was agreed that we should remain inside our present apartment for the next couple of days until we see how the situation develops.

This evening Roy Brown in Calgary called about the kidnapping of Chris George. Mitch Clark and the people at Mount Royal College are strongly in favor of us leaving Gaza right away. Roy was also leaning in this direction. However, at that moment Salah came to the door and told us that Chris had been released unharmed. This gave me some ammunition in my discussion with Roy, and we were able to postpone the decision to leave until Monday. I am sure that by then things will have calmed down and life will be back to what passes for normal in Gaza.

The effects of the kidnapping were interesting. It is claimed that the perpetrators were members of the Palestine Popular Army, an elite faction of the PLO. If this is true, their action received total condemnation, and many local Palestinian organizations spoke out against it. This is very encouraging, and we doubt there will be similar incidents in the future. It was also reassuring to discover the Embassy and our colleagues are concerned for our safety.

June 25th 1989

Selim Abu Ramadan came into our diploma program a few weeks ago. He was a quiet young man who worked hard with a minimal amount of prompting. So, I was surprised to hear that he had been arrested by the soldiers. He was missing from class for about a week, and then I heard he had been released but was injured.

Today he came to the Centre to say that he no longer wished to participate in the program. When asked why, he avoided giving a direct answer. I did not pursue the issue, feeling the truth would emerge in its own good time.

His injuries were readily apparent. He had sustained a blow to the side of his head just behind the right temple. This area of his skull seemed flattened and new skin was forming over a flesh wound. He also had a broken wrist.

Selim told me he had been arrested and beaten by the soldiers. They asked him about his work, and he told them he was a student. They said that if he was a student, they wanted to see him write. As he began to write, a soldier deliberately struck him on the right wrist with a club. The blow was delivered with sufficient force to break the bone. The soldiers went on to say that when his arm was healed, they would return to arrest him again. Perhaps this is the reason he does not want to continue in the program.

June 29th 1989

On June 26th Rhona, Jenann, and I travelled to Tel Aviv to attend a party hosted by the Canadian Embassy in honor of Canada Day. As usual, we stayed at the Carlton Hotel where we changed from our travelling clothes into our party outfits. As Rhona's clothes were black, she chose to complement them with a black and white *keffiya*.

The party was held at the residence of the Canadian Ambassador in a fashionable suburb on the coast north of Tel Aviv. When we arrived the affair was in full swing, and there seemed to be about 150 people in the garden at the rear of the house. We were greeted by Michael Mace who is the Charge D'Affaires since the Ambassador is in Washington. Other people greeted us including John Campbell, the Australian Ambassador, and most of the staff from our embassy. Many people were curious about Gaza, and we spent an enjoyable time relating our experiences.

After a while, Rhona's *keffiya* was noticed by a group of Israeli officials. They were outraged, and some even left the party. One of the Israeli ministers gave Rhona a lecture which consisted of Israeli propaganda about the history of the present situation. An Israeli woman attacked her verbally, becoming quite irrational. Rhona remained calm, made her points and was friendly and polite in the face of these assaults.

Later, I joined the conversation with this woman. However, It was largely a one-way street as she seemed quite incapable of listening to others. At one point, she shouted, "Fifty Israeli soldiers have been killed during the intifada and every one was like my son!" "This is terrible," I agreed. "But what about the 500 Palestinians who have also died?" "They do not matter — they are all terrorists," she said. I then asked if it was permissible for the Israeli soldiers to kill children. "Yes," she replied unequivocally. I was so shocked by her response that I repeated my question. "Yes! Yes!" she said again. "Because they are not children, they are terrorists."

Meanwhile, Jenann had an interesting interaction with another woman who was hovering in the background during this conversation. "Who are these people from Gaza?" she asked, pointing in our direction. "They are working on a Canadian project," Jennan said. "Would you like me to introduce you?" At this offer the woman backed away, shaking her head and saying, "Everybody in Israel knows the Canadian Embassy is pro-Palestinian."

June 30th 1989

This month one Israeli and 22 Palestinians were killed. The total number of deaths for the first six months of 1989 is nine and 151 respectively. During this period, 37 Israelis and 1,422 Palestinians were wounded. In June, there were four strike days and the entire Gaza Strip was under curfew for a period of seven consecutive days.

A Day In The Country

One Friday in June we return early from the Centre, change out of our teaching clothes and follow Salah's car to the farm owned by his family. We drive for a few kilometres down the beach road with its spectacular sand and blue-green breakers crashing onto the shore. Here, men and boys are the only people playing and enjoying the sea.

Eventually, we turn left and head inland down a winding road, passing an Israeli settlement built on land expropriated from Salah's farm. Further along we come to the beautiful little mosque built at the roadside by Abu Kamal, Salah's father. Here we turn off the paved road and drive a short way along a dirt track leading to the farm gate.

The tenant farmer, Fayez, has two wives but no children. I think his wives are the happiest women I have seen in Gaza. They get along well together, and the fact that Fayez is probably sterile means that they are not burdened with children on top of all the other farm work they are expected to do. Furthermore, the house and agricultural work is halved by the fact of there being two of them. By Gazan peasant standards they have it made!

As we walk into the small paved courtyard, mattresses are brought out and set in the shade for our comfort. The rooms inside the single story buildings are primitive. There are cement walls and floors, a bed, a cupboard, a picture of the Dome of the Rock hanging crookedly from a nail driven into the wall, and a Singer treadle sewing machine. This last item, along with the television placed on the bed for viewing, is the pride and joy of its owners and I am requested to take photographs with the women posed beside it.

We first go to visit the grave of old Abu Kamal who died on Land Day. It is a simple memorial set in a small, walled garden behind the mosque. The white headstone is engraved in Arabic, with rectangular marble slabs placed step-like below and in front of it. Peter and I have brought flowers which we place by the grave, as Salah and the family express their appreciation for this small act of recognition and respect. Mellika tries to contain her grief, but when I hug her we both have a quiet cry. We still miss the old man.

People begin to arrive at the mosque for the Friday prayers. They come in cars, on donkeys, and bicycles, and I believe there is even a camel in the parking area. The prayers are essentially a tape recording of one of the most famous muezzin's in Egypt and are broadcast across the countryside by means of speakers placed atop the minaret.

Peter spends the time with Fayez, while Salah attends prayers. I return to the courtyard with the women who serve a smorgasbord of *salata*, stuffed vine leaves, *bamia*, and rice. We are joined shortly by a shy, pretty young Bedouin girl who lives nearby. Beneath her long skirt and cover-up blouse I can see that she is wearing jeans and a t-shirt. Her fresh young face is framed by hair swept back from her face in a pony tail. She smiles and responds quietly to my questions but has no idea what to say back to this strange foreigner. She has probably never met an *azjnabiyya* before.

After the main meal is finished, the two wives start to make the popular, large, flat rounds of crispy bread in one of the small

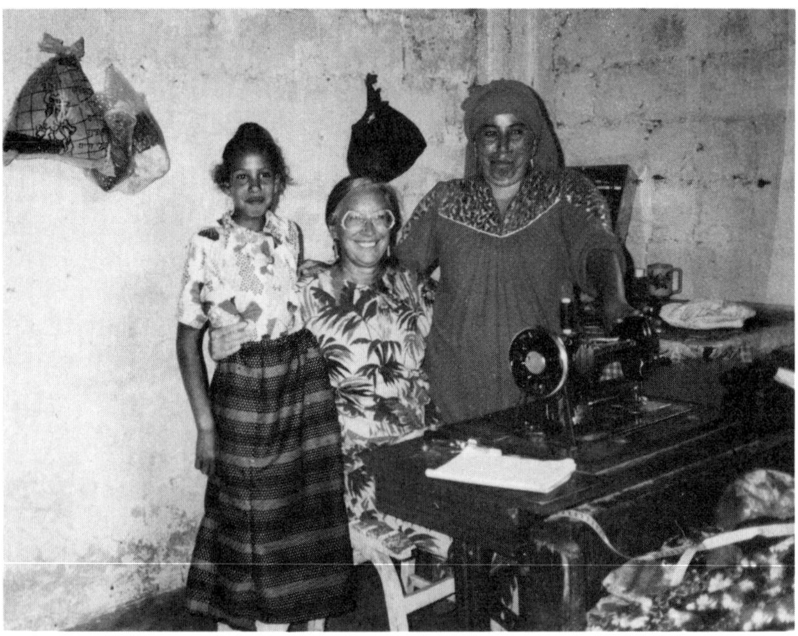

Rhona and two friends pose by the sewing machine which is the treasured possession of the farmer's wife (right).

breeze-block cement rooms that has a dirt floor and corrugated tin roof. A traditional clay oven stands in the middle of the small room, but this is not what they are going to use today to make the bread. Twigs and dried, dead leaves are taken in handfuls from a huge pile by the door and pushed beneath an inverted, wok-like cooking pan. The dried fuel is ignited and fanned to get the fire glowing hot. As the smoke begins to rise, it combines with thin rays of sunlight streaming through small holes in the corrugated metal roof, giving the illusion of a waterfall. Indeed, for a minute I am convinced it must have started raining outside. The scene from the doorway is very biblical, with the two women sitting on their haunches, the firelight glowing on their faces, and celestial sun-rays shining down on them. It reminds me of old paintings from the Holy Land and the stable where the Christ-child is described as being born. It is one of the most beautiful memories I have of Gaza.

From a bowl of prepared dough, one of the women tears off a handful and shapes it into a ball. I watch carefully as she rolls it out flat on a small wooden board and then passes it to her companion. The flat rounds of dough are then tossed back and forth across the hands and forearms, gradually increasing in size until they look like enormous pancakes about 16 inches in diameter. The task is performed with such skill that it looks easy. I have been assigned to rolling out the dough on the wooden board, but when they see me watching them they invite me to try my hand at throwing the dough back and forth. I am totally inept, much to their amusement.

Their laughter is not unkind, but I think they are puzzled by a woman who says she has raised children but who doesn't even know how to make bread pancakes. They have no real understanding of educated women. I suspect they think we're phonies.

As I sit and watch, assisting when asked, I am reminded of a previous occasion when we visited a family in the Rafah refugee camp. It had been during my early days in Gaza, and I was not so familiar with the accents of the camps. For almost an hour, I had sat in the women's quarters, struggling with the language. During a pause, one old *Haga* had turned to me in annoyance and said quite angrily, "Why don't you learn to speak Arabic?" I had replied that indeed I was trying, but that I found it a difficult but beautiful language.

"It isn't difficult at all!" she responded. "Why! The children all speak it without a problem!" She reminded me of the Queen of Hearts, and I half expected to hear her shout, "Off with her head!"

The *Haga* had no idea how you go about learning anything or the studying and memorizing that is involved. I doubt it would have made much difference if she had. Education, from her perspective, was a waste of time. Why do you need books and education to raise children and slave away at housework? Telling her I was a lecturer from a university cut no ice at all.

In contrast, the two farm women indulged my apparent incompetence rather kindly on the whole, encouraging me with *shatra* (clever).

Next on the agenda are rides on the donkey-cart with Salah's children, Ahmed, Rami, and Karma. I am pleased I had the foresight to wear the traditional Palestinian dress given me by the Bad Boys, for it covers me very adequately in this rural part of the country where tradition is strict. Karma sits huddled close to me, with my arm around her, and I pull the scarf-veil well over my hair and face as we set off along the dirt track threading its way between fields of vegetables and citrus groves. I am surprised at how difficult it is to balance on a two-wheeled cart! The Palestinian women do it with such style and dignity. I desperately try to hold onto the cart with one hand and Karma with the other as we bump along between the fences made of prickly-pear cactus. We meet and pass other donkey-carts, and farmers on foot, exchanging the greeting, "*Essalaamu alleykum*" as we go by. Sometimes, in the scrub by the side of the track, Bedouin have constructed shelters of twigs, branches, and that ubiquitous miracle of Western technology — plastic sheeting. These are their homes. I marvel at how they survive the very wet, cold winters.

The boys are exuberant at being allowed to play peasant. It is totally appropriate for them to be in charge of the driving, even though they are so young. Mostly, they seem to see the occasion as an opportunity to abuse the poor donkey, for they beat it repeatedly and several times thrust the driving stick into the beast's anus to make it go faster. My admonitions go mostly unheeded since I am female and an *ajnabiyya* to boot. They need the firm hand of their father Salah. On our return, I am gratified to see the farmer chastise them when they again start to beat the poor animal.

A walk through the orange and lemon groves with the family, the farmer and his wives, brings our visit to its conclusion. The land originally extended down to the sea before it was claimed for the Israeli settlement with its ugly red-roofed houses impinging incompatibly on the biblical nature of the scene around us. Soon we are prevented from going further by barbed wire and security fences, so we turn and stroll back through the groves.

The farmer and his wives inundate us with gifts of the delicious flat bread, oranges, and lemons and we leave feeling, as always, overwhelmed by the Arab generosity and kindness.

On our return to the apartment, we find a driver from the Centre waiting with messages from the Canadian Embassy in Tel Aviv and the University in Calgary. Ironically, while we have been enjoying a relaxing day with Palestinians out in the country, the embassy and university staff have been desperately trying to locate us. Feeling completely safe with Salah, his family, and Fayez and his wives, it had never occurred to us to notify anyone of our planned day in the country. We are shocked to learn that an international worker for the Save the Children Society has been taken hostage. His whereabouts and situation are unknown. Fearing that we have suffered a similar fate, our compatriots are relieved when we report in. It is a jarring, embarrassing conclusion to an otherwise idyllic day.

Salah is concerned that all Palestinians are being judged on the basis of this isolated incident, and does his utmost to assure the Canadians that we are valued and safe. Nonetheless, we are instructed by the embassy to consider moving into the UN Beach Club facility for a while. The university orders us to pack our bags and leave immediately. We do neither, and in the end negotiate to remain in our apartment for the next forty-eight hours, by which time we are sure the matter will have been cleared up.

Thankfully our intuition turns out to be correct. A few hours later the kidnap victim is found walking along the beach road, shaken but unharmed.

The Assistant

She climbs the four flights of marble-tiled stairs one at a time, step-and-a-hop, step-and-a-hop, using the arm and leg remaining to her on the left side to haul up the primitive prosthetics which are in lieu of the right arm and leg she lost to the cause of one country's expansionism and another's resistance. In present-day intifada terminology, she is called a hero. To those of us less tolerant of patriarchal rhetoric, she is one of the innocent victims of war, of whom women and children often comprise the greatest number, being rendered both physically and psychologically disabled by this predominantly male activity.

Yet she does not invoke pity — far from it. Rather, incredulity and admiration are foremost in an observer's mind as she negotiates the four flights of stairs sometimes twice or more each day. The elevator, installed for differently-abled people like herself, has not functioned for at least a year. The Israeli engineer who is able to perform the repairs is too fearful to come to Gaza because of the current hatred and conflict between the two national groups; a Palestinian with the ability to do the job is not to be found.

She remembers it all. The old town had been under curfew for days, the citizens allowed out for only one hour in every period of twenty-four in order to get food. She had gone down to the street to play with her younger sister, and there in the gutter she had spotted what she thought was a treasure that would solve the hardships of her family. It was gold-colored; the size and shape of a large egg. Believing it to be real gold she picked it up to take to her father so that he could sell it for more money than her childish mind could imagine.

Her curiosity was piqued by the covering cap. What might be inside? She began to remove the cap; as she did so there was a strange hissing sound of escaping air which attracted the attention of a passerby who called out in alarm, telling her to throw the grenade quickly, quickly! Misunderstanding his admonition, and believing herself to be obeying his command, she threw it to the ground at her feet.

There was an explosion she describes as being like the end of the world. She felt herself hurled into the air and then falling. She remained conscious. Strangely, she recalls no pain at this point. Her family carried her into the house where they tried to stop the bleeding with the only medication to hand: iodine. She remembers looking down and seeing her hand dangling from her wrist, and her shattered leg a mass of torn flesh and mangled bone. She was eight years old.

Her father set out carrying his maimed child to the small, local hospital. The curfew had been reimposed, necessitating his taking to the backstreets for fear a passing patrol would spot him and shoot. Eventually, he reached the hospital. The casualties were too numerous for the limited services and staff available, and the doctors advised immediate amputation of both hand and leg. She was taken to the primitive operating theatre, laid on the table and, with no anaesthetic, subjected to the horror of watching her limbs cut off. It is at this point that she first recalls feeling pain, when the doctors stitched the flaps of skin over the stunted remains of her young body. Mercifully she at last fell unconscious.

She remained in hospital for a year, recovering slowly, receiving physiotherapy, learning to walk on crutches. Thanks to the concerned intervention of a Palestinian UNRWA worker she was permitted to attend an UNRWA school close to her home, rather than the regular public school some distance away. This was unusual for she is not from the refugee population which receives services and assistance from UNRWA. She did well in school and later was to earn a degree from a university in Cairo.

I ask her where anger comes into this story, and she replies that only once has she felt angry, and that was when she was rejected for a teaching position in Saudi Arabia. She had arrived for the interview unobserved by the selection committee, and had sat in the waiting room while they examined her papers. A committee member emerged from the office and informed her that she was accepted. He handed her some papers and directed her to take them to another office down the hall. Delighted, she proceeded to follow his instructions, thus revealing her limp. He called out to her in surprise. The committee had not known she was handicapped; how could they employ a handicapped woman? What would people say? They could not have this in Saudia.

In our interview, this is the only point at which she expresses outrage. She does not blame the Israelis; it was just her "unfortunate luck," she says in her own way of expressing her Muslim acceptance of fate. But the Saudis are fellow Arabs; they should know better and do more to help their less fortunate sisters and brothers in Palestine. She does not forgive them for rejecting her on the basis of her disability.

Compared to many handicapped women in the Occupied Territories she considers herself fortunate. She is independent, holding a job with considerable esteem as a teaching assistant in a university-level program in rehabilitation studies. She is also the sole source of income for her family of two parents, and twin teenage brothers and a sister all still in school. Although unmarried, she would like to have a husband and children. However, the chances of this happening seem remote in a situation where Western concepts of self-advocacy and recognition of personhood for handicapped people are low on the list of a populace whose prime concern is a battle for human rights and the restoration of a nationality that has been forcibly suppressed.

There are other cultural inhibitors. She tells me that several men have approached her family seeking marriage. However, she is in a "Catch-22" situation. The men have known of her earning capacity and would have liked to either boost their own incomes or have access solely to hers; but she fears that marriage will mean the termination of her employment, there being no effective unions or adequate legislation to protect women in this society from such discriminatory practices. Thus, she says, once the men knew that marriage might jeopardize her income, the offers were withdrawn.

She receives charitable funding for the purchase and maintenance of her prosthetics. It comes from the PLO offices in Jordan, a fact that causes her endless difficulties. The military government will not permit her to receive the money in Gaza, it being deemed from a terrorist source. The fact that the disability was caused by what many people might interpret as state-approved terrorism in the form of military oppression, seems of no concern to the occupying authorities. To be fitted with her right arm and leg, she must first apply for a pass from the military government to enable her to travel to Jordan. She has to plan weeks in advance, apply and wait for approval, go for interrogation, and then arrange her travel. At the end of it all she is grateful to return with third-rate mechanical limbs.

On returning from her last trip for fittings and parts, she proudly showed me her new arm. The sole visible improvement so far as I could discern was the fact that the simulated skin color was a slightly better match and constructed of a softer plastic. But no, I had not seen everything. Looking closer, she showed me how the thumb and forefinger seemed slightly flexible. And then the real marvel of this new monstrosity: reaching inside her blouse she located a piece of string, and hauling on it with all her energy, the gap between the two digits closed sufficiently to allow her to hold a pen or pencil. She was delighted. I was appalled at the indignity of the procedure in an age of technology that sends probes to distant galaxies but ignores the needs of earthbound humans. By 11 in the morning, the hideous string no longer functioned; by two o'clock in the afternoon the ball-joint in the wrist had broken and I found her in the office struggling with the dangling appendage in the sleeve of her blouse; by the following day she had abandoned the whole thing in favor of the old, primitive prosthetic, and I was on the verge of weeping or screaming or both.

Her status as a hero of Palestine is a label whose identification is a single event afforded her the day of her mutilation. What is not recognized is the daily, and for her, lifelong heroism that is climbing four flights of stairs, step-and-a-hop, struggling in and out of servis taxis, an agonizing two-mile walk home on a strike day, and uncertainty about her long-term future where, with no rights to a pension of any kind, she fears becoming dependent upon the goodwill of her brothers and their wives whom she says may not necessarily feel kindly toward her once her productivity ceases. Her fears may not be unfounded, for Arab researchers have found that disabled people are a source of shame for their families.

There is, however, a terrible irony in her present situation when cultural aspects relating to the status of women in Gaza are considered. One has to begin by asking what would her quality of life have been had the accident not happened. What does the non-handicapped Palestinian woman have to look forward to? This is a culture that remains both tribal and traditional; where the ideals of femininity require silence, obedience, and immobility. These characteristics are maintained by secluding females in their homes and mostly excluding them from dealing with society-at-large. It would be impossible in this culture for a woman to ride a bicycle, for example. The restrictive, requisite sack-like garments are designed to restrict women's movements to nothing more than steps about one foot apart. It is not unusual in some smaller towns in the Gaza Strip for women to come to a complete standstill if they see a man approaching in the street, for fear that they will be viewed as sexually provocative.

Our assistant cannot therefore be pitied on grounds of immobility, since culturally this is a male ideal of female beauty. Had she not lost her limbs she would most likely have been sought after for marriage at an early age (fifteen for females is not uncommon in Gaza) by a male cousin in all likelihood considerably older than herself. Furthermore, it is quite possible that she could have become some man's second or third wife, with a status that rendered her pretty much the servant to everyone in the family. It is unlikely that she would have been allowed to complete her education in Egypt, far from the protection of male members of the family, for fear that she would be perceived as having committed some unforgivable offence for which her family had abandoned her, thus rendering her worthless and subject to all manner of abuse.

Her terrible disfigurement therefore, while precluding marriageability, at the same time has permitted her safe participation in an economic domain denied to most women in her culture. As a wage-earner she has status within both her work domain and her family environment. Far from the servile role ascribed to daughters, daughters-in-law, and women in general, she is respected, consulted and obeyed in many family matters. She therefore enjoys a freedom and autonomy largely unknown and inaccessible to the majority of her "sisters" in traditional Muslim cultures where fertility appears to predetermine the restrictive role of women to a life of hardship, illiteracy, drudgery, poor health care, and polygyny.

The tragedy of our Palestinian assistant lies in the fact that the loss of her limbs and thus her desirability as a female in a traditional culture have afforded her status as a *person*. She exists. She is visible. She can move relatively freely in the male-dominant world of economics and employment. Viewed from this perspective one might question who, in the final analysis, is more handicapped — our handicapped but independent colleague, or the fully able-bodied women destined for early marriage and a life of anonymity and invisibility.

This is the kind of dichotomy that persists for women worldwide, whereby their sex is their destiny. History gives testimony to the fact that they have been judged first on their femaleness, not on ability. If they are perceived as feminine (pretty and compliant) their work is treated flippantly; if they are viewed as unattractive to males (plain and assertive) their work is treated as an expression of frustrated maternity and sexuality.

Our assistant's appalling mutilation might therefore be seen as having contributed in a bizarre way toward her career fulfillment in a society that still has much ground to cover in terms of redeeming its female population from the bondages of gender and fertility.

(This essay with minor changes was first published in *The Journal of Practical Approaches to Developmental Handicap*, 1990, 14(2). It is reprinted here with the kind permission of the Editor.)

CHAPTER TEN

July – August 1989

July 4th 1989

Today there is a strike. There was a burning tire and shooting at the intersection about 100 metres away. We have spent the majority of the day with Azzad and Ahmed waiting for Iyad to be released from Ansar Two.

Azzad and Ahmed were in court yesterday when Iyad's case came up. For the third time, the key prosecution witness, a soldier, did not show up. Azzad spoke with the prosecutor and managed to persuade him to agree to bail on this occasion so that Iyad would not automatically be returned to jail to await his next appearance in court. Bail was finally set at $1,500 (US) and Iyad's family somehow managed to raise the money. I have been told that even if the accused appears for the trial, the money is never refunded.

Now more than 24 hours later, the Israelis have still not released Iyad. To date, he has been in prison for 45 days on suspicion of throwing stones at the soldiers. His trial has been re-scheduled for August 13th.

July 6th 1989

Iyad was finally released from prison at 9 p.m. on July 4th. This was during the curfew so nobody was able to meet him, and he had to walk home alone. If he had been stopped by an IDF patrol, he could have been re-arrested for breaking the curfew.

We managed to get a message to Iyad telling him to head for our apartment which is near Ansar Two. We put on all the lights as a signal, and at about 9:30 p.m., I saw Iyad limping down the street. He called out to me, and I went down to let him in. Although he was smiling, this normally smartly-dressed young man was in poor physical condition. He was dirty and sweaty and dressed in worn and torn prison clothes. We all kissed and hugged in the Arab style and had a very emotional reunion.

After we brought Iyad into the apartment, Azzad and I went into the study to try to telephone for somebody with a car and a curfew pass to take him home. As we were telephoning, somebody hurled a fist-sized rock through the study window. One of the local *shabab* had seen the lights on and heard the commotion as we were greeting Iyad. He (they) decided that by having what sounded suspiciously like a party, we were not being supportive of the intifada and so punished us. I am outraged by this incident and feel we are now being abused by both the Israelis and the Palestinians.

Azzad's telephone call was successful. After about ten minutes, an ambulance with a flashing light pulled up outside the house. All three young men climbed in and drove off through the empty streets to Iyad's home where his family was anxiously awaiting his return.

Today there was a terrible incident on a bus travelling from Jerusalem to Tel Aviv. As it was passing through the Judaean Hills, a young Arab man approached the front of the bus, shouted "*Allahu akbar*!" wrested the steering wheel from the driver, and drove it into a deep ravine. Fourteen Israelis were killed and a further 27 were badly injured. The world will scream that the perpetrator of this heinous act is a terrorist, but what drove him to such desperation?

July 11th 1989

Today a group of the former diploma students held a party in our apartment. They were celebrating for a variety of reasons including Iyad's release from prison and the visit from Amman of Mona, one of our former students who had married a Jordanian. It was good to see them all together again.

Tomorrow, we are going to spend a few days in a hotel in Tel Aviv. We need to get out of Gaza as we have been here for two months without a break. The Feast of the Sacrifice begins tomorrow and this marks the end of the annual pilgrimage to Mecca. It is a five-day holiday similar in length to the feast at the end of Ramadan.

July 15th 1989

The political situation continues to be quite tense with numerous killings on both sides. After the recent bus disaster, a number of Palestinians were killed in retaliation. Yesterday an elderly Israeli was stabbed to death by two 16-year-old Arab teenagers in an argument about the payment of wages. So far this month 15 Israelis and 16 Palestinians have died violently.

Almost on a daily basis, the Voice of Israel reports that a suspected collaborator has been murdered in the Occupied Territories. Undoubtedly, this is reported to give the impression that the PLO has to resort to murder and intimidation in order to prevent the population of Gaza and the West Bank from cooperating with Israel. It is a strategy designed to undermine the role of the PLO as the sole legitimate representative of the Palestinian people.

It is the lack of education of the Palestinians which lies at the root of the murders of the collaborators. Their culture and tradition place the extended family or tribe as the focal point of a person's loyalty. The idea that one might be more loyal to one's country than to a second cousin, for example, seems absurd to most Palestinians. Consequently, Israel has never had any difficulty in finding informers who will spy on a neighboring family in return for money, a gun, or privileges which would set them above other families. Many sources estimate that there are thousands of these paid informers in the Gaza Strip alone.

I believe that the so-called murders of the collaborators fall into three categories. The first are the true informers who have been discovered by the neighborhood intifada committees and executed. The second and third are those people who have been labelled as drug dealers and prostitutes. I think the former are largely killed as a result of inter-family feuds, while the latter seem to be women who have lost the support of their families for a variety of cultural reasons.

In spite of these terrible murders and the ensuing Israeli propaganda, there is one thing which reflects very well on the Palestinians. Given that there has been no locally-supported police force in the Gaza Strip since the beginning of the intifada, there is little crime. There are Israeli police present, but very few Palestinians would ever go to them to report a violation. I try to imagine what the United States would be like if there was no recognized police force for more than a year. In my opinion the ensuing looting, raping, and killing would create a crime wave of mammoth proportions. It is a credit to the self-discipline and religious beliefs of the Palestinians that there has been relatively little crime in the last year and a half.

July 20th 1989

Hatem was summoned for an appointment with the Military Governor of Gaza yesterday. An Israeli newspaper had printed a photograph of the handicapped children's visit to Washington. In the picture, a handicapped Palestinian child is shown with Jean Kennedy Smith, and he is giving the "V" for Victory sign. The Military Governor seemed to interpret this as an act of hostility against the State of Israel. Hatem was called in to explain why he had trained the children to do this after the authorities had been so kind in allowing them to travel to the United States. Hatem explained that children do not learn this behavior from the teachers at school but from their siblings on the streets of Gaza. It seems difficult to believe that such a spontaneous and widely-used gesture could have caused so much concern in the Military Governor's office.

July 23rd 1989

Today we returned to work following a strike called by the Hamas organization. The Voice of Israel reported that it was a commercial strike, i.e., only the stores were closed. They went on to say that only three people were wounded by gunfire, even though the Palestinians claimed that dozens were injured. We observed that there was a full strike in Gaza yesterday and from the amount of shooting we heard from Beach Camp, one would have thought there would be more than three casualties in that single location.

About mid-morning, I was asked to see a 15-year-old student who was mentally retarded. He told me that yesterday he and his twin brother, who is also mentally handicapped, were emptying garbage from their home into the receptacle on the street corner when they were arrested by the soldiers. They were handcuffed, blindfolded, and beaten with clubs. I saw the welts and bruises on his arms, shoulders, back, and legs. My feeling was the blows had been administered with great force in a manner which would maximize the pain but minimize the physical damage. In other words, this handicapped teenager had been subjected to a professional beating.

July 25th 1989

This morning I was awakened by the doorbell at about 5:30 a.m. I got up and answered through the intercom. It was the soldiers. I was angry at being disturbed and still only half awake, so in Arabic I told them to go away. In response, they smashed in the street door, entered the yard, and started to kick in the door at the bottom of the stairs. I went downstairs closely followed by Salah who was coming from the apartment above.

When the door opened we encountered two young soldiers pointing their guns at us. Furious, I said, "What do you want? It is 5:30 a.m. and I was sleeping." This was the first time I had spoken English, and obviously they had thought it was a Palestinian talking to them through the intercom. One of the soldiers started to apologize, but the other was more belligerent. They asked Salah to show identification and demanded he remove the writing that had appeared on the wall overnight. Knowing he and his family were at risk, Salah agreed to clean the walls.

I suppose I must have looked aggravated while this was going on because after the soldiers had questioned me and I explained my situation, they backed off and said that Salah didn't have to clean the walls.

In retrospect, such an incident is demeaning to all concerned. First, I cannot speak out because if I do, the soldiers will take out their anger on any Palestinian I am with. Secondly, Salah is forced to be compliant or his family will suffer. Finally, the soldiers are forced to impose group punishments for "offences" they know have not been committed by the individuals they are detaining. From a psychological standpoint, there are no winners in this kind of confrontation.

July 28th 1989

I have the feeling that in a strange way the intifada has finished. In effect, without their knowledge, the Palestinians have been outmaneuvered by the Israelis. With the skillful and selective use of excessive physical violence and economic pressure, Israel has blocked every move by the Palestinians. They have deported all the would-be leaders, killed or imprisoned the activists, and co-opted the leading families without their being fully aware of what was really happening. In the giant chess game for control of the area, the Palestinians are in checkmate but don't realize it yet.

July 31st 1989

This morning the whole class visited the Lababidi Centre. (It was formerly the Beach Camp School, but it has been renamed in memory of Fahed Lababidi.) The centre was in good condition and was functioning well. This was the first site visit for the new students, and they enjoyed it very much. One of them asked me what I meant by the term "a deprived environment," so I had them walk across the playground and look through a classroom window in the UNRWA school. There, they saw the bare, empty room with its dirty plaster walls and old battered desks. "That," I said, "is a deprived environment!"

Later in the day, Hatem and Aida put on a lunch for all the employees of the Society. It must be a daunting task to prepare *maftoul* for some 240 people. This seems to be one of the periodic responsibilities of community leaders in Gaza.

At lunch, we were joined by some new arrivals, an American professor and his teenage daughter. The professor told us he had been in the U.S. Marines and that entering Gaza reminded him of being in a war zone. He said the Israeli commanders are deploying personnel and equipment in a manner which suggests battle readiness. However, he was at a loss to see the enemy.

July 31st 1989

This month 17 Israelis were killed, the vast majority in the bus attack near Jerusalem. This represents an almost 200 percent increase in Israeli deaths since the end of June. In clashes with the soldiers, 27 Palestinians also died this month. Furthermore, 31 Israelis and 225 Palestinians were wounded.

Although there were six strike days, we were not put under daytime curfew during the month of July.

August 3rd 1989

Today at the Sun Centre I met the Consul-General from the French Embassy. He remarked that it was time for a second intifada, seeming to imply the first one had wound down. This comment was an incredibly forceful statement from a diplomat and probably reveals the strong relationship between France and the PLO.

Two small incidents in the last 24 hours reflect the general atmosphere in Gaza. First, I saw a troop carrier moving down the street near my apartment, watched by a small girl who was about eight years old. As it passed, a soldier waved to the child who turned and ran home as fast as her legs would carry her. It seems this girl had learned, perhaps by both direct and indirect experience, never to trust Israeli soldiers.

In the second incident, two troop carriers were passing along Ittalatini Street in the direction of Ansar Two. Each contained about six soldiers and a Palestinian teenager. The boys looked to be about 14 years old. They both seemed to be handcuffed, and one was being beaten with the business end of an uzi.

August 9th 1989

This is the first strike day since July 30th. It has been the longest period without a strike since I came to Gaza almost a year ago. Earlier this morning, we saw a burning tire in Sabbra and over a period of an hour heard about eight shots fired in the street behind our apartment. Rhona saw a small group of *shabab* run through the garden, while military vehicles were patrolling the main street on the other side of the wall. Jabalia Camp remains under curfew for the fourth straight day. The situation today might be described as "warm."

I have spent most of the day trying to telephone the Canadian Consulate to get information for one of our ex-students who is trying to leave the country to study in Calgary. It took four hours of dialling before the line was clear, and then I was asked to call again at 2 p.m. It seems virtually impossible for a student to get out of Gaza to study in Canada. This young man, who has been accepted by Mount Royal College, miraculously found a Canadian sponsor who happens to be Jewish and will guarantee him the $10,000 required by the Canadian Consulate before they will issue a student visa. Now the officials in the consulate say he must obtain a letter from the Israeli authorities in Gaza saying he has never been in jail. I cannot think of a more unreasonable requirement given that the authorities seem to be rather indiscriminate in arresting people between the ages of 15 and 25 years.

Yesterday two American officials came to the Centre because they wanted to meet some ordinary Palestinian people. Hatem arranged for them to spend an hour with our diploma students. It was a very interesting meeting, and our students did extremely well, especially since the whole session was conducted in English.

The Americans were a young woman named Sarah who is an assistant to Senator Mitchell, the Majority Leader in the Senate, and Debbie, a recent university graduate who has just started working at the American Embassy in Tel Aviv. They seemed quite unaware of the real situation in Gaza and made rather naive comments on American foreign policy. I was impressed by the fact that the students did not accept these statements and saw them for what they were — hogwash!

This session reinforced my view that American foreign policy is heavily influenced by the supporters of Israel to the extent that the former country seems unable to act unilaterally on the Palestinian question. U.S. aid for the Palestinians is comparatively small but even this is viewed with suspicion by Israel. If an American politician makes a statement which is critical of Israel, he (it is always a man) withdraws his comments or alters his position within 24 hours. Such is the strength of the Jewish lobby in Washington. Given this scenario, it is difficult to believe Sarah and Debbie's assertion that the U.S. is making giant steps toward solving the problems of the area.

The students were very effective in that they expressed strong emotion but did not become offensive or hysterical. They countered the points made by the Americans with rational arguments. One can only hope Sarah and Debbie were affected by the students' responses and realize the word "terrorists" is totally inappropriate when applied to the *shabab* of Palestine.

Rhona made herself very unpopular with our visitors by making two comments. When they asked the students about the Palestinians ending the intifada Rhona said this was the wrong question. She suggested it should be changed to "When will the occupation end?"

Later, Rhona asked Sarah and Debbie to leave a personal message with the students. They seemed to be put on the spot as this question made it difficult for them to hide behind their official positions. While Sarah refused to answer, Debbie told the students to be moderate and not to hate. I wonder if she would say this if she had lived all her life in Breiyuj or Beach Camp and had no hope of ever getting out.

August 13th 1989

Two days ago, we witnessed a strange incident from the balcony of our apartment. A blue van was passing our apartment when it suddenly screeched to a halt. Two soldiers jumped out and ran down the street toward us. They stopped at the house of the chicken man which is just opposite. It seems they mistakenly thought they had seen *shabab* hiding in the garden. We had been sitting on our balcony facing that direction for about 20 minutes and had seen nothing. One soldier jumped on the wall and then on to the roof of the garage. From there, he had a bird's eye view of the garden which is quite heavily treed. Not seeing anybody to arrest, he fired at random to flush "the enemy" out of the bushes. We saw him fire three short bursts of live ammunition into the garden.

The soldier's positioning was very interesting. There he was standing on the garage roof, clearly outlined against the sky; a perfect target for "the enemy." I am certain that even the most basic of army training teaches soldiers not to make themselves "sitting targets" for the enemy. Apparently, this young man was so confident the Palestinians did not have the weapons to harm him that he could safely forget his basic training.

The two soldiers and several colleagues who had joined them went into the house to search it. We heard another shot fired and then saw the tin roof of the house raised as the soldiers searched through the building. Two or three women and about six small children were allowed to leave and took refuge in the house of a neighbor. Soon more soldiers arrived and it looked as though they were going to arrest some men, but in the end, they left without further incident.

I think the soldier put the lives of those small children at risk by firing randomly into their garden. Perhaps he didn't care because, if he killed somebody accidentally, there would be little retribution. The Israeli media would probably say that a child had died under mysterious circumstances, and the IDF were investigating the incident. In situations like this, they sometimes imply that the child died due to the negligence of its parents.

Yesterday we went for lunch at Iyad's home. Although we were very happy to be there, it was obvious from the food which was served that the family is going through hard times. Like many other Palestinian families, they are feeling the effects of Israeli economic policy in the Occupied Territories. Iyad's father is pessimistic and believes the intifada is ending in victory for Israel. He says the local people are starving and completely at the mercy of the Occupiers.

Today Iyad returned to court for his trial. It was his word against that of an Israeli soldier, so he was found guilty. At Omar's urging, Iyad's Palestinian lawyer tried to influence the severity of the sentence by showing the court a letter I had written saying Iyad planned to continue his studies in Canada. Perhaps as a consequence, the judge gave Iyad a suspended sentence of two years, fined him $1,500 (US) and sent him out of the country for a further two years. Given that he has already spent six weeks in jail, this seems a rather heavy sentence. But Iyad is quite happy for he expected to be sent back to jail.

August 18th 1989

We appear to be experiencing a new type of oppression — tax collection. I have seen the collectors arrive at a house in a van escorted by two trucks full of Israeli soldiers. The four or five tax collectors are in civilian clothes but carry uzis. They enter the house, and if they do not get their money, they confiscate goods such as furniture, television sets, and stereos. It was even been reported that they take children's bicycles.

Two nights ago we witnessed another such incident. At about 11 p.m. the tax collectors and soldiers arrived at a corner near us, took five or six men from an apartment building, and confiscated their identity cards. Then they made the men get on the back of a large truck belonging to a Palestinian in the same building. They also took this man's identity card and made him drive the truck to the house of one of our neighbors.

The men were then forced to enter the house, remove furniture, and load it onto the truck. The vehicle was eventually driven off somewhere, presumably to unload, and returned some time later. Another neighbor's house was entered and the process was repeated. When the men returned from this trip, they were given their identity cards and allowed to return home.

In one week we return to Canada for a month. We will spend a week in England en route, attend Melanie's wedding in Vancouver, and then go to the University of Calgary for a series of meetings.

August 19th 1989

Today some of our former students took us for a picnic by the sea. The scenery was beautiful; a farmer's field overlooking the Mediterranean. A delicious meal of *maftoul*, chicken, fruit, and pop was prepared by Azzad and Mohammed. After the meal, we sat and sang songs before deciding to walk down to the beach.

On the way, we were harshly reminded of the realities of the military occupation. To get to the beach, we needed to cross a narrow, paved road. As we approached it, some soldiers were driving by in three trucks. When they saw us, they screeched to a halt and about a dozen of them jumped out to confront us in a very aggressive way. They started to shout at Azzad, asking him in Hebrew what he was doing. Without waiting for an answer, they harshly told everybody to go back.

When we started to protest they said that Rhona, Jenann, and I could go to the beach but not the Palestinians. I asked why, and they said that it was a closed military zone. This was blatantly untrue as two weeks previously we had walked on this beach, and from where we were now standing could see two people and a donkey cart near the sea. Rhona continued to protest to no avail. As we became concerned the students would be beaten or arrested, we decided to go back. The soldiers continued to shout and jeer at us as we retreated.

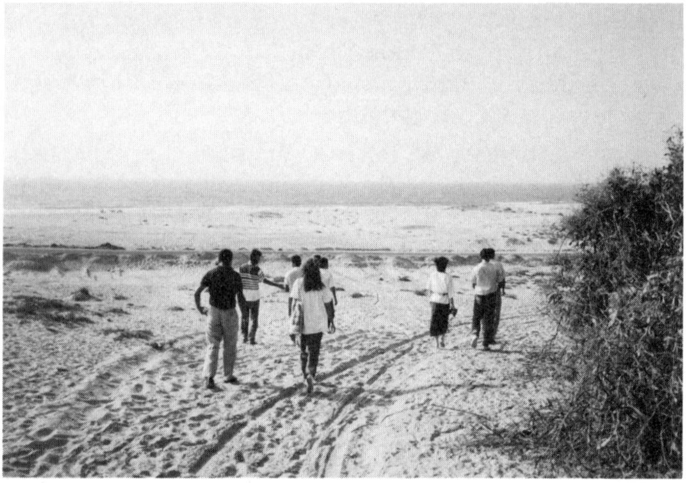

Going for a walk on the beach with a group of our students. A few minutes later we were surrounded by the IDF.

August 25th 1989

This morning we left Gaza and travelled to England. At Ben Gurion Airport I bought today's edition of the *Jerusalem Post*. On the back page, there was a report on the death of a Palestinian teenager. It said he had been arrested by the Border Police who were taking him to jail. However, as he was getting out of the jeep, he had a heart attack and died.

August 31st 1989

So far this year, 27 Israelis have been killed and 77 wounded. This compares with 202 Palestinians killed and 1,873 wounded during the same period.

There were no daytime curfews in the Gaza Strip during August, but six strike days were observed.

The Tinkerman

I didn't know where his home was. The cart, laden with every possible household item you could imagine, would sometimes appear near the Centre, and at other times in streets way over toward the Nasser and Sheikh Radwan suburbs. Some people said he lived in the squalid Beach refugee camp; others said they thought he was really quite well-off and lived in Rimal suburb but didn't want the costs and taxes of a regular shop. No doubt there were elements of truth in all the stories, this being Gaza.

Everything on the cart was enclosed in a wire mesh cage to keep it from spilling off into the street. The fluted, painted roof gave a touch of carnival to what was essentially a mobile hardware store. The little dark-brown donkey plodded mournfully along, up hill and down, at one steady pace, his owner perched on a seat at the front of the cage-like apparatus. In a way, both man and beast seemed to have similar expressions and attitudes. Both worked at their monotonous task with an air of resignation and acceptance; the pace never varied come rain or shine. In the winter downpours, the cart would be driven on to the sidewalk to shelter beneath a garage or workshop awning and wait out the storm.

I first spotted the tinkerman from the balcony of our new apartment one strike day.

"*Sabon* Tide!" (Tide soap) he would call, but he never had any when you went down to the street. The call had become just a way of attracting attention, though originally he did sell Tide. People had come to refer to him locally as the Tide Soap Man. He was so well-known around the town that people were familiar with his inventory, and it didn't much matter that he didn't sell Tide any more.

I knew exactly what I was looking for when I ran down to the garden door and waved him to stop, but he either ignored what I said or replied "*Aywa*," (Yes) to all my inquiries while moving slowly around the wagon opening the mesh doors to reveal a regular Aladdin's cave of kitchen and household goods. Reaching in and poking around, digging beneath tea-towels I suddenly came across a set of real English china tea-cups on the next layer; even further down were aluminum, non-stick cooking pots. Meanwhile, he extracted all manner of items to attract my interest and money. Toys and balls, insect killer, glass cleaner, washing-up bowls, wooden spoons, glassware, hair ribbons, combs, coffee sets, cheap perfume, toothpaste... all were produced by his sleight-of-hand as we both rummaged through the mobile department store.

Everything was incredibly cheap, but it would have been unthinkable not to bargain. It was part of the procedure, and even on the occasions when I couldn't get him to budge on his price, I felt satisfied that we had at least followed the proprieties. By Western standards, I always ended up with a bargain, though I would scowl and complain that he was charging me a high price just because I was an *ajnabiyya*. We both knew it was part of the game, and there were never hard feelings.

"No, never!" he would say with a grin. "You live with the Palestinian people, and so I give you the Palestinian price." I would put the few sheqels into his hand, ask his permission to pat the donkey, and return through the garden door as the cart, transformed like Cinderella's coach to its former mundane, familiar shape, moved slowly down the street to the cry of "*Sabon* Tide! *Yalla, Sabon* Tide!"

Children And Politics 4

There is a knock on the door to our new apartment. It is five-year-old Karma from upstairs.

"Are you busy today or can I visit you?" she asks in her clear, child's Arabic that forever leaves me feeling like a non-starter. She has seen Peter go and visit her father in his office and, following the code of her culture, knows that now will be her best chance of visiting while the men are occupied elsewhere. "*Ahlan wa sahlan,*" I reply and she hops over the step and walks into the sitting room. The ritual formalities I have learned allow us to move gradually into our conversation. I serve her Cola and cookies, and practice the familiar phrases of welcome. Today she is being very grown-up and asks me how I am and if I have had news of the family in Canada, while she nibbles daintily on her biscuits.

The introductory phase of the visit satisfactorily completed, she moves directly to her request for a comb, and we embark on our grooming routine. She climbs onto the couch and combs through my hair, clipping it up in different styles, braiding and unbraiding while we talk casually. She is fascinated by my ring combs, and then notices I am wearing sandals she has not seen before.

"How do you fasten your sandals?" she asks and jumps down to watch a demonstration. She claps her hands in delight and says, "*Mumtaz!*"

And then it is drawing time. We go into the office for crayons and paper. I already know the probable outcome, but wonder if this will be the day when she draws something other than the Palestinian flag. I now have a drawer full of Palestinian flags which are the standard fare from Karma, her brothers, and just about every Palestinian child who draws pictures for me.

Today there is to be a slight variation, for she wants to see our Canadian flag. She copies it faithfully beside the Palestinian one she has completed, and joins the two together with the word "Peace" in beautiful Arabic script, her skillful control of the pen far superior to our expectations of young children in the West.

CHAPTER ELEVEN

September – October 1989

September 28th 1989

We have just returned to Gaza after spending a month in Canada. Melanie was married on September 3rd, and then we went to Calgary for several days of meetings relating to the educational program in Gaza. Canada seemed incredibly sane and civilized compared with the daily mayhem here.

Driving through the checkpoint at Eretz, the soldier looked at us as if we were so many pieces of garbage. Even though it was not yet time for the regular 8 p.m. curfew, Gaza was like a ghost town, the streets completely empty. Evidently, the United Leadership has said that no cars should be driven after 6:30 p.m.

Today I listened to the news on the Voice of Israel radio station and, it felt as though I have never been away. Prime Minister Shamir said his government is ready to negotiate a peace settlement with any Palestinian who does not support the PLO and who will accept in advance that there can never be a Palestinian state. In addition, the Minister of Justice said that Palestinian prisoners are being treated too well and must be given harsher punishments.

On a personal level, we have learned of the fate of several young friends. Samir, the least political of our former students, was arrested two weeks ago, and his whereabouts are unknown. Anwar, one of our current students, has been sentenced to 18 months in jail for participating in a local intifada committee, and Ehab, the son of Mohammed Abu Hamda, is in Ansar Three for 14 months because he was writing political slogans on the walls.

Same old Gaza, same old Israel!

September 29th 1989

As of 2 p.m. today, the Gaza Strip has been sealed and declared a closed military zone. Nobody is allowed in or out except the soldiers who of course have free access. Journalists are not allowed in without special permission, and they must be escorted by a military officer at all times. The purpose of this action is to prevent problems during the celebration of the Jewish New Year. The restriction is expected to last for three days.

An interesting item was reported on the radio this morning. For some weeks, a group of Israelis and Palestinians have been jogging together in an area near Bethlehem. They have been wearing t-shirts on which the words "We Want Peace" are written in three languages. This morning they were arrested and their jogging trail was declared a closed military zone. A journalist who was with them was also jailed until he apologized. For what? Perhaps the army is afraid that peace might break out.

October 2nd 1989

This weekend has seen an upsurge in the number of casualties. The Voice of Israel reported six Palestinian deaths following violent clashes with the army. Although there were no reports of people being wounded, one can safely assume the number to be in excess of 30. There is new writing on the wall opposite the house, and Palestinian flags have been thrown across the telephone wires further down the street. We have not seen these local signs of resistance for some months.

October 5th 1989

Yesterday came the sudden announcement of a five-day strike. The announcement from the United Leadership said that there will be a strike for six days except Saturday. On Saturday people will be allowed to stock up on food, and the stores have permission to stay open until 5 p.m. The move is to illustrate an increased resistance to the Israeli occupation. Certainly this month has started in a particularly bloody way with seven Palestinians killed in five days.

October 6th 1989

It is dusk on the second day of the projected long strike. The evening is cool and quiet with only the sounds of our neighbors' voices and the bells on the harness of a passing donkey cart to break the silence. We haven't heard of any serious problems, although we have been harassed by an IDF foot patrol who rang our door bell and jeered at us through the intercom and at the gate. This morning we were startled by a stun grenade which the soldiers threw into the garden opposite for no apparent reason. A typical strike day in Gaza.

October 8th 1989

Yesterday we worked, but today we are back on strike for another three days. This strike period coincides with the Israeli holiday of Yom Kippur. The Israelis have sealed off the Gaza Strip and the West Bank. Although it is quiet on our street, Radio Monte Carlo has mentioned troubles in Breiyuj and Mughazi camps — 19 people injured.

Almost overnight the weather changed and summer has ended. It rained today for the first time since the beginning of March, and the air is considerably cooler.

The children have found a kitten in the garden and brought it into the house. Rhona and Karma are looking after it. I call it the terrorist cat because it is so wild compared with its Western relatives. It must weigh about six ounces. It is all fur and sinew with large eyes and even bigger ears. Its cry is unbelievably loud, and it literally attacks any food that is offered. I could see it moving into a Western home and absolutely terrorizing larger and more domesticated cats. It would certainly survive very well in such surroundings.

October 11th 1989

Yesterday we had lunch with Ahmed Abdullah Hammad who is our new Arabic teacher. Ahmed is employed as a teacher in a nearby UNRWA school and lives in Jabalia Camp with his wife, mother, and eight children. His home is typical of those in the refugee camps. It is partially open to the elements, being hot in summer and very cold in winter. The walls are constructed from breeze blocks and concrete, while the corrugated iron roof is anchored to the rest of the building by large rocks. A large sheet of clear plastic was laid out on the tile floor near the entrance to the house, and it was here that lunch was served.

After lunch, we settled back on cushions while Ahmed told us the story of his life. While in one sense the story is highly personal, in another it is the archetypical tale of the Palestinian refugee.

It began in 1948 when he was one year old. His family lived in a village near Ashqelon, Majdal in Arabic, but had to flee at the outbreak of the war. One mile from their home, en route to the next village, they were bombed by an Israeli plane. Ahmed's three brothers were killed, and Ahmed was badly wounded. As it was thought that Ahmed was also dead, he was left with the corpses of his brothers while his wounded mother was evacuated to an Egyptian field hospital in Majdal.

As the men were digging a grave for Ahmed and his brothers, they heard the baby begin to cry. This saved him from a premature burial. At that moment, there was another air attack and the men fled, leaving him alone by the side of the road. After some hours, an old woman who was passing by recognized Ahmed and took him to his old aunts. As he was very badly wounded, an uncle took him to the hospital in Gaza where the doctors wanted to amputate both of his legs. The uncle refused and took him to a private practitioner for treatment.

Meanwhile, Ahmed's mother was lying close to death in the Majdal hospital. The doctor who was treating Ahmed managed to get a message to the mother that her youngest son was still alive. On hearing the news, the mother began to take the treatment and made a miraculous recovery in order to be with her son.

Life was very hard for them. During the first year, they slept in the open under trees and against walls. After UNRWA was founded, they were given a tent and this seemed like a real home to them. At first, they existed by collecting manure from the streets and selling it to the farmers as fertilizer. Later, Ahmed's mother began to get work as a washerwoman for some of the rich people in Gaza, and so they managed to survive.

Eventually, they were able to build a more permanent home in Jabalia Camp and Ahmed attended school. He did very well and later attended a teacher training college. When he brought his first wages home to his mother, she refused to accept them saying that he should save the money to marry and give her another family of children to take care of. This he did and there are now eight children in the family.

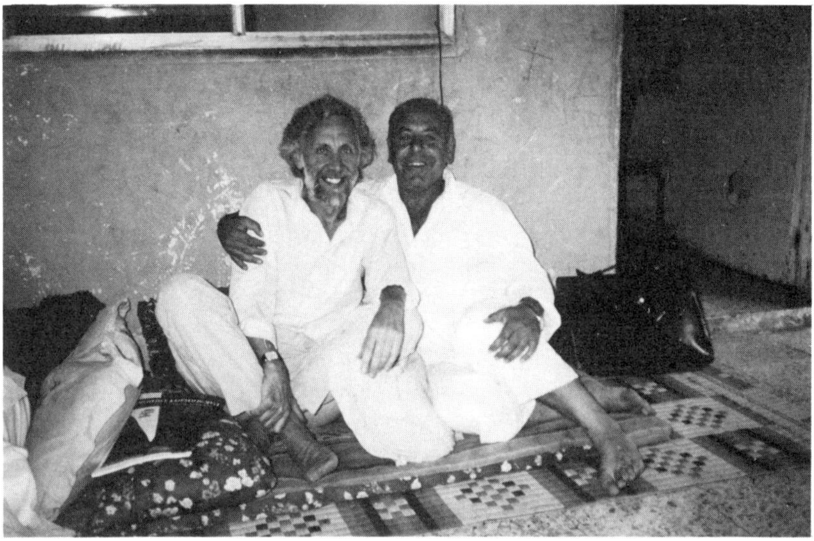

Jabalia Refugee Camp: Peter and Ahmed Abdullah Hammad

His mother has never forgotten the children she lost. Sometimes she still sits and cries for them. She has insisted that Ahmed's sons bear the names of his dead brothers. Now her only wish is to return to the ruined village near Ashqelon.

Because of the melodramatic tone of the story, one might be tempted to dismiss it as largely fictional. However, this would be a mistake, for it is a tale which is representative of the tragedy of the Palestinian people. In the beautiful lush countryside a few kilometres outside the Gaza Strip, the foundations of Ahmed's house in the overgrown ruins of his village can still be identified. You can also see the holes in his mother's leg; remnants of a fearful wound.

October 18th 1989

For the last three days we have been experiencing the fiasco of a television crew from the Canadian program "W5" visiting us. Their visit followed about six months of telephone conversations about our lives in Gaza. When the crew arrived, it was soon evident that they were not interested in us or the program. Probably out of politeness they interviewed Rhona and Aida at the Lababidi Centre and spoke with our students for about half an hour. It finally became clear that they saw our purpose as providing introductions to people who might be useful to them and organizing transportation around the Gaza Strip.

The television crew desperately wanted take a sensational story back to Canada. They spent most of their time with an American physician who has been in Gaza for about two weeks. They had no insight into the real heroism which was before their eyes as each day Sabah El-Hato, Sakher Kandeel, and Adel El-Bhaissi battle their severe physical handicaps with incredible courage. The crew showed no interest in either the life-affirming work of the Mothers' Program or the CIDA project which attempts to provide a Western-style college education under such trying conditions. In the case of the latter, they declared that it would not be of interest to a Canadian audience.

October 20th 1989

The situation remains "warm." So far this month, at least one Palestinian has been killed every day. Two days ago a 13-year-old died in Khan Younis and a three-year-old was killed in Beach Camp. The latter has been under curfew for three days, and we have heard plenty of shooting both from that area and the neighborhood to the north-east of the Centre.

October 21st 1989

Two recent items in the *Jerusalem Post* were very enlightening. In the first, an Israeli soldier was court-martialled because he ignored his officer's orders and shot at two Palestinians, killing them both. His sentence was two years in prison. In the second report, a Palestinian was convicted of throwing a Molotov Cocktail which caused no injuries. The punishment in this case was 15 years in jail plus the demolition of his family's home. I wonder how the Israeli authorities rationalize what clearly seems to be a double standard in the judicial system.

Yesterday we went to the wedding of our student, Sakher. It was a typical Arab wedding with many people, much music, and the bride and groom sitting on a raised dais rather like a king and queen. At regular intervals the bride changed clothes in order to show off her trousseau. The female guests were all invited to dance, including Rhona. She did very well, and this was much appreciated by Sakher's family. The wedding was somewhat unusual for Gaza in that Sakher is a man who is quite severely handicapped.

There was a strike today in Gaza, but the van from the Sun Centre went around as usual to collect the administrative staff from their homes. On the way back to the Centre, the van was stopped by the soldiers. Selim, the driver, Yewsif, the accountant, and Nasser, the psychologist were told to get out. While these young men stood facing a wall with their hands up, the soldiers searched and beat them. The incident was witnessed by many of the female staff who remained in the van. Although they were then allowed to continue on their way, no reason was given for this action by the soldiers.

October 23rd 1989

Recently, the story of Beit Sahur has been uppermost in the minds of Israelis and Palestinians. The people of this mainly Christian village which is situated near Bethlehem have staged a tax revolt against the Israeli government. In response, the Israelis decided to punish them.

To date, the village has been under continuous curfew for almost a month. Every day the tax collectors with their guns and army escort go into Beit Sahur and search the houses systematically. Today's *Jerusalem Post* reported that so far the authorities have confiscated $2 million (US) of household goods and 23 cars. The punishment continues. The residents of Beit Sahur managed to smuggle out a message for the media. It read: "We refuse to pay for the bullets which kill our children."

October 25th 1989

Today we went to Jabalia for our Arabic lesson. Everything went well except that our lesson was punctuated by gunfire from IDF soldiers in the street outside. This is such a common occurrence nobody in Ahmed's house paid any attention.

Yesterday's *Jerusalem Post* contained another example of the double standard in the Israeli system of justice. A settler who had killed a teenage Palestinian girl was given a seven-month suspended sentence, while a teenage boy who had "intended to throw" a petrol bomb at an IDF patrol in Rafah was sentenced to nine years plus a three-year suspended sentence.

October 31st 1989

Some men were arrested at the Sun Centre this morning. A car stopped just outside the gates, and men in civilian clothes got out. It was obvious they were members of the secret police since they were carrying uzis. They were looking for one of the drivers and quickly arrested him. At that moment, Ahmed and Emad, two other drivers, and Yewsif, the accountant, were leaving the Centre to go to Tel Aviv. They were stopped, beaten, arrested, and driven off for questioning.

The news ran through the Sun Centre like wildfire. I became concerned about some letters Yewsif was carrying to be mailed in Tel Aviv. Among them was an article about the psychological effects of the intifada. I had co-authored this paper with two Palestinian colleagues. As this research data gives a negative view of the Occupation, I was worried the secret police might arrest my colleagues and deport me. Rhona seemed ready to go back to the apartment right away and start packing. However, an hour later, the letter was discovered on a secretary's desk. She had forgotten to give it to Yewsif before he left!

This month there were no Israeli deaths, but 32 Palestinians were killed. This brings the total number of intifada-related deaths this year to 27 Israelis and 238 Palestinians. In the same period, 84 Israelis and 2,199 Palestinians were wounded.

There were eight strike days this month, but no daytime curfews. The night curfew continues and is imposed at 8 p.m. each evening.

Return To Gaza

Our plane arrives at Ben Gurion airport in the late afternoon, and it is already dark by the time we retrieve the luggage and go through customs. Back home in Canada, the evenings are still quite light at five o'clock, and we do not feel any apprehension about the onset of darkness. But here, it is different. The drivers from the Centre where we work will be hard pressed to get us back into the Strip before the eight o'clock curfew — a regular nightly imposition, and just one of many for the Palestinian people living under military occupation.

We emerge from the passenger building into the deepening dusk and almost immediately spot Abed and Emad standing in the crush of Israelis. As always, they seem somewhat uneasy in a crowd which eyes them with suspicion.

Whatever the two drivers feel, having to wait amid a crowd of people they see as their oppressors, it does not in the least affect their pleasure and warmth when they see us. Abed, the chief driver, stands waving with a big smile of amazement. Returning to Arab friends is always a big deal, as if they are surprised that you have appeared. There is much expression of thanks to Allah, handshaking, and Arabic blessings at our safe return. It is a nice formality; an acknowledgment that really, we should take nothing for granted and ought to be thankful for every day or minute lived in safety and with friends.

Our bags are loaded into the minibus from the Centre, and then we are on the road. By now, it is completely dark, and we have just over one hour to get into the Strip. Abed drives like a bat out of hell. I shut out thoughts of head-on crashes and mangled bodies by taking a Calmex travel pill and sliding down on the back seat with my eyes closed. I prefer a state of being semi-comatose to that of being fully-conscious of the hazards we narrowly avoid.

We reach the checkpoint with about half an hour to spare. The soldiers are the usual scruffy-looking bunch. They're not pleasant, but they let us through without a hassle. Abed and Emad are used to the surly treatment: the barked questions and the thumb-jerk telling them to get moving. Sometimes I wonder what it would be like to try and talk to one of the more polite soldiers, but I know better. It would soon turn hostile; his officer wouldn't like it and he'd get into trouble; his macho colleagues would deride him later, and it would put our relationship with the Arab people in jeopardy.

The closest I have ever come to talking to a young IDF soldier was on the campus of the university at Tel Aviv. We had just bought some psychology text books, and the young man offered to help us carry them out to the street where we would later be picked up by Emad. We asked what he was studying, and he explained that right now he was preparing for his three years of national service in the army. We asked him about his perceptions of what was happening in Israel and the Occupied Territories, and he said he didn't think Israel needed Gaza, but it must retain the West Bank. He supported the mandated national service because he felt Israel was in a very vulnerable position geographically. He referred to a recent international conference in Sweden, on the control of chemical weapons, especially in the Middle East. This was very important, he said, because he knew that Arab nations like Libya were producing chemical weapons.

I found it difficult not to respond by asking him what he thought Israeli soldiers were doing with tear-gas in Gaza. The used tear-gas canisters I had seen carried explicit instructions to the effect that they were lethal if fired indoors. Yet we saw soldiers on more than one occasion fire them directly into apartments. The results can be found in the lists of injuries and deaths of women and children published by groups such as the Association of Israeli and Palestinian Physicians for Human Rights. The action has been condemned by Amnesty International, and of course denied by the Israeli government. From our conversation, I knew that, like ourselves in pre-Gaza days, and, I suspect like most people in the West, the soldier would not consider tear-gas to be a lethal chemical weapon. Such discussions inevitably seem to conclude in a dead-end debate of what constitutes a chemical weapon and what doesn't, or which ones are permissible and which ones forbidden. I knew it would be one more exercise in futility.

At the check-point we know that the soldiers would prefer we were not there. We try to remain calm, polite, and distant. Sometimes we don't quite manage it, but tonight we don't want to cause any trouble. They will only take it out on our Palestinian drivers. In any case, it is almost curfew time and none of us wants to become target practice for an IDF patrol.

The city is dead silent. If we didn't already know that Gaza is densely populated, we would think we had driven into a ghost town. A few street lights illuminate the familiar walls, apartment buildings, shops, and mosques; but there is neither sight nor sound of human life. Windows are dark and shuttered. Occasionally, we see a pack of wild dogs rummaging in the garbage bins, but this is the only sign of life.

Abed reaches up and turns on the interior light of the van. The curfew is not the only regular evening imposition. The United Leadership of the intifada has decreed no vehicles are to be on the streets after 7 p.m. Transgressors with no valid explanations are likely to be stoned by groups of children or masked youth hiding behind high garden walls. Our protection is the emblem of the Society for the Handicapped painted clearly on the front and sides of the bus, and the light that will show Peter and I to be foreigners but not Israelis. I have already put the large, veil-like scarf over my hair, pinning it below my chin and up at the side in the Palestinian style. Nonetheless, we are all aware of each other's increasing tension as we drive at speed down the dark streets of Gaza.

Eventually, we see our house, the three-tiered stuccoed, cream-colored building protected by its high garden wall. This is where we live with our extended Muslim family; the Canadian filling in a Palestinian sandwich. The place is in darkness. We ring the bell at the gate and hear Salah's familiar voice asking, "*Min al bab*?" Who is at the gate? He seems incredulous that we have returned from Canada and hurries down to welcome us. We climb the two flights of marble-tiled stairs up to our apartment. Peter takes the keys from Salah and opens the double doors to the carpeted hallway. Abed and Emad bring up the suitcases, deposit them in the bedroom and leave in haste. It is ten minutes to curfew time.

I wander through the rooms opening doors and windows to bring in fresh air after a month away. Everything is there; nothing has been disturbed; our plants have been watered and the whole place freshly-cleaned. Somebody has been thoughtful enough to leave some food in the fridge.

We step out onto the large front balcony lit by a full moon. It is the same moon we see back home in Delta, now ten thousand miles away. The sky is full of stars, and a mile away the Mediterranean laps gently onto a beach which, in a free country would be a million-dollar asset to the economy. The serenity is disturbed by the rumble of approaching heavy vehicles, and a convoy of tank-like machines and Jeeps thunders by in the street below.

It is eight o'clock; we are now under curfew. It is all so familiar. We are home.

The Adoption

We had never intended to let Biss move in on our lives the way he did. We were sensible, intelligent people who knew when enough was enough. The last thing we needed was to take on another responsibility when we were already coping with as much as we could. What we didn't realize was that Biss had other plans based on his ability to recognize a pair of ex-patriates who were an easy target.

A cry like a banshee sent us running to the front door. There, clinging spread-eagled to the screen mesh, all teeth and claws and wild eyes, was Biss. At the time, we were uncertain what he was. He was in such awful condition that we couldn't decide whether he was some exotic rat, or a starving but determined kitten. He let out another scream for good measure. He had an incredibly loud voice.

What to do? Peter, already concerned about how we would feel at leaving the humans we knew and loved, advised ignoring the animal until it got tired and went away. I'm sure he knew it was the beginning of the end when I cautiously opened the screen door and Biss, as we were to name him (very uncreatively, for it means "cat" — male gender — in Arabic), ran into the apartment. We gave him a dish of milk and then carried him out to the garden and shut the door firmly behind us. That was enough of that. We agreed this was very wise.

Next day after work, the banshee was back on the screen door. We sighed as Biss eyeballed us determinedly through the mesh. One more dish of milk was served. "It's probably got fleas," Peter said. He was right. But Biss had drunk his milk and was exploring the living room, alert to any possible danger. He seemed very highly-strung, though we attributed this to his survival needs outdoors. He was terribly skinny and his ears were red raw, scorched from being exposed to the sun. Still, he allowed me to pick him up and cuddle him, a fatal move, for that was the end of us. Biss was there to stay.

We bathed him in warm water with some Kwellada shampoo we'd brought from Canada, and got rid of his fleas. During the day, before the onset of winter, he would sleep under our desks in the office in a plastic washing-up bowl lined with a soft cloth, taking time out when he was awake to bat around the fuzzy ball we'd tied to a chair. At night, we put him out on the balcony in a large Arab cooking jar turned on its side, and he'd sleep there on his little blanket until we got up the next morning to let him in.

Later, as the weather grew cold, we let him stay inside at night. There'd be a gentle bump as he sprang onto the bed, stepping carefully around our sleeping forms. In the morning, we'd wake up to find him snuggled between us under the covers, his head on the pillow, forepaws on Peter's shoulders.

He was incredibly spoiled. Feline-loving friends in Canada sent a care package for him comprising a catnip mouse, Nine Lives tins of food, vitamin pills, foamy balls, a flea collar, and other goodies. It was all pretty outrageous considering the lot of the human population. Pets were a luxury, and as far as the Palestinian people were concerned animals were no use unless you intended to eat them or put them to some practical purpose.

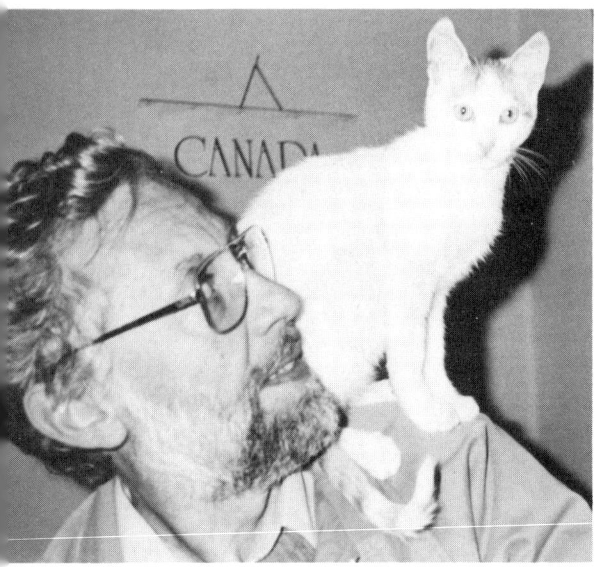

Peter with Biss, our hardy little feline companion.

Some of the local superstitions about cats were interesting and in many instances generated considerable fear of the animals. People said they had evil eyes and were untrustworthy. Visiting the educated family of one of our students, the father, whom we had found quite rational in all other ways, entertained us with the story of a local sheikh who had once owned a cat. One day, so the story went, the cat had sprung on to a chair and started to talk. The student's father impressed upon us the fact that this story was definitely true. He believed it, he said, and wanted nothing to do with the creatures because they were from the devil. Other people believed that when cats purr they are reciting the Koran.

Biss did serve several useful purposes during his time with us. He got rid of our mice, reduced our stress levels in his own way and served as at least one constant in a daily life that was so unpredictable we rarely knew which day of the week it was. Every day when we came home from work he'd be near the gate waiting. We'd call to him and talk to him as he trotted jauntily ahead of us up the stairs to the apartment and stood waiting at the door.

He had his routines. A call of "din-dins" would bring him running from anywhere, and he often took an after-dinner sleep on one of the chairs or on someone's lap as we worked in the office at home. Later, he would racket around the apartment wreaking havoc with paper garbage, crashing out of control into doors, and doing forward rolls into the television set. Eventually, he also learned how to plunge us into darkened silence by accidentally-on-purpose becoming entangled in the electric cables and unloosening them from the wall sockets.

Then there was ball-retrieval. I've never known a cat to chase a ball, bring it back and drop it at your feet or into your hand the way Biss did. I'd only known dogs to do that.

At about ten o'clock every night after we'd retired, he'd have one last session of tearing around the apartment like something gone mad, pausing now and again on our bed, panting like a dog with his mouth open and his tongue hanging out. Then that would be it. We reckoned he figured us to be Big Cats, and if the Big Cats were into sleeping, so be it. He'd go into the kitchen and have a drink of water out of his cup, use his toilet tray down the hall and then settle down. He disdained a saucer after he was big enough to jump up onto the kitchen counter and check what was in the sink. He always wanted to sip out of the tea mugs in the sink so in the end we gave him one of his own.

In the mornings, he doubled as an alarm clock. He seemed to know when six o'clock rolled around and you'd feel his whiskers on your face. His way of getting us up and moving was to walk quietly around on the bed and then throw himself down flat up against your body and start grooming. Sometimes we got his rough-tongued "kisses" like sandpaper on our cheeks. He was always right on time though. Once he'd got us on our feet, he headed for the kitchen where his morning routine involved jumping up on the counter, leaning his forepaws on the window sill, looking down at the pigeons on an outside ledge, and hissing at them. Then after his breakfast we'd put him in the garden for the day. Quite often he'd go and visit Umm Kamal downstairs where he got extra tidbits because she thought he had a nice face.

Twice we thought he was going to die. The first time he seemed to catch the flu that was going around the human population. He stopped eating and sat huddled by the electric heater on a woollen jump-suit. His energy level deteriorated each day. He refused to even have a sip of water and became so thin and weak that he could no longer even climb onto a chair. There was nothing we could do. After about three days, we were sure he would not be alive the next morning and Peter said we must burn the jump-suit after we buried him. But he began to rally and in a couple of days was his old havoc-wreaking self, dancing out from behind chairs on his hind legs, his front paws flaying the air as he tried to bat our legs and ankles.

The second time he got sick seemed to be from what I later figured must have been a snake bite. One of his hind feet was bleeding. When I examined it I could see a couple of small punctures underneath on the pad, and a small hole on top. It puzzled me for weeks until one of the boys upstairs said there was a snake in the garden. Biss fussed with his foot for several days and would not let me touch it. He limped around on three legs as the injured foot grew alarmingly in size. We kept hoping it would get better, but it continued to swell, and Biss again went off his food.

Then Peter remembered seeing a shop with VETCO written on it, on El-Waehda street. I put on a pair of leather gloves and sat in the car with Biss screaming and struggling on my knee while Peter drove us to the doctor. Somewhere en route, the swelling burst and blood covered the sleeve of my blouse. At the VETCO shop Peter went in and spoke to the veterinarian. He was a young, educated man who spoke excellent English. We placed Biss on the counter, and everyone else in the store left immediately; they probably thought we were crazy bringing in a cat for treatment. The vet usually dealt with useful animals such as goats and donkeys.

We and Biss were taken into a room that served as the clinic. It seemed to double as a storage room and was full of dust and grime. A single old metal-framed kitchen chair was set among storage shelves, and here I sat down with Biss. It took the two of us, Peter and I, to hold him down as the young man squeezed out the accumulated poison, blood, and puss. Biss screamed horribly, but we all three talked quietly to him, like doting parents with a pediatrician! The wound was sprayed with antiseptic used for sheep and goats, and then with a soluble-plastic covering for protection. The vet charged us 20 *sheqels* (about ten dollars) which was probably a fortune by Gazan standards, but we didn't mind. He had done a good job.

Biss minded, of course. I think he associated the car with bad things after this, and screamed himself hoarse all the way home. He drank half the water in his tea mug afterwards. We were always amazed that he didn't hold these things against us, but he never did. He seemed to understand we were trying to help him. Biss was back to racketing and climbing in no time, as spoiled as ever.

When we took time off to travel we would take him to stay with Fadi, one of our students, a kind young man who liked animals. Fadi's father used to say that theirs was the only home in Gaza where the animals got better treatment than the people. We would pack Biss's toys, blanket, tea mug, and cans of food into a tote-bag and truck him over. He visited several times with Fadi and was always in good shape when we returned. We could tell all was well because he would allow Fadi to pick him up and fuss over him; he was very picky about who he allowed to do that.

As the time for our departure from Gaza drew nearer, we worried about him. Fadi had agreed to take him, so we knew he would be all right. In any case, we reckoned, in our specio-centric way, that we'd given him nine months of fun and affection and a good life he wouldn't otherwise have had. He'd simply have to learn to adjust.

Back home in Canada, his framed picture stands among portraits of friends and family. There he is, sitting on the counter in the kitchen, looking seriously at the camera. And it is only now that we understand the truth. We didn't adopt Biss at all; he adopted us and gave us nine months of fun and affection. They were nine months of a good life we wouldn't otherwise have had, and now that he's moved on we'll simply have to learn to adjust.

First Winter Rain

Today is the sixth of October and we have our first rain since March. It arrived early this morning, heralded by a cool breeze unusual for the time of day. The breezes normally arrive in the early-to-mid afternoon, cooling down the rooms after the intense heat of the day. But today, just before six in the morning, the venetian blinds on the windows were disturbed by the untimely draft, accompanied by a gentle swishing sound. The air smelled suddenly different from the familiar early-morning trash burning odor that usually roused us, and we both instinctively tensed, sensing an approaching change.

At first we attributed the swishing sound to the palm fronds on the tree outside the window, but it increased in intensity and the smell of damp earth permeated the room. Outside we could hear the delighted screams of the children next door, and we jumped out of bed and ran to the window. Below us the children had run into the garden and were standing with sun-browned arms outstretched to the grey sky, their faces turned upward to feel the coolness on their skin. Across the street a family-laden horse and cart had pulled on to the sidewalk to shelter under the awning of the chicken shop. All around us the balconies gleamed as though freshly-waxed.

The feeling and reactions of the children reminded me of times back home in Canada when the first snow arrived just before Christmas. It suddenly felt a million miles away.

CHAPTER TWELVE

November – December 1989

November 2nd 1989

There is a strike today to commemorate the Balfour Declaration. Gaza seems very quiet. Sara Roy is visiting us and will be staying for two weeks. She is conducting interviews and collecting material for her upcoming book on the Gaza Strip.

Yesterday Azzad left for Canada. We have not heard from him yet but expect he arrived safely. He is the first one of our students to be able to study in Canada. On his last day in Gaza, we were invited to his home in Jabalia to say goodbye. Seven of our old students were there as well as a group of his other friends. I am very happy he has been able to leave Gaza, and we hope to see him in Canada when we return next summer.

November 10th 1989

There was a strike in Gaza yesterday to commemorate the beginning of the 24th month of the intifada. The situation in our area was more lively than it has been for a while. We heard tear-gas grenades being fired, accompanied by much whistling and shouting from the *shabab*, and saw three teenagers behind a wall throwing stones at passing vehicles, including army Jeeps. There was of course much military activity with army personnel carriers driving up and down the streets at regular intervals.

Tonight we were invited to dinner at the home of Abdel-Latif Abu Midain who is helping Sara with her book. He and his family live in a delightful house just around the corner from us. It is decorated tastefully in the Arab style and has a beautiful garden with flowers, patios, and climbing honeysuckle. Abdel-Latif is an educated man who has a degree in economics from the American University in Beirut. After dinner, he showed us many deeds to land which his tribe owned in the Gaza Strip. The deeds were from the Ottoman

Empire and described the price as quantities of gold in French liras — no doubt a vestige of Napoleon's presence in Gaza during his Egyptian campaign. The occupying forces do not recognize these deeds and have confiscated the land in the name of the State of Israel.

November 12th 1989

There were two very interesting announcements in Leaflet #48 of the United Leadership. The first said there are to be three days of demonstrations as a prelude to Palestine Day on November 15th. This is to be a national holiday with many celebrations. It seems likely the Israelis will pre-empt this by putting the Gaza Strip under curfew.

The second announcement was more ominous. It was written in English and stated that the Israelis have started to dress as tourists and priests in order to surprise and kill the masked people who are the neighborhood leaders of the intifada. The United Leadership, therefore, can no longer guarantee the safety of foreigners. In other words, foreigners might be killed if they are suspected of being Israelis in disguise. This certainly raises our anxiety.

November 14th 1989

Yesterday an Israeli Jeep was ambushed on the coast road about three kilometres from our apartment. Both occupants of the Jeep were killed and their assailants escaped. As there is so much violence in Gaza, it is difficult to comprehend that these are the first Israeli soldiers killed in the Gaza Strip since the beginning of the intifada. People are asking if this means the Palestinians are escalating their resistance to include firearms. No longer will the soldiers be able to drive around Gaza without fear, knowing they have only to face a few stones. Instead, they will never know where the next bullet is coming from.

Today was totally chaotic at the Centre and indeed in the whole of Gaza. Celebrations were planned for Palestine Day which is tomorrow. Starting at about 11 a.m. people went wild. Cars drove down the street honking loudly, and there was a noisy party at the

Centre with singing and dancing. In the streets, the *shabab* were giving out balloons and stoning cars if the drivers were not "happy." On the other hand, the soldiers were trying to prevent the celebration and were detaining and harassing people for driving with balloons attached to their cars.

On a more serious note, there was a considerable amount of gunfire today. At about 6:30 p.m., I heard a long volley of shots close to the house. Since coming to Gaza, I haven't heard so many shots fired at one time; I couldn't count them. I don't know what happened out there in the twilight. Neither will the outside world, for the Gaza Strip has been closed off once again.

November 17th 1989

On Palestine Day we were under curfew so there were no celebrations. Instead, on the Israeli television news, we saw soldiers kicking in doors and storming into houses to pop balloons. I suppose the officers saw this as an effective way of preventing any celebrations. Perhaps the Israelis have become so obsessed with eradicating all symbols of the Palestinian nation that they do not realize the senselessness of mounting a campaign against balloons!

Today Aida and I tried to go to the Sony factory in Tel Aviv to work on a videotape of the Centre's educational programs, but we were prevented from leaving the Gaza Strip. The Eretz checkpoint was closed, and we were ordered back. We were planning to attend a UN conference on special education in two days in Amman, Jordan, but it looks as though we will be detained by the Israelis.

November 28th 1989

The checkpoint was re-opened on November 19th, so we have just returned from a week in Jordan — with terrible colds. Still, we had a very interesting time. We attended the UN conference in Amman where we met Queen Noor and Prince Ra'd.

The conference wasn't very successful, comprising mostly of rich people *talking* about providing services to handicapped people rather than *doing* anything about it. Later, we took a holiday for three days, visiting Petra and the Wadi Rum as well as the historical site at Mount Nebo which is reputed to be the burial place of Moses. We also visited the mosaic floors at Madaba and the crusader castles of Karak and Shubak.

We were happy to escape from Gaza for a few days, but it was depressing to return. We discovered that while we were away our area was under curfew for three days even though the general situation has been very quiet. The intifada seems on the decline once again, and some people are saying the Israelis have won.

November 30th 1989

There were six strike days and five daytime curfews in November. The night curfew continues in force. Since the beginning of the year, 30 Israelis have been killed and 88 wounded. The corresponding Palestinian figures are 251 and 2,381.

December 2nd 1989

I need to qualify my previous statement about the intifada being on the decline. While this is true, there is still a good deal of resistance. It may be more accurate to say that this phase has been won by Israel, but the undeclared war continues to its tortuous end. Every day the repression increases, and we hear of more casualties.

Yesterday Israeli soldiers discovered what they refer to as a "gang" in Nablus. Although these young men were not firing weapons, they were carrying them, and this was sufficient reason for the IDF to open fire. Four Palestinians were killed and three others were seriously wounded. There has been an outcry among the Palestinian people with spontaneous strikes occurring in many areas. As we returned home from work, Ittalatini Street was covered with debris, and there was a burning tire in a nearby intersection. Mellika told us there had been a violent confrontation. Fortunately, nobody was seriously hurt.

December 4th 1989

This is another strike day and marks the period leading up to the second anniversary of the intifada. Gaza remains "hot," and there are rumors that yesterday in Beach Camp a ten-year-old child was shot in the head and killed. People are also saying there will be many strikes and curfews in the next week or so.

Yesterday from my office window at the Sun Centre, I noticed some trouble between the soldiers and some school children. A few minutes later I spotted a group of adults from the orphanage next door carrying a teenager who had been shot in the leg. A car was preparing to take the boy to hospital, but it did not leave the parking lot, presumably for fear of being intercepted by the soldiers. It was difficult to tell how badly the boy was injured, and in the end, I don't know what happened to him. This is the kind of everyday event we have come to tolerate. We have been brutalized into accepting the shooting of a 14-year-old boy as normal.

This evening Rhona and I heard a couple of shots fired in the street outside our apartment. When we looked out we heard the sound of many people chanting as if at a funeral. Then a figure emerged from the darkness into the light of a street lamp and hurled a couple of stones toward an unseen target further down the street. At the same time, we heard the derisive whistles which usually accompany any armed intervention by the soldiers.

A few minutes later a convoy of three vehicles approached from the opposite direction. It appeared to comprise a police Jeep and two civilian cars. The Jeep continued, but the cars stopped at a barricade which was partially blocking the street. Suddenly figures leapt from the cars and began to fire pistol shots in all directions. The noises and flashes from the barrels of the pistols gave the impression of firecrackers being thrown on Halloween. But here, the intent was much more deadly. After a few minutes these people jumped back into their cars and sped off. As far as we could see nobody was hurt.

We don't know the identity of the people in the cars but believe them to be Israeli settlers in Gaza. These civilians are allowed to carry weapons and sometimes react violently in the face of even symbolic resistance by the Palestinians. If a person is killed during these clashes, the settlers are sometimes brought to trial. Such a prosecution is always controversial and causes much dissention among the Israelis themselves.

December 7th 1989

Last evening the military authorities imposed an indefinite curfew on the Gaza Strip so today we are forced to stay home. The streets are deserted except for the occasional military vehicle or Israeli car which roars by. I am curious to know what is happening in the refugee camps.

After a relatively quiet two-month period since our return from Canada, Gaza has again erupted. The violence and demonstrations began about a week ago in response to the killing of the so-called "Black Panther Gang" in Nablus and are probably continuing as a prelude to the second anniversary of the intifada. Israeli sources are saying that nine Palestinians have been killed and more than 100 have been wounded in the first six days of this month. The dead include a 17-year-old schoolboy who was killed in a demonstration on Ittalatini Street about 200 metres from our home, and a ten-year-old girl from Beach Camp who was shot in the back of the head as she walked home from school. The casualty figures do not include the five members of an armed guerilla band who crossed the border from Egypt into the western Negev where they encountered the IDF and were shot to death.

I am surprised by the current upsurge of resistance because I was beginning to think the intifada was dying down. One of the first moves by the Israelis was to close all the schools in Gaza. This suggests that, despite the removal of huge numbers of the leadership, the young people are still prepared to fight on. In fact, the great strength of this truly popular uprising may be that the external leadership in Tunis has limited influence while the local *shabab* have so little to gain by surrendering to the Israelis.

Yesterday rumors of a curfew began. We had already expected a three-day strike, but when Sabah went to the hospital for her physiotherapy treatment, the doctors told her they had been given special passes to travel during the curfew.

Despite the threat of curfew, we went to Jabalia for our Arabic lesson with Ahmed Abdullah. Carey Denholm, a visiting professor from Victoria, British Columbia, came with us and went to visit the house of Moussa, one of our students. Jabalia was very tense, and there was plenty of shooting. While we were taking our lesson, a teenager was shot in the hip near Ahmed's house. This was Carey's first experience of violent clashes between the military and civilians, and like most people, he found it quite frightening.

We left Jabalia as it was getting dark. Some boys were setting up a roadblock to try to "liberate" their section of the camp. They were quite cheerful and waved us through, pointing out that we were heading in the wrong direction for the Eretz checkpoint. I believe they took us for journalists who were returning to Israel before the regular evening curfew came into force. It was a disconcerting journey, and all of us were relieved to arrive home safely.

As we were eating supper, the curfew was announced on the radio. And at 3 a.m., we were awakened by the soldiers announcement that it was forbidden to go out on the street until further notice. So here we remain.

December 11th 1989

The curfew was lifted yesterday, so this morning Carey Denholm, Sabah, and I visited the various sites for the upcoming practicum. One of them was the UNRWA School for Blind Students. It has been closed by the military authorities. This means students are not allowed to attend, so the teachers were sitting around with very little to do. We were told that all schools in the area had been closed to prevent the students from throwing stones at the soldiers. This ban includes the blind students!

December 13th 1989

We are feeling rather overwhelmed by the local culture because we have been taking Carey around to say his goodbyes to people. I feel as though I have been speaking Arabic nonstop for the last two days. This afternoon we were in Jabalia and visited the Abu

Rass family and the nearby home of Salah. We met his wife and new baby daughter who is very cute. While we were with the Abu Rass family, the news came through that tomorrow one of their sons will be released from Ansar Three. There was great joy in the family with many cries of "Thank God!" and "Congratulations."

Lately, I have had a very interesting time visiting people who have been injured in the intifada. Our purpose is to perform initial brief assessments on survivors of bullet wounds to the head or spinal cord. Our university is planning to develop a program to provide rehabilitation services for these unfortunate people.

In Nusseirat Camp we saw a 17-year-old boy who was shot, along with more than a hundred others, in the large demonstration about seven months ago. One eye was destroyed, and the boy had a large concave hollow where his forehead should be. In some ways his recovery seems quite miraculous for he is able to move all his limbs and is attending school. However, he complains of physical weakness, and his family says his personality has changed since the shooting. Now, he is much more emotionally labile and loses his temper in response to even minor stress. These of course are the classic symptoms of injury to the frontal lobe of the brain.

In Breiyuj Camp we met a 15-year-old who was shot in the left side of the head. The bullet fragmented, and he underwent three operations as doctors tried to remove pieces of the bullet from his brain. Obviously such an injury caused widespread damage. The boy's right arm and leg are paralyzed, he has great difficulty with speech, and his memory is seriously affected. Before the accident, he was in senior high school, but now he can no longer read. Given his injuries, it was surprising to find him in such good spirits.

The visit to the Sheikh Radwan neighborhood was a fine example of Gaza as the Twilight Zone. The house we visited is situated near a large army station and essentially consists of two garages. At the front of the space there was a small shop, and behind this a bedroom. To the left of the bed was a large gas ring on which a pot of corn was boiling. To the right was a hole in the wall which was perhaps one metre high and half a metre wide. This rough opening provided access to the next building. For our interview, Carey and I sat on the bed while the patient and Khaled sat on stools, with the women crouched together on the floor.

The family's story was poignant. We were shown a large picture of the 19-year-old son who had been killed by the soldiers last spring during the 23-day curfew in Sheikh Radwan. The mother was very tearful and everybody said her son was not dead but *shahid* (a martyr). Another son who lives in Jabalia Camp evidently received 17 bullet wounds in his body. Although he survived, the family reported that he is now heavily medicated to control both his emotional lability and his hallucinations.

The man we had come to see was in very bad condition. Some months ago he had been making a bomb when it exploded. Following the accident, his right leg was amputated at the hip. His left leg was also shattered. Although it was not amputated, the knee was ruined and the leg will no longer bend. There are still pieces of shrapnel in his leg and holes which continue to ooze a watery fluid. In addition, his artificial leg does not fit properly, and he is experiencing constant pain and irritation caused by the prosthetic limb. At this point, our only intervention option is to put him in touch with Ali Shawwa's clinic. Hopefully, other services will be provided when our own program begins.

December 17th 1989

Last Thursday a group of people from the Centre — Carey, Cheryl Rubenberg, Yewsif, Emad, and I — needed to leave the Gaza Strip for a variety of reasons. While we were in the line-up at the checkpoint, a man in civilian clothes, who had no identity tag, asked us to pull over. The Palestinians told us he was an Israeli income tax official.

We were directed to a nearby enclosure where there were about 100 cars and trucks which had been confiscated by the tax collectors. As we were waiting for our file to be called up on the computer, we saw a former driver from the Centre who now had his own taxi. He showed me a paper which the tax people had just given him. It said he must pay $2,500 income tax. As this amount is probably more than he earns in a year, he has no chance of paying it off in the foreseeable future.

After the tax people reviewed our file, they would not allow us to leave Gaza because Hatem had refused to deduct income tax from his employees' salaries. Apparently, Hatem believes that in the present situation it is not his responsibility to collect taxes for the state of Israel.

I was quite polite with the tax people, but let them know they would face problems if they detained a group of international consultants who had various appointments in Israel and the West Bank. In the end, they said we could leave on this occasion, but until Hatem had complied with their directives, they would not allow any other van from the Centre to leave Gaza. It was quite obvious that the tax collectors expected to be thanked for their magnanimous gesture. I was pleased that none of our group exhibited symptoms of the Hostage Syndrome. It was our right to leave, and we didn't need to thank people who are trying to curtail our freedom.

During our visit to the West Bank, Cheryl Rubenberg recalled her husband's analogy of our work in Gaza — "teaching college courses on the train to Auschwitz" — all we can do is ride the train with them and share their journey. At least our being here may give the people hope.

December 19th 1989

Yesterday there was a strike called by the United Leadership of the Uprising. At about 2 p.m. we heard a commotion in the street. A group of soldiers and a bulldozer were busy destroying a wall. This was near the location where our one masked person unsuccessfully throws stones at vehicles, hitting perhaps one in 30 and causing little damage. Nevertheless, the IDF had moved in once more to inflict group punishment.

Many of the neighbors voiced some gentle protests, and eventually the old man who owns the house came out and started to walk away from his home. "I'm going to Hell because it couldn't be worse than living in Gaza," he said. The walls of two homes were destroyed before the soldiers admitted they had made a mistake in demolishing the one belonging to the old man. The masked man had never been on his property, having only thrown stones from the empty lot next door. There is little chance the old man will get his wall replaced by the authorities.

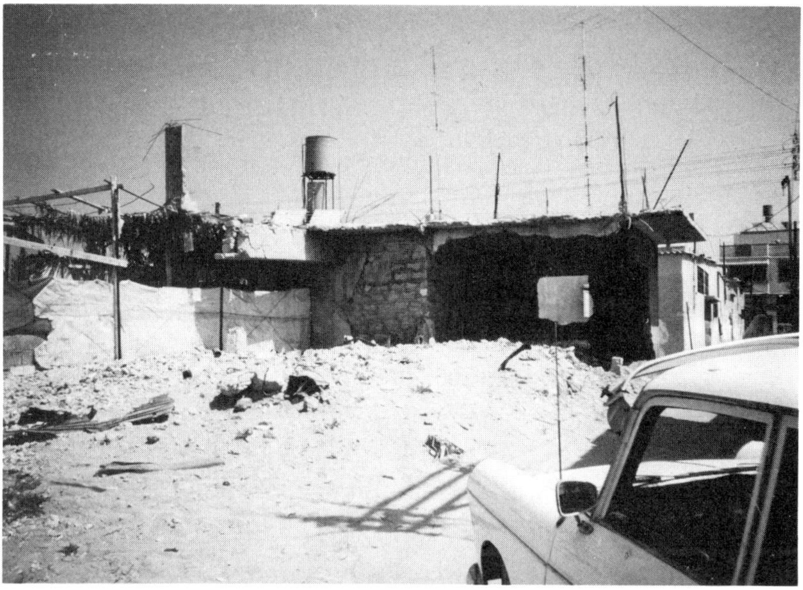

Beach Refugee Camp: The remains of a house destroyed by the Israeli Army. One of its former occupants was suspected of resistance.

December 21st 1989

Today it was noted in the *Jerusalem Post* that 19 Israeli soldiers have committed suicide in the last year. The article commented that many of these deaths are due to the brutalization of the young men while they are serving in the IDF. These tragedies are not usually reported, and when they are the suicides are said to be for "personal reasons." I cannot imagine anybody committing suicide for impersonal reasons!

There was an announcement yesterday that a prisoner in the Gaza Central Jail had committed suicide in his cell. The suicides of prisoners are always viewed with suspicion, and in this case, the family claims that the man was tortured to death.

The report of the death provoked widespread disturbances in Gaza, particularly in the Rimal area where the man lived. Streets were blocked by large rocks and chunks of old appliances from the garbage dump, while about 50 *shabab* gathered at an intersection chanting and waving the Palestinian flag. The soldiers were plentiful, but they sensibly kept their distance so the casualties were minimized. When I drove Rhona home at lunchtime, our street was littered with rocks and other debris, suggesting there had been demonstrations when the young people were leaving school.

December 26th 1989

This year we escaped from Gaza for Christmas. On December 24th, we took a service taxi to Tel Aviv and stayed at the Carlton Hotel for a couple of days. We ate Chinese food, watched Western movies in our room, had Christmas dinner at the Hilton, and shopped in the bookstores. It was not like Christmas at home, but we successfully avoided the depression of last year's festive season.

December 27th 1989

This is yet another strike day. This morning I phoned the Canadian Embassy in Tel Aviv to invite Michel Desalaberry for lunch during his visit tomorrow. However, he told me he intended to come today and would bring Flora MacDonald, the former Canadian cabinet minister, with him.

We waited for them at the Centre. They were due to arrive at 2:30 p.m. but hadn't shown up an hour later. The staff at the Centre were waiting to leave, so in the end, we said *khalas* (enough) and everybody went home.

As we arrived at our apartment, we noticed a car with diplomatic plates had stopped at the gate. We hurriedly left the van and found Michel and Ms. MacDonald waiting for us. They told us they had arrived at the Centre just after our departure and decided to try to catch up with us at home.

We had an enjoyable time together. As Rhona said, we have seen Flora MacDonald so many times on television that she seemed very familiar to us. Later, we were joined by Salah, Wasfia, and Tony Charters, an Englishman who is temporarily in charge of the Save the Children office in Gaza and the West Bank. The group broke up about 6:30 p.m. as the people from Tel Aviv had to leave Gaza before the evening curfew came into effect.

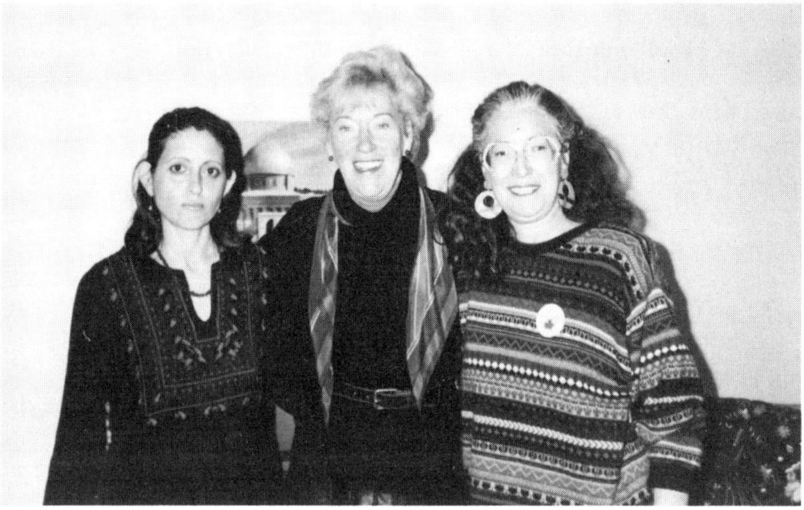

(from left) Wasfia, Flora MacDonald and Rhona in the apartment on Ittalatini Street.

December 31st 1989

Today marks the end of the year for which I have collected data on the situation in the Occupied Territories. While I do not believe my figures are totally accurate, I am sure they reflect conservative estimates of casualties.

This month there were four strike days and three daytime curfews in the Gaza Strip. The night curfew remains in force. During 1989, there were 56 strike days and the entire Gaza Strip was under curfew for 28 days. Specific areas were under curfew for much longer periods. For example, in the Sheikh Radwan neighborhood, people were once under house arrest for 23 consecutive days. The dusk to dawn curfew was in effect for approximately ten months of the year.

The number of casualties has mounted slowly but steadily during the year. In December, no Israeli deaths were reported, but three people were wounded. In the same period, 27 Palestinians were killed and 369 were wounded. This means that in 1989, some 30 Israelis and 278 Palestinians were killed in intifada-related violence, and 91 Israelis and 2,741 Palestinians were wounded.

At this point, it might be interesting to compare my figures with those of the Palestinians. Yesterday Rhona and I went to visit Iyad's father for a turkey lunch in honor of Christmas. While we were there we met a Palestinian administrator from the Ahli Arab Hospital. She said 3,400 people had been treated for intifada-related injuries at Ahli during 1989. This figure includes 1,109 children under the age of 15 years. The administrator was speaking about the medical records of one hospital in Gaza, while from the Israeli media I have gathered data concerning the whole of Palestine. Given the discrepancies in the two sources of information, the real human cost of the occupation may be much worse than is generally known in the West.

Flight To Freedom

The early morning sun streams through the library windows as I sit at my desk. For once I am grateful to have had the responsibility for the first lecture of the day, starting at half-past seven. That done, I can now sit quietly and alone. My lecture notebook lies open before me, the final sentence in a paragraph trailing into a nothingness caused by the sound of a distant jet. The noise immediately arouses the anxiety I have been carrying all night, and I look toward the window, half hoping to see a passenger plane, westward bound. It is a totally unrealistic expectation, for passenger planes do not fly over Gaza. The scream of fighter planes, the throbbing of helicopters, and drone of spotter planes are the only aircraft sounds one hears in this occupied territory.

Today Azzad should be on his way to Canada if all has gone well. His flight was scheduled to leave from Ben Gurion airport at 8:30 this morning. I glance at my watch. It is 8:45. I wonder if he has made it safely past the check-point at Eretz, through security at the airport, up the stairs, and into the passenger waiting lounge. Did he remember everything we told him to do? We gave him so many instructions on the appropriate way to behave, and the rules that everyone must follow. I wonder how it must feel to know that you are leaving behind 20 years of a culture that has come to depend solely on charity, for a new life where none of your hard-learned survival skills from the refugee camps will make much sense. I wish so badly that I could at least have seen him through to the departure gate.

Yesterday afternoon, when classes were over, he had invited us to have a final lunch with him at his home in Jabalia Camp. There, surrounded by his friends, an uncle, and well-wishers, we had seen him for what we hoped would be the last time before he embarked on his new life as a student in Canada. He would leave behind his spartan little cement-block house and the members of a family to whom he had never felt very close.

Early in his life both his parents had died and left him an orphan. He had not been treated well by his remaining relatives, and there had been some traumatizing incident which he would not discuss. Whatever it was, it had forced him to survive independently from a very young age, and although family members lived nearby, he refused to share the same dwelling with them and had built his own quarters.

He showed me the portrait of his mother hanging over the door. She looked kind, with the beauty of a mature woman. Azzad does not indulge in sad nostalgia or self-pity, but his feelings surface occasionally when he perceives others not being respectful about their parents. Not having had parents of his own, he sometimes finds it difficult to understand how there can be disagreements in the kind of relationship for which he secretly longs. I had long since stopped protesting at his calling me "mom." The mother in me worried about him. He had always reminded me of my youngest child Calvin who, like Azzad, seems to have a special vulnerability that haunts me from time to time.

At the lunch, there had been a good deal of horsing around among his friends. They were laughing, slapping each other on the back, smoking, and shouting. They also took photographs with my camera. While this was all going on we had slipped a small gift into Azzad's bag. It was a wallet containing some Canadian bills and change in case there was a hitch when he arrived.

Azzad had sensed my anxiety and concern for him, and after eating, we took a walk together over to the home of his fiancee. As we strolled across the sandy wasteland that separated the refugee camp from the village where his fiancee lived, I checked everything out with him. Was his ticket safe? Did he have enough money? Had he packed a toothbrush? He recited everything patiently back to me, calling me *yama* (mom) and telling me I must not worry. I had told him several times that if he did not manage to get out, then I would believe it was impossible for anyone ever to get out and break this wretched cycle of human misery and degradation. He had given me a hug and told me not to cry.

Now, sitting in the library, the thing I most dread is a visitor sent to tell me that Azzad did not get away. The clock ticks toward nine o'clock, and I sigh and return to my lecture notes. He must be in the air now, and the ominous messenger has not materialized.

Suddenly, I hear footsteps coming up the stairs. I hope it is one of the accountants in the next room, but I do not hear the familiar rattle of keys. The footsteps stop outside the library; the doorknob turns quietly and the door opens. I am convinced it will be Azzad. Instead it is Ahmed, but he is looking even more serious than usual. My heart sinks. I look at him in silence, dreading the words I am going to hear. Without speaking he fumbles around inside the jacket he is clutching together across his chest, pulls out a plastic bag and places it on the desk.

"This is from Azzad. He wants you to have it, but you must not wear it in Gaza!"

"But Ahmed," I respond, "Where is Azzad now? Did he get out safely?"

Ahmed does his imitation of going into shock. His mouth drops open, his eyebrows shoot up to his hairline in horror and he says, "But of course! He left very early this morning, exactly at four o'clock as you told him to. He had arranged for a car to take him to the airport, and he has gone to Canada! What did you think had happened?"

I turn to the gift Ahmed has delivered. Inside the plastic bag is a banned t-shirt displaying the colors of the Palestinian flag. I bury my face in it and cry with relief. "*Hamdulillah*!" I say. For once Ahmed, a confirmed atheist, knows better than to challenge me on what he sees as superstitious nonsense, and closing the door quietly behind him, leaves me to my tears and the morning sunshine.

Palestine Day

We had been told that the day was to have been one of public celebration ordained by the United Leadership, but instead we were placed under full curfew until further notice. Celebrations had taken place the previous day, but under rather unusual circumstances. *Shabab* in the streets had stopped cars and ordered them to accept balloons to fly from their windows, accompanied by rhythmic horn-honking. A refusal to accept the free balloons was taken as non-support for the liberation of Palestine and punished by stone-throwing. There was therefore general acceptance of the balloons. Drivers then ran the risk of being apprehended by the soldiers who would beat cars and/or their occupants for daring to show open support for Palestine. It was a rather bizarre situation.

We sent our students home early after celebrations at the Centre. Most of them were hysterically happy, and it was obviously futile to attempt a return to serious lectures after several performances of the *dibka* national dance and patriotic songs.

Returning home, I went downstairs to visit Umm Kamal on this special day. It was cold, and she had remained in the bedroom with an oil heater in front of her knees as she sat by the window knitting, taking advantage of the pale afternoon sunlight.

The room was dim apart from the window in the curved corner of the room. This was the room where Abu Kamal had been laid out on Land Day earlier in the year. Things looked pretty much the same. The huge bed with its bolsters and dark, richly-colored quilts and covers of burgundy and brown. The room reminded me of paintings from the Renaissance period in its richness of deep tones and the high ceiling which emphasized the lines of the tall wardrobes and long window drapes.

Around the walls were photographs of her sons. One now lives in Germany where he owns a restaurant and has a German wife and two small children. They try to come and visit the family in

Gaza once a year. Another son lives and works in Saudia with his wife and older children. They also visit each year. Salah, of course, lives upstairs with Wasfia and the three children. He is the only son who has remained in Gaza, trying to earn a living as an architect.

Umm Kamal sat with her head covered by the scarf. When it is time to pray she excuses herself and pulls the scarf lower over her forehead creating her own private praying space as she follows the ritual of reciting the Koran, nodding her head right and left, touching her lips and forehead with her hand. I never saw her read anything other than the Koran, and she would invoke the assistance of Allah for all manner of enterprises. Once, when she was altering a skirt for me, she recited the opening words of the Koran before applying the scissors.

I noticed people doing this in many circumstances when they were fearful or anxious that some instrument or piece of technology might not work properly. I was trying to start our old car one day without much success, when a man walked by and muttered, "*Bismillah Il Rahman Il Rahhiim.*" The car started.

Today Umm Kamal was very subdued. Her legs and diabetes had been giving her problems and she finds it difficult to stand or walk even on the best of days. Though she knew they were bad for her she still liked to eat sweets and would ask me to bring her some *Knafa bi gibna* (honey with cheese) whenever she knew I had had guests. She regularly rebuked Wasfia and Mellika for making coffee with too little sugar. It was all a far cry from the awareness of diet and health that are part of the North American drive to live as long as possible.

I sat down quietly near her, and we exchanged the necessary greetings and gave thanks to Allah. We talked about the Palestine Day celebrations yesterday, and I remarked that I was surprised nobody had shouted *Allahu akbar* from the rooftops last night. She sighed and said the soldiers would shoot anyone who did that, and then she drifted into reminiscences about the 22 years they had spent under Israeli occupation. We both felt sad and despondent.

She asked if I thought the Israelis would ever leave them alone. Usually I try to be optimistic, but today I answered honestly that no, I didn't think they'd ever go away. She remained focussed on her handiwork, sighed deeply and said, "*Aysh n'amil, ya* Rhona, *aysh n'amil*?" What can we do?

I replied quietly that I really didn't know, and that I was sorry. I finished drinking the coffee, gave Arabic blessings, and left her to her room of memories.

Negotiation In The Wadi Rum

It was time for us to take a break from Gaza, and we decided to visit Jordan once again. This would be our third visit to the small, Hashemite kingdom of Hussein I. We would return to the hidden, magical city of Petra, and then move on further south to see the Wadi Rum, the setting for many of the early scenes in the film *Lawrence of Arabia.*

For our journey south from Amman we hired a local car and a driver-guide named Omar. Everything had gone quite well until our last evening in Petra when Omar had come to the hotel to check what time we wanted to set out the following morning. Betraying his Muslim faith, he had been drinking alcohol, and the normal inhibitions of his culture were rapidly eroding. After arranging our departure time, we stood up to leave, at which point Omar, after delivering effusive compliments, decided to try and kiss me. I was surprised, taken aback, and angry. My uncovered hair and perfectly appropriate conversation by Western standards had yet again been interpreted as signals of sexual availability. More than anything, we felt annoyed at being put in the position where now it was necessary for Peter to discipline Omar in some way, and for me to return to covering myself with the large white scarf-veil which I had come to detest. In Amman, I had felt comfortable without it. Many of the Arab women in the city went uncovered, and there were plenty of foreigners dressed Western style. Being on the road with this pathetic, unhappy man was obviously a different kettle of fish, and it was time to apply the strict rules and traditions we had learned so well in Gaza.

When we were ready to leave in the morning, Peter went downstairs without me to find Omar. He was ready, waiting, and on his best behavior. Nonetheless, the previous evening's transgression had to be dealt with, and Peter told him we did not require his services, that we would travel by bus from then on.

Omar was immediately reduced to a grovelling mess, begging Peter not to dismiss him. His boss would be bound to find out and fire him, and there was so little work in Jordan he might never get another job. Peter had finally agreed to retain him, but on probation only. Omar pleaded with him not to report the incident to his boss. Peter said it would depend on Omar's behavior for the remainder of our trip, leaving him in a very uncertain frame of mind.

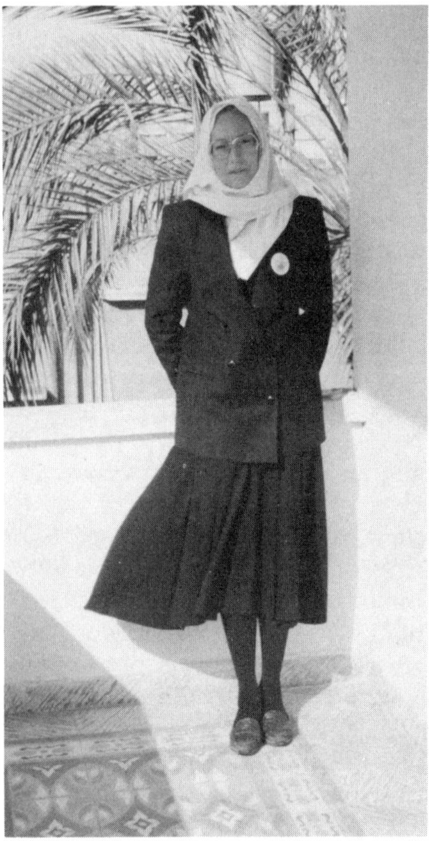

Rhona as she usually appeared in public. Her dressing in this manner was usually attributed to Peter being a "good man."

The men's business settled, I dutifully followed Peter downstairs to find Omar being the epitome of good Arab manners and courtesy, obviously subdued and anxious. We hated the whole business, but mistakes in intercultural understanding are inevitable and not always comprehensible. There is usually something to be learned from them, and in this case I now understood that so-called differences in attitudes between Gaza and Jordan were obviously fairly minimal once you left the sophistication of the capital. I also remembered having a conversation in Canada with an Arab gentleman from Beirut who, in response to my question as to why he refused to allow his two grown daughters to have their own apartment, explained that he had read a book (written by a man) which claimed that any woman would succumb to the advances of a male after five propositions. He was totally bemused by my outrage. To him, if something had appeared in print, it had to be true. Now, with the incident involving Omar, I understood why the women in the Arab cultures I experienced are kept pretty well under house arrest. They are paying the penalty for potentially delinquent male behavior.

The journey to the Wadi Rum was uneventful, and the scenery along the desert highway fairly unspectacular until we saw rocky outcroppings of the Wadi shimmering ahead in the distance. Heading south toward Aqaba, we came to an inconspicuous junction and turned left on to the road into Wadi Rum. This road ran parallel with a railroad track which apparently connected Aqaba, through the desert, with the cities of the Arabian hinterland. It is this line which T.E. Lawrence and his troops attacked, and the skeleton of the abandoned train is purported to still stand exactly where the events happened, thus blocking the direct route through Jordan to Saudi Arabia.

When we reached the government resthouse located in the middle of Wadi Rum, we hoped to be able to ride to some of the mountainous outcroppings on camels. Omar had solicited the help of Alfi, the young manager of the resthouse, in finding Bedouin camel-owners who might take us in. However, it was still quite early in the morning, and neither people nor animals seemed to be in evidence. When the camel men were found, they seemed reluctant to comply with our request and quoted outrageous prices. My comment to them that we did not wish to buy camels, only to rent them for a few hours' exploration, met with barely a glimmer of amusement, but they got the point. Instead of camels, we were offered a driver with a beaten-up Toyota pickup truck. It wasn't the romantic scenario we'd envisioned, but it was better than nothing, and obviously nobody was going to budge on the camel request.

The driver, who seemed to have been dragged out of bed, became agitated because he could speak no English. However, everyone assured him that we spoke Arabic just fine (*Ya Salaam*! I thought to myself), and so we climbed onto the truck bed and clung to a rail which had been rigged up at the front, safari style. I had no idea what "four-wheel-drive" was in Arabic, but I was sure the truck didn't have it, and there was an awful lot of sand ahead of us. Still, we now knew with the certainty of experience, that if anything happened, the local people would get us out of it safely.

Sure enough, we had barely been on the sandy track for ten minutes when the truck crunched into a deep sandy pocket and stopped. Neither of us felt any need for concern, and so we jumped down, enjoyed the scenery, and learned how to get a stuck truck unstuck in the desert. The driver collected coarse desert grasses and small twigs, packing them underneath and slightly ahead of the wheels. Then he started the engine and revved hard while we pushed behind. It took a good half hour of gathering and packing, but then the truck leapt forward and out of the sandhole to everyone's cries of "*Hamdulillah*!"

Ahead of us the valley floor rose gently between the sheer sides of two mountains until all that was left was the line of a horizon beyond which, maybe a hundred miles away, lay the border of Saudi Arabia. I wanted to walk to the line of the horizon to see what lay beyond, but I already knew that this was the seduction of the magnificent Wadi.

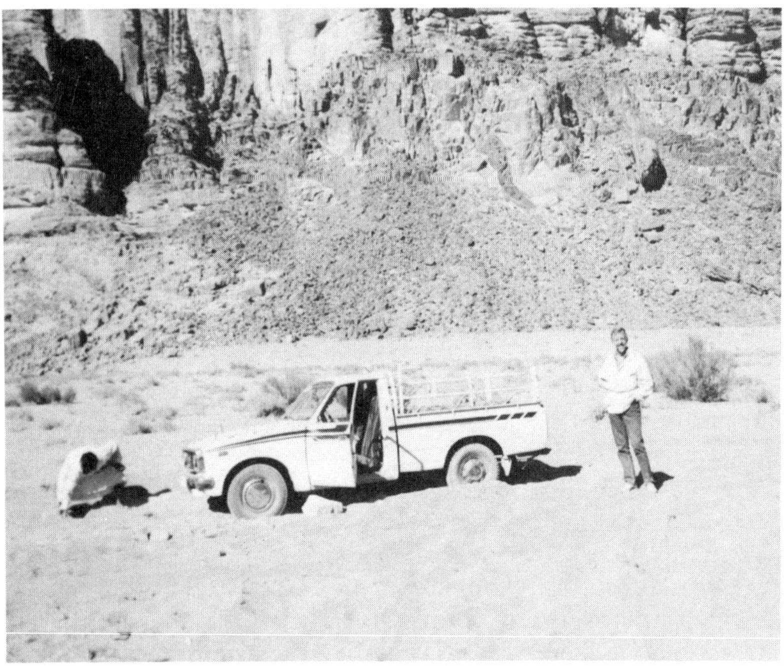

Wadi Rum, Jordan: Peter standing by our truck which is stuck in the soft sand.

Everything was incredibly still and silent, with the sky a clear azure dome above the desert. Although the sun was high in the midday sky, it was still cool enough that I needed to wear my thick Canadian jacket which I was now glad I had carted around, secretly cursing the bulkiness of the thing, but feeling that I might just need it, for deserts are not always hot places. Now I could give myself a smug little pat on the back.

The driver stopped the truck after a twenty-minute drive, and we jumped down. I walked behind Peter and our Bedouin guide toward one of the many fabulous outcroppings of rock that have made the Wadi famous. The incongruities were with us again; things always took unexpected twists and turns like the dry stream beds that criss-crossed the desert. So now, here we were on a moonscape of silence in the Wadi Rum, with Peter and the Bedouin guide discussing psychology as we hiked to the cliffs ahead. The man was describing how his brother flew into terrifying rages at the slightest provocation and was asking for advice. Peter explained how in his work he tries to help people with this kind of problem by talking with them and encouraging them to tell what it is that makes them so angry. The concept was alien to the Bedouin, who was looking for an instant solution.

After listening and asking more questions he finally said, "But why bother with all the talking? Why can you not give him some medicine that will immediately stop him from being so violent?" The men continued the discussion quietly, their voices barely intruding on the silence that surrounded us.

We reached a cleft in the steep, jagged side of a huge outcrop, and the Bedouin climbed up to a ledge and beckoned us to follow. The cleft was high and steep, and the ledge we were on was barely eighteen inches wide as we nudged ourselves slowly and cautiously along. Then, looking up, we saw on the sheer wall across the cleft a strange sight. There were some markings which reminded me of the Nabatean hieroglyphics we had seen in Petra, but then a little higher on an overhang was the imprint of a pair of quite small feet. But this was solid rock, and the footprints were vertical, and at least ten feet from any foothold, on a sheer cliff face! The driver-guide smiled with pleasure at our exclamations. We questioned him about the origin of the footprints, but it was the usual exercise in futility which we had previously encountered at sites of interest.

Once you strayed off the beaten track of the major sites, little seemed to be known about the human historical past except in very broad terms. We had to be content for now at having ventured up to see the carvings, and hope for information at another time and place.

We drove back across the broad valley where the large battle scene in *Lawrence of Arabia* was filmed. The Bedouin told us he was a camel-boy extra in the movie. If this were true, he couldn't have been more than about five years old, so I figured it was just tourist talk; he'd probably told the story so often that he himself now believed it. No matter. The government resthouse was in sight once more, and we had to get moving if we were to reach Amman before nightfall. However, our departure was to be delayed.

Alfi and Omar were sitting in the sun waiting for us. We said we must leave now, but then Alfi invited us to drink tea or coffee with him in the resthouse. There was something in his manner that made us hesitate to argue; something else was involved, though we were not sure what. Whatever it was, we knew it would be interesting, and so we agreed to have a beverage and were led inside while Omar waited by the car, still looking fearful and dragging on endless cigarettes.

First, Alfi questioned us about the trip into the Wadi. Was it to our liking? Was the guide satisfactory? We talked about the beauty of Jordan and the kindness of the people, and then Alfi asked about our work in Gaza and said complimentary things. The coffee appeared and, as we sipped from the tiny cups, the conversation changed tack and became serious.

Alfi said Omar seemed very nervous today. Omar was a good man and yet Alfi had never seen him so upset. We now realized what this was all about. While we had been off exploring the Wadi, Omar had had time to relate his tale of woe to Alfi who would now act as his negotiator to try and placate Peter into not reporting the incident that had occurred back at the hotel in Petra. Using an intermediary was common Arab practice and one that Peter knew well how to deal with, for slamming his fist on the table he shouted that Omar did a very bad thing that was *haraam* (shameful). He went on to tell Alfi what had happened, saying that what Omar did was not the behavior of an honorable Arab. Alfi gave a thin smile of acknowledgment, and said that the tragedy was that some people at the hotel who did not like Omar put whisky into his orange juice to make him drunk and get him into trouble. We all knew this was a farce, but it couldn't not be treated as such. Peter said that this too, then, was very bad, and retained his look of displeasure while I, fully scarved, quietly tried to add my two-bits' worth.

I said that Omar, like many Arab men, did not understand Western women. If a Western woman spoke to a man it did not mean she was in love with him. If Omar believed in the Koran, I continued, then he must treat all women respectfully, not just the Arab women.

Alfi listened, nodding his head. Turning to Peter he explained that Omar now was very afraid that he would lose his job. Peter remained non-committal. Alfi got up and left us for a few minutes. When he returned he presented us with two sets of posters and photographs of the Wadi Rum, one for each of us. Peter looked at them and expressed approval. He said we would accept one set, and not report Omar to the boss if all went well on the journey back to Amman. This was good enough. Alfi sighed and smiled and brought in Omar who was told the outcome of the negotiations. We all shook hands and everyone agreed that everyone else was perfectly wonderful. International relations were restored and everyone's honor remained intact.

As I settled down in the back of the car for the long ride back to Amman along the Desert Highway, I took a last look at the Wadi fast-disappearing in the late afternoon light. I could never decide, on these excursions, what had been the most interesting event: the sights we had seen or the human interactions that transpired wherever we went. I wondered from time to time if life in Canada would seem incredibly dull when we returned.

CHAPTER THIRTEEN

January – February 1990

January 1st 1990

We begin this year in the same way we began 1989 — under curfew! Today is the 25th anniversary of the founding of Fatah, Yasser Arafat's faction in the PLO. To prevent demonstrations, there are many soldiers in our area and presumably in the rest of the Gaza Strip as well. A new soldiers' station has been set up on the roof of a block of flats which are kitty-corner to our apartment. We have been under surveillance every time we go out on our balcony. In addition, there is an almost continuous stream of military vehicles up and down the street, along with an increased number of foot patrols. I doubt there will be any disturbances today.

Perhaps the Israelis are being extremely cautious at this time because of the popular uprising which has just overthrown the government of Nicolae Caecescu in Romania. It is possible they think a similar thing will happen in the Occupied Territories. I don't think so, for the Palestinian culture prevents the people from organizing on a large scale. For example, they will not let women participate, nor are they really committed to any concept which is external to their own families. The idea of nationhood is understood only in a very superficial way.

January 5th 1990

Already this year I am craving Western food. The situation in Gaza is quite grim. While it is possible to get the basics, and we are not starving, the circumstances are similar to Britain during the Second World War. The food we have is of low quality, and our diet is poor. Today we went to the supermarket, and it was almost empty. We managed to get jam, a little cheese, teabags we don't like, and a chocolate bar. Beef and chicken can be bought, but the meat is usually tough and stringy. Tonight I want English fish and chips, a seafood curry, hot rice pudding, and apple pie!

January 16th 1990

Yesterday the schools re-opened for the first time in about a month, and immediately the soldiers in our area were very active in clashes with students. At about 7 a.m. yesterday, Rhona was out on the balcony when two stun grenades were thrown from a speeding Jeep. These weapons work well, so Rhona was quite confused and frightened by the incident. It was difficult to understand why the soldiers threw the grenades because there were no problems, and the street was full of children walking to school. Shortly after this, a Jeep with a loudspeaker came by announcing that eight local schools had again been closed indefinitely. I doubt if they ever had time to open!

The schools around the Sun Centre remained open. As the first shift of children was returning home at 11 a.m., problems began to develop. From our office window, we watched the soldiers set a trap for some teenagers who were shouting at them and whistling derisively. I didn't see people throwing stones or burning tires. Nevertheless, we saw the soldiers give chase and arrest three teenage boys on the property of the orphanage next door.

The boys were treated roughly. One was immediately thrown to the ground, then picked up by his hair. All three were subjected to occasional punches to the head, and one was kneed in the genital area. None of the boys offered any resistance while being arrested and abused.

The prisoners were put in the back of a Jeep which waited for a few minutes before taking them away. While it was waiting, a soldier from another unit came over, climbed into the back of the Jeep, and beat up one of the boys. In other words, he deliberately walked at least 100 metres down the street to beat up this boy. Soldiers like this one seem to love being in Gaza because it gives them a chance to act out their most violent and destructive feelings. Unfortunately, they also act as role models for their more-normal colleagues and undoubtedly try to influence them to behave in the same manner.

Despite the protest of an elderly woman who appeared to be the mother of one of the boys, they were taken away. They will probably be put in administrative detention for six months. If they go to trial and are found guilty, they will be heavily fined and imprisoned for perhaps 18 months. As far as I could see, their only "crime" was to provoke the soldiers with derisive whistles.

January 18th 1990

Today it was quite tense in the schools near the Sun Centre. Most of them have been allowed to remain open. However, some of the girls' schools have either been closed or threatened with closure. Given the restricted role of females in Islamic society, it is difficult to understand why they are being punished.

Just after the local elementary school finished for the day, I saw an army Jeep cruising near the school. It circled the block a couple of times and then stopped at the school gates. The area was very quiet as most of the children had gone home. However, there was a small boy who looked less than ten years old standing against the wall. A soldier went over to him, took him by the shoulder, and put him in the back of the Jeep. I couldn't believe my eyes! I had just witnessed the arrest of a child who, as far as I could see, was completely innocent of even childish mischief.

I have been reading for some time of the soldiers arresting young children who are then charged with throwing stones. To get a child released from custody, the family must pay a large fine. The Palestinian newspaper, *El-Fajr*, regularly reports fines of up to $1,500 (US) for these alleged offenses. Perhaps I have witnessed such a case.

January 25th 1990

On January 22nd, we were visited by a group of people connected with the Canadian Embassy. They came to see our program and meet the students. Included in the group were Michel Desalaberry (First Secretary), Barbara Gibson (Head of the Middle East Desk at External Affairs in Ottawa), Brenda Minnis from the Embassy Small Grants Program, and a man from the Canada-Israel Committee.

The group met with our undergraduate students for about an hour. The session began with Michel presenting Mount Royal College pins to the four students who had successfully passed the TOEFL examination. The highest scorer was Adel El-Bhaissi, and he received particularly enthusiastic acclaim from the students.

Last year, Adel had his leg amputated due to cancer. The authorities often prevent him from keeping medical appointments in Tel Aviv. He is still quite ill, and we hope this achievement will be a psychological boost to his recovery.

There followed a discussion between the Canadian-Jewish visitor and the students. I think this man was courageous to come to Gaza and confront a very difficult situation. Unfortunately, he espoused some of the worst aspects of the Israeli position. He saw the Palestinians as being primarily responsible for the current situation, and believed a solution would come only when these people learned to behave themselves. During the debate, he mentioned he had a brother in the IDF, and this made me speculate as to where his loyalties might lie. This man is very intelligent and articulate, so our students did very well in holding their ground in the discussions, especially as English is their second language.

February 2nd 1990

Today we travelled to Jerusalem to buy textbooks for the program. We were taken by a driver at the Centre. It was an uneventful journey, but to our surprise he did not know his way around the city. This seems to be the case with many of the drivers who appear to have little experience of the world outside the Gaza Strip. It seemed incongruous to be helping a Palestinian find the main post office in East Jerusalem.

On the way home, we entered Gaza when people were leaving the mosques after Friday prayers. As we passed the big mosque on the main road near Jabalia, I noticed some men were reading papers which were perhaps leaflets from the leaders of the uprising. An Israeli personnel carrier passed by, and a few rocks were half-heartedly thrown. Suddenly, the situation became very tense and our driver put his foot down to get us away from the hundreds of people who started to pick up stones. At this point, I saw a boy who looked about seven years old crying out in pain. He was put into the back of a Palestinian car which sped off. It seems the boy had been wounded.

A few seconds later we saw the car again. It was travelling very fast in the direction of the Shifa Hospital. As it came to the military checkpoint in the main street of the Tufah neighborhood, it veered off in order to by-pass the soldiers. The driver knew he might be arrested if he were found carrying a wounded person in his car.

February 10th 1990

At 6 a.m. this morning our neighborhood was put under curfew. We do not know the reason for this. I called Hatem, and he sent Abed who has a pass to drive during the curfew for humanitarian reasons. He picked us up, and although the soldiers stopped us, we were allowed to proceed to the Centre where it was pretty much business as usual.

This afternoon there were visitors for lunch. Pauline Nutting is a British surgeon and Ben Aloffs, her partner, is a theatre nurse. They met in Beirut where they both worked for several years. Currently, they are doing a four-month stint at the Ahli Arab Hospital. I really admire people like this who give up lucrative positions in the West to give much-needed help in the developing world where they often work in the most appalling conditions.

I asked Pauline about the current situation at Ahli. She said they were dealing with from three to ten bullet wounds daily. She was most distressed about a ten-year-old boy who was brought in two days ago. He is still in a coma, after being beaten by the soldiers.

February 16th 1990

Today there was a strike called by Islamic Jihad. It was also a Friday — our day off. We were awakened at 7 a.m. by the doorbell; it was the soldiers. I went down to the street, and as usual, the scene was quite bizarre. A patrol of the dreaded Border Police were trying to get people to come out of their houses because someone had written on the walls during the night. This was the first time there has been any writing in over a month. The soldiers were very angry because people were not answering their doors. One of them climbed the wall of the house opposite ours and threw big rocks at the door while shouting loudly for the occupants to come out. Meanwhile, his companions were collecting rocks and throwing them up to him.

Rami had already gone to answer the door, so by the time I got there, he and Salah were bringing paint to erase the writing on our wall. As usual, I stood out on the street, hoping my presence might minimize the abuse Salah would have to suffer. When one of the soldiers saw me speak to Salah, he started shouting at me. I suppose one is not even allowed to speak without their permission. Although I was scared and angry, I spoke calmly in English. I told him I was a foreigner and didn't understand Arabic. As he didn't understand English, he became confused, resorting to cursing under his breath and scowling at me.

It has been an interesting week. Today Hatem left for Washington and Calgary in the hope of finally bringing back some long-promised money for the Society which is in a very difficult financial situation. He asked me to be in charge of the school while he is away. Although I am honored that he would entrust the operation of the Centre to a foreigner, I am not looking forward to the extra workload.

February 23rd 1990

Yesterday I witnessed an incredible scene from the window of my office at the Sun Centre. It began when a group of teenage boys set up a barricade in the street. It included wrecked cars and some burning material. Then they started to whistle and shout to attract the soldiers. After a while, a personnel carrier appeared and the boys ran away. The vehicle had a plough on the front and was able to break down the barricade.

Some ten minutes later, a group of about 20 teenage boys returned to a piece of open land next to the school. Here they began to chant pro-Palestinian slogans until the IDF re-appeared. The soldiers began to shoot from the street, and all the boys immediately ducked and then ran away. They hid behind the wall of the school and continued their chanting. One or two of the leaders ventured out cautiously and threw a few stones. The soldiers were standing about 200 metres away and so were out of range of these missiles. They continued to fire sporadically at the boys until it became clear that these *shabab* were out of range of the bullets. The boys continued to chant, and the soldiers seemed reluctant to leave the street to chase them. It looked like a stand-off.

In the interim, the soldiers rounded up a group of middle-aged and elderly men and made them remove the remains of the barricade from the street. The men did this meekly and without protest. This seems to be the story of the intifada, with the defiant youth screaming in protest, while their beaten elders collaborate, bereft of the will to resist.

The stand-off continued on the empty piece of land by the school. As the soldiers became frustrated, their discipline started to wane. They began shouting obscenities at the teenagers, making vulgar signs, and challenging them to come and fight. The teenagers stood their ground, now clearly directed by their leaders. It was one of those rare occasions when the Palestinians showed more discipline than their rivals who were made to appear indecisive and ineffective.

February 24th 1990

As we left for a vacation in Egypt, we got a glimpse of Gaza as the Soweto of Israel. It was 5:30 a.m. and not yet light, but the service taxi stands in the downtown area were at their busiest. The shops nearby were doing a roaring trade in selling sandwiches and cans of pop. The customers were the thousands of men who rise at 4 or 4:30 a.m. each day to travel to Tel Aviv to find casual work at a rate of less than half that paid to a Jewish person for doing the same job.

The drive from Gaza City to the Eretz checkpoint was very beautiful in the pre-dawn light. A new crescent moon hung over the rooftops, and the silhouettes of palm trees and minarets contrasted sharply with the lightening sky. The central market was beginning to stir. A family sat huddled around a glowing firebox and two or three donkey carts were approaching the city, their owners wishing to make an early start on their trading. These were glimpses of a rural life that has changed little since the time of the Ottoman Empire.

There were also hundreds of service taxis heading for Eretz. Here, they were stopped by the soldiers, checked, and perhaps allowed to continue. The young soldiers are often arrogant, knowing the power they hold over each man wishing to work in Israel. If they don't let a man leave the Gaza Strip, there may be no food for his family that day. The soldiers worked sluggishly, the road jammed up with five lanes of cars, and slowly at regular intervals a single vehicle passed through the checkpoint and began the 50-mile journey to Tel Aviv. Once there, many of the men will stand in the human markets at places like Rishon Le Ziyyon, waiting to be hired. In the early evening, they will come back to Gaza, for Palestinians are not allowed to remain overnight in Israel. Many return home bone-weary, knowing they will be on the road again within a few hours. To the State of Israel, the Gaza Strip has become a "native township."

The School

The hot afternoon sun beats down on the arid landscape, dotted here and there with a small town or village. We have passed through areas of intensively-cultivated sugar cane by the banks of the River Nile, but in this area the Eastern Desert reigns supreme, with dunes and dry gullies stretching away to the Red Sea coast.

It has been a fascinating day visiting the remains of ancient temples which must have been stunning in their prime. Ahead of us, a two-hour drive to the south, lies Aswan. The Nile, on our right, flows north to Cairo and the delta, its placid waters the vehicle for an assortment of contrasts. The *feluccas* of the local people drift dream-like, their triangular sails billowing gently in the minimal breeze. Their grace and charm are overwhelmed by the enormous, clumsy-looking ships which are floating versions of the Hilton Hotel or Holiday Inn. Poverty and affluence, adaptation and exploitation, harmony and intrusion are all juxtaposed on this stretch of water that is the lifeline of Lower Egypt, Nubia, and the Sudan.

The magical quality of this region is missing in northern Egypt. Here even the light seems different, softer. The people are just as poor, I suspect, but theirs is a rural poverty rather than the seemingly unconquerable poverty of the urban horrors that are Cairo and Alexandria. Perhaps there is less unemployment, and more land and space for the people; perhaps these are the critical factors. There is none of the persistent, unpleasant harassment of street vendors selling souvenirs, or camel boys desperately pursuing tourists around the historic sites. This is much more like, say, Greece, where the people seem able to make enough money to be satisfied, and have time to feel happy.

Jamal, our driver, is typical of the people we have encountered in and around Aswan. His English is minimal but gets him by with most tourists. However, when he discovers that we speak some Arabic he switches happily into his native tongue. It has been a pleasant, relaxed day, and he has been very sensitive to our needs. On the outward journey he had played some tapes of Arab music in the car, and I had casually asked if he had a tape of Umm Khalsoum, the revered singer-queen of all Egypt. He didn't, but after dropping us off at the magnificent temple near Edfu, Jamal went shopping. When he picked us up some two hours later, we found he had bought a tape of Umm Khalsoum to play on the way home.

Over lunch in Edfu, he tells us he has been a driver for fourteen years. Because of his dark skin, he is readily identifiable as Nubian. He is thirty years old. We ask him about education in Aswan and get a reply that, as usual, is paradoxical. On the one hand, he seems rather ashamed to admit to having only an elementary school education. "*Mish kwayyis*!" (not good), he had said. Education is very important. But on the other hand, he could not see the relevance of a higher education in driving a taxi, sailing a *felucca* or cutting sugar cane. The choice of work in Aswan is so very limited, why does anyone need education beyond a little reading and writing?

Jamal wants to marry a foreign woman. He says they are prettier. "How much do you pay for a wife in Canada?" he asks Peter, who tries to explain that the idea would be *haraam* (shameful) in Canada, for women are not like cars and furniture, they are human beings. Jamal looks totally puzzled. I expect he thinks North American men must be incredibly weak if they cannot chuck their weight about with women.

For my part in the discussion, I take him up on the "pretty" business. We come across this prejudice all the time. Arab men think Western women are always prettier than the native women, and it simply isn't true. It's a form of cultural stereotyping, and their prejudice is all to do with skin color. Where Westerners strive for a deep tan, the Arab equivalent is to make your skin look as light as possible. It is all quite ridiculously sad.

Jamal says that if he could get a visa, he would go to Canada or any other country tomorrow. I wonder if this is true. We have heard this so often in Gaza, and in those instances where we have assisted students with form-filling and information, we have found that as the chance of leaving increases, some get cold feet and decide to stay. It's understandable, especially in a culture where the physical closeness of family is so highly valued. Moving away causes a great deal of distress. The common practice, in Gaza at any rate, is for another floor to be added on to the existing house for each son as he marries, brings home a new wife, and starts a family. Families stay together.

To our left among the sandy hills and gullies, I suddenly see a primitive-looking, cream and blue structure standing in isolation below a rocky ridge. Two skinny-looking trees make an ineffectual effort at providing shade.

"What is that?" I ask Jamal.

"A school," he replies.

"Is it possible for me take a picture?" I inquire. Of course it is, for Jamal will do anything to ensure that we have a happy day. I expect him to pull over to the side of the road while I search in the bag for my camera. But suddenly we are lurching off across the sand. Jamal insists everything is all right. He maneuvers along the narrow tracks until we are prevented from going further by a deep gully. Jamal stops the car, tells us to please wait, and sets off walking across the desert toward the little school now only a few hundred metres away. He has us figured out and knows that we enjoy interacting with people much more than the average tourist.

We get out of the car and wait in the hot afternoon sun. Some breeze wafts across the sand from the Nile, so it is not unpleasant. I will not take any pictures until I get the go-ahead from Jamal, as he will know what etiquette is required in this situation. He disappears into the school and emerges after a few minutes with two men and a small child. He points to where we are waiting, says something to the men and then we see him beckoning us. We are delighted at this opportunity to actually visit the little school and so set off to join him.

He introduces us to an imposing-looking gentleman who is wearing sunglasses, a white *galabiyya*, and a blue scarf swathed in a turban around his head. This is the principal. Then we meet the other three male staff members and the caretaker who has been assigned the task of making us Arab mint tea on a small butane camp stove set near the clay water jar beside the two unsuccessful shade trees. The small child seems to belong to the caretaker, but is too young to attend the school formally.

A rickety table and two benches have been set out under the awning of the cement porch. Blankets have been suspended between the cement pillars of the porch. Today they are rolled up, but presumably they are used as sun-blocks when the weather becomes very hot, as it will in only a few weeks' time.

While the tea-water is being prepared, we sit and talk to the staff. We share information on teacher training, qualifications, number of students in school, the area it services, examinations, and special education. As we talk, there is barely a sound from the two classrooms except for quiet whispering now and then. One of the teachers produces an atlas and finds Canada.

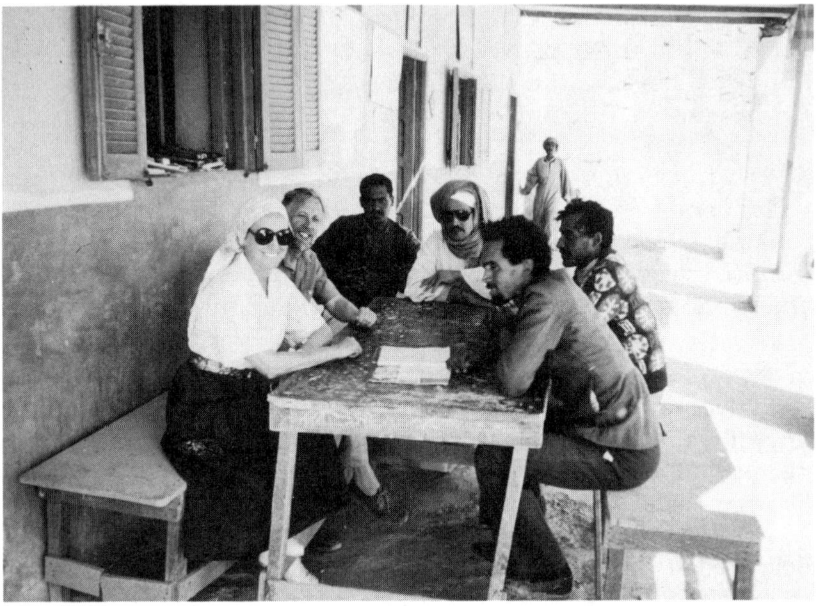

Near Aswan, Egypt: Rhona and Peter meeting with the teachers at the country schoolhouse. The principal is the man with sunglasses and a turban.

"Show us where you live," he asks. We look at the west coast of our homeland and there locate the word "Vancouver," written in Arabic script.

"It is a very big country," the teachers say. We agree. Although these men have had some education, we have the feeling we might just as easily have said we were from Mars, it is all so far away from what they know. Jamal seems quite proud at having produced tourists who are interested in Arab people, and has done his P.R. work, for we are invited to go and visit the nearby village which the school serves. We are genuinely regretful that we do not have the time, for we have to catch a plane in only a few hours' time. We tell them we will try to come again, and would like to visit the children before we leave.

As we enter each of the two classrooms, the children stand respectfully. There are about twelve of them in each of the two rooms. They are shy but delightful, and try to understand our Arabic, telling us their names and which subjects they like best in school. Inside the classrooms the children are segregated; girls sit on one side of the room, boys on the other. All wear the long white *galabiyya* over ordinary clothes. Despite the heat, many of them seem to be wearing high-necked sweaters beneath their robes. Their schoolbags hang on the backs of their chairs or are placed on the fixed wooden bench that is attached to the ancient desks. Some of the bags are made of canvas or cotton; many are plastic, and one little girl has a tote decorated with a large picture of what looks like a young Arab wearing a cowboy costume. It reminds me of the villages we have passed through, where the walls are

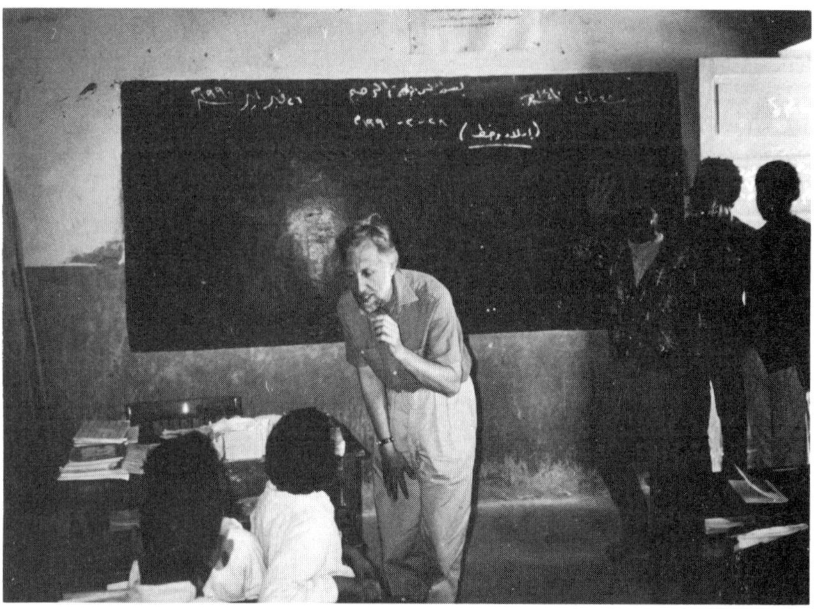

Near Aswan, Egypt: Peter talking with a child about Canada while a friendly teacher waves at the camera.

decorated, not with scenes of local daily life, but with jet planes and other icons of Western technology. I suppose this is one impact of televised, osmotic education.

The dusty floor is made of cement. Blue framed and shuttered windows give air and visual access to the outside, but there is nothing to see except desert, and so they are placed high up in the wall. Obviously, there are none of the concepts of children's curiosity that we cater to in the West. However, there is also a practical aspect to the architecture for the shutters are closed on one side of the classrooms, keeping out the warm sunshine, while on the opposite wall they are wide open to allow in the breeze.

Maps and charts decorate the walls, but there is not a single picture, nor any examples of the children's work on display. The one large blackboard and the maps seem to be the only visual aids in the classrooms. On a small cement platform at the back of one room lies a set of faded textbooks which have long abandoned their covers, if indeed they ever had any. They look as though they were recently retrieved from one of the ancient tombs!

Now that the formalities of tea-drinking and conversation have been accomplished, I can take photographs and everyone is very pleased. The teachers, principal, janitor, and children crowd into the small rooms to be included. We promise we will try to send the pictures somehow, or will bring them ourselves, *inshallah*. And then we must take our leave.

We walk back across the sand to the car which has been left unlocked with our passports and money inside, for this is not Cairo where everything has to be carried safely on your person. Here, in the small villages, you can leave anything around, and it will not be stolen. Jamal had been incredulous and somewhat offended (but forgiving) when I had told him I was worried about leaving the car unlocked.

I turn and take one last picture of the school in the desert as the principal and the janitor wave goodbye and go back inside. As we drive back to Aswan, I reflect on what we've experienced today. I wonder how I'm going to feel and act when I return to teaching in Canada and the union starts telling us we must fight for better working conditions!

CHAPTER FOURTEEN

March – April 1990

March 8th 1990

Three or four days ago Rhona and I returned from Egypt where we had an exotic vacation, visiting Cairo, Alexandria, Fayoum, and Aswan.

Just prior to our leaving Gaza, the intifada intensified and continues to be "hot." For example, Rafah was under curfew for eight consecutive days. On one of these days, the media reported that 70 people were wounded.

Today the area around the Sun Centre was like a battleground. I was trying to run a teachers' meeting, but we couldn't hear each other across the table due to prolonged gunfire near the school. People in the neighborhood said there was a group of about 100 demonstrators — women and children led by masked youths in paramilitary outfits. Rhona saw the soldiers shooting tear gas and stun grenades right into the middle of the crowd of children. She also saw flashes from the barrels of the guns as the soldiers fired. Wasfia said that on our street the soldiers retreated temporarily when they were pelted with stones. One of my students who is from Rafah said that this morning he counted a group of 77 soldiers inside the camp.

The media remains completely silent about these events. Neither the Voice of Israel nor the BBC World Service has mentioned the Gaza Strip for some time. Instead we hear of the endless machinations of the Likud Party as they try to avoid peace negotiations.

March 17th 1990

For about a week, we have had soldiers stationed outside the house. They are preventing Israeli Government cars from travelling down Ittalatini Street, presumably because they cannot guarantee their safety. The *shabab* have become very active in stoning all cars with the yellow Israeli license plates.

I was awakened in the middle of the night by gunfire. I think about ten shots were fired, perhaps more. This morning I noticed there was new writing on the walls. I suppose that during the night the soldiers had surprised the masked teenagers while they were writing announcements of the next strike days and other political slogans. I don't know if anyone was killed or wounded.

It seems that the soldiers are acting under different orders these days. Although they often fire their guns, they do not seem to be as intent on killing people. In support of this hypothesis, the official casualty list is considerably lower than it was at this time last year.

Two days ago Israel's National Unity government fell to a vote of no confidence. Basically, the Labour Party withdrew from the coalition and enough of the smaller parties joined them to outvote the Likud group. It seems abundantly clear that Mr. Shamir has never had any intention of negotiating with the Palestinians. An article in the *Jerusalem Post* said the Prime Minister's ambition is not to move one millimetre nearer to peace during his political career.

March 20th 1990

This is the second of two successive strike days which have been fully observed in our neighborhood. Yesterday's strike was called by Islamic Jihad, while today it is the United Leadership's turn.

On March 18th, there was another terrible incident near the Sun Centre. At about 10 a.m., the usual demonstration was taking place at the school just behind the Centre. The *shabab* had brought garbage from the dump to block the street and a group of them were standing near the wall of the school whistling at the soldiers and chanting Palestinian slogans. I expect that stones were also hurled in the direction of the soldiers.

At this time, I was in one of the classrooms watching a student who was teaching a group of three or four handicapped children. It was difficult for the children to focus on the lesson because of the noise of the demonstration. At one point, we let them look out of the window for a few minutes so they could see what was happening. After this, the children returned to their seats and continued with their lesson.

Meanwhile, Rhona was leaving the Centre to do some food shopping. Our car was parked on the street in front of the school and as Rhona walked toward it she saw a group of soldiers in the intersection some 30 metres away. From their uniforms, she recognized the Border Police, and one of them, a sharpshooter, was down on one knee taking careful aim at the group of Palestinian teenagers. An officer was leaning over the sharpshooter, presumably giving him instructions.

Rhona said she knew the soldier was going to shoot one of the *shabab*. She wanted to shout and tell him to stop, but she was afraid he might think he was being attacked and shoot at her instead. Suddenly there was a deafening roar as the soldier fired at his target. Afterwards, Rhona re-lived her period of indecision as if it had lasted for many minutes. In reality, the shooting was probably over in less than a second; she could have done nothing to prevent it.

After this, events became confusing. We heard that a high school student had been wounded. Sabah, our assistant, reported seeing an ambulance entering the school grounds. Rhona saw the traffic come to a halt on El-Waehda Street while an ambulance drove past with its siren wailing. Finally Khaled, the Assistant Director at the Centre, told me the student had been taken to Telashomer Hospital in Israel because his wounds were so serious.

The next morning the Voice of Israel reported widespread "rioting" in Gaza on the previous day. The announcer said that during a demonstration in the Rimal district, an 18-year-old youth was shot. He later died from his wounds. This was the incident which Rhona had witnessed.

Later in the day of March 18th, two Jeeps full of soldiers stopped at the gate of the Sun Centre. They wanted to confiscate one of the Centre's vans in order to drive around Gaza undetected. A messenger was sent to ask me to intervene, but I was upstairs, and it took me some time to reach the gate. In the meantime, Elias, the Business Manager, explained to the officer that we were a school for handicapped children and needed all our vans to transport the students to and from their homes. The soldiers reluctantly agreed and grudgingly drove off in search of another vehicle. I have heard of the soldiers using this method to capture unsuspecting Palestinians but have always thought it was a myth. Evidently, I was wrong!

March 29th 1990

The Gaza Strip is under curfew in preparation for Land Day which is tomorrow. The rumor is that the curfew will remain in effect for three days. The IDF have set up a soldiers' station on the roof of an apartment some 200 metres down the street from here and the Israeli flag flies over Ittalatini Street once again.

Yesterday we had a group of about 30 visitors in the Centre. They are British Quakers from Woodbrook College in England. They had an educative hour with our students who, with some very forthright speech, punctured the visitors' "nice" view of life. Afterwards, the Quakers presented a cheque to the Society and some toys for the children.

March 31st 1990

This is the third day of the curfew but we expect to be allowed out tomorrow. These days seem to have been very quiet, but since we are not allowed out on the street and reporters are not allowed into the Gaza Strip except under the supervision of an IDF officer, we really have no idea what is happening outside our own neighborhood.

April 6th 1990

Last Tuesday I went to Tel Aviv with Hatem to buy some equipment for the Mothers' Program. These expeditions are usually interesting because we get to meet ordinary Israelis in informal situations. This trip was no exception.

At the business machine dealership we met a man named Moshe who is about 40 years old. He is of course a reserve soldier, as every Jewish male in Israel under the age of 55 years must spend about seven weeks a year in the army. Moshe has had several tours of duty in the Occupied Territories.

He told us about a time when he was on duty in Hebron. His colleagues had collected a group of Palestinian teenagers and were holding them in a detention room. The boys were made to stand spread-eagled with the palms of their hands flat against the wall in front of them. Then a group of soldiers with sticks stood in the middle of the room. They shouted at the boys, "Who eats donkey shit?" If the boys did not shout "Arafat" in response, they were beaten with the clubs. This is significant because it is the first time I have heard an Israeli soldier mention such an incident, thus substantiating the Palestinian stories I had previously dismissed as rumor and propaganda.

Last evening we went for Ramadan breakfast at the home of two of our students who live in the Nasser district. We took a visitor with us, Jim Graff, president of the Near East Cultural and Educational Foundation of Canada (NECEF). He is a philosophy professor at the University of Toronto who has become interested in the political situation of the Palestinians. NECEF is the organization which raised the scholarship money for Azzad and Iyad.

Rhona and I both liked Jim very much but found him to be caught up in the world of diplomacy. When our friends expressed some rather forceful ideas about the occupation, Jim took a conservative position, insisting the Palestinians must be patient because the situation is slowly changing. He listed a number of diplomatic initiatives in support of his argument, but as Rhona pointed out, these haven't made the slightest impact on the lives of the 650,000 Palestinians who are trying to eke out a living in Gaza. Their situation remains without hope. ▪

April 11th 1990

Today there is a strike called by Islamic Jihad. Although the situation in Gaza City has been relatively quiet in recent days, there have been major problems in Rafah and Khan Younis. Rafah was under curfew for several days last week after a Palestinian was killed by the soldiers. Khan Younis has also been closed following an incident at a mosque.

The trouble began when soldiers spotted a youth trying to attach a Palestinian flag to the minaret of the main mosque in the town. As the boy was trying to escape, he was shot and wounded. The injury caused him to fall to his death. To make matters worse, the soldiers then ordered the mosque to be closed even though this is the holy month of Ramadan. This action provoked large demonstrations and the corollary retaliation. The end result has been that our students from Khan Younis have not been able to attend class for several days.

April 12th 1990

Today when we arrived home from the Centre we discovered the intercom system at our gate had been smashed in, the main gate to the house had sustained much damage, and all the panes of frosted glass had been broken. Our neighbors explained that there had been the usual problems in the street at about noon. The teenagers were returning from school and stones were thrown at the soldiers. The soldiers thought the *shabab* were hiding in our garden, so they damaged the intercom and the gate in efforts to gain access to the property.

The soldiers eventually forced their way in and searched the house. The only people at home were the two old ladies downstairs. When confronted by the soldiers they merely said "*Ahlan wa Sahlan*" (welcome), and returned to reading the Koran. The soldiers continued their search, but of course the teenagers were not hiding in either the house or the garden.

April 22nd 1990

We seem to be in a period of strikes and curfews. Currently, there is a two-day strike called by the United Leadership and on April 16th we were put under curfew because it was the second anniversary of the assassination of Abu Jihad. There has been a call for an escalation in the intifada.

Our neighborhood is more active than at any time since the beginning of the intifada. I am not sure if this is true of the entire Gaza Strip. Every day at about 11:30 a.m. when the children return from school clashes begin near the house. The soldiers are stoned, and they respond by chasing or firing at the *shabab*.

These students take enormous risks for they run out into the street and throw stones at the army Jeeps from a distance of about two metres. I am surprised by the depth of anger in the voices of these children. They scream their insults and seem to have a kind of reckless courage, given it is always the uzi against the stone. When adults tell the boys to be careful, they reply calmly and seriously that they want to die. In some ways this is not surprising for their lives in Gaza are almost totally without hope.

This week we moved to the new college building — after a three-year wait! It is quite spacious and a vast improvement on our three or four small rooms at the Sun Centre. Much work remains to be done on the building, and we are barely functional at the moment, but soon this location will provide an excellent setting for the university program.

April 28th 1990

Rhona and I have just returned from three days in Jerusalem and Tel Aviv. We took advantage of the Eidd El-Fittr holiday and bought souvenirs in the Old City before shopping in Tel Aviv and sending parcels to Canada in advance of our return. We will be returning home in about two months.

While we were away, there was a dreadful incident in Jabalia. On the first day of the Feast it is the custom to visit the tombs of the intifada martyrs who are buried in the graveyard of this refugee camp. Following this year's visit, the people marched on the soldiers' station which is situated in the middle of the camp. Here the people met with an extreme reaction, for the *Jerusalem Post* reported that three were killed and more than 150 wounded. The IDF said two people died and more than 100 were hurt, while local sources claimed four deaths and hundreds of injuries. By anybody's reckoning, this was one of the worst incidents since the beginning of the intifada. Interestingly, a similar event occurred in Nusseirat Camp on the first day of last year's Feast.

April 29th 1990

Last evening, there was a radio announcement to the effect that the Gaza Strip is being placed under curfew for a period of two days. During this period, it is Remembrance and Independence Days in Israel so this is the probable reason for the curfew. However, when I referred to my journal, I discovered that we were not under curfew at this time last year. I wonder why we are being punished this time around.

Children And Politics 5

From our office window in the Centre we watch as a young boy of about sixteen hauls an assortment of debris from the nearby garbage dump and shapes it into a barrier across the street, creating a hindrance to the army Jeeps which regularly patrol the area. We have seen this strategy dozens of times. It has almost become a game between the two groups who seem quite resigned to the familiar ritual. When the barricade is finished, the soldiers will stop passersby, confiscate their identity cards, and order them to clear the street. The routine will start all over again as soon as the army Jeep is out of sight.

I become bored watching the barricade construction and leave the office to do some hasty shopping before the stores close at noon. Downstairs, as I am getting into my car, I hear the crackle of an army radio and a Jeep stops a few yards away. The soldiers are unaware of me as they get out and hold a discussion, all the time looking down the cross street to where I know the teenager is still making his barricade. I still don't think anything more than identity-card confiscation is in the works.

One of the soldiers, who looks no older than the Palestinian boy at the barricade, drops to his knee, and I am suddenly very alarmed. I have seen this before, and it means the soldier is aiming at a specific target. He pauses and glances away from his gun-sight to whatever it is he is aiming at, while his colleague leans over him, apparently giving instruction. I cannot see the teenager from where I am, but I know he is still there and may be unaware of what is happening.

I want to shout. Sometimes the presence of a foreigner can inhibit the soldiers, but I am afraid that if I do shout, the soldiers might think they are being attacked from behind, and one of them already has his finger on the trigger.

The rifle shot is deafening as I sit cowering in the car, hands over my ears. I want to get away from what is happening. I start the car and drive off. I reach the main street where traffic is coming to a halt as an ambulance from a nearby clinic screeches its way past me to the street where the youth was making his barricade.

On the evening news, I hear that a teenager was shot dead in Gaza for blocking a road and shouting anti-Israel slogans. I cannot sleep for nights. The mother in me sees the nightmare of somebody's son, barely out of high school, trained out of any human feeling to the point where he can kill someone else's son in cold blood. Meanwhile, the other willingly relinquishes his life to martyrdom, his portrait prepared ahead of time for the book of so-called heroes which is discreetly circulated with pride throughout the homes and institutions of Gaza.

I find it sufficiently bizarre to hear Palestinian mothers announce with pride that their sons are martyrs. But what do the Israeli mothers say?

Children And Politics 6

A few days after the shooting incident, I go into the vegetable shop on the street where the boy was killed. As I enter the store, I am accosted by two teenaged boys on their way home from school who speak to me quietly in Arabic. They seem not to want to be overheard. Politely they ask if I will answer some questions and I agree.

"You are from Canada?" they begin.

"Yes."

"Please, Canada lady," they say, "Please help us to get to your country. We will work at anything. If we stay here there is no hope for us; we have no future."

The death of the teenager is still wracking my emotions. Now I feel more impotent than ever, for I know the impossibility of what they are asking me to do. I have gone through this before, helping fill out immigration forms that I know are an exercise in futility. There are too many criteria to meet; criteria with which I cannot really argue.

"Can you speak any English?" I begin.

"No, but we will learn."

I go through the list I know only too well. They can do some carpentry work but that is all. Like the dead boy, they do not stand a chance.

I try to be encouraging as the tears run down my face. I tell them what I truly believe.

"Education," I say. "That is your best chance of getting away. Go to school when you can, and study hard. That way you will also be helping your country."

They are dejected but not angry; they say they understand, and then leave the shop with the blessing, "*Ma'essalaama*" (with peace). It will be another sleepless night for me. No one can help the dead, and I can't even seem to help the living.

CHAPTER FIFTEEN

May – June 1990

May 12th 1990

Today I had a rather frightening experience in the old city. I was with Tom Oakland, a visiting professor from Texas, and we were travelling back to the college after visiting the Dar es Salaam institution. As we were passing through one of the very narrow streets in the Zeitun quarter, our way was blocked by what seemed to be an ordinary white Puegot taxi. Then a group of terrified *shabab* came sprinting down the street past us. Some of them attempted to get into cars, while others tried to enter the buildings on either side of the street. As men suddenly leaped out of the white Puegot, I noticed the sun glinting on the metal barrels of the revolvers they were carrying. I immediately realized that these men were soldiers who had disguised themselves as Palestinians in order to surprise the *shabab*. We heard people screaming and the sound of shooting nearby, and witnessed the arrest of one young man. There was pandemonium in the narrow street.

I tried to reverse down the street to get us out of danger, but the situation was more complex than I thought. At the point where I tried to turn around, I scraped the car against the walls in a couple of places. Then I drove like crazy through a maze of alleys toward Omar El-Mukhtar Street from where I expected to be able to drive to the college without further difficulty.

The area, however, had just been put under curfew. There were neither people nor cars on this main street of Gaza City. Looking left toward Palestine Square, I could see large groups of soldiers and personnel carriers. The length of the street looked like a battleground. I took a chance by driving quickly across Omar El-Mukhtar and into another maze of narrow streets, this time hoping to reach El-Waehda Street and drive north out of the downtown area.

But there were also problems on El-Waehda Street. We encountered a large traffic jam caused by a barricade erected across the street. Now we could not move at all because we were surrounded by other vehicles also trying to leave the area. Soon the soldiers arrived to remove the barricade, but they were pelted with stones, pieces of cement, and other debris which rained down from the rooftops of the buildings on either side of the street. Again there was much shouting and screaming. Cars were honking, and mothers were trying to drag their protesting teenage sons into the houses.

Eventually, the barricade was cleared and we were able to proceed to the college. This has been perhaps my most frightening experience since I arrived in Gaza. None of the incidents were particularly unusual but previously I have always been able to extricate myself within two or three minutes. This time the unrest was so widespread that we seemed to be in the midst of it for a long time. In reality the journey from Dar es Salaam to the college took no more than 20 minutes.

May 20th 1990

Today at 7 a.m. Rhona and I were listening to the news in English on the Voice of Israel. The announcer was reporting an incident that had just happened at Rishon Le-Ziyyon on the outskirts of Tel Aviv. Workers from the Gaza Strip were waiting to be hired for the day when a man in army fatigues asked for their identity cards. He then made them sit on the ground before opening fire with an uzi. Israel radio reported that four people were killed and ten wounded.

When we got to the college, nobody knew of the incident because it had not yet been announced on the Arabic stations. The morning started as usual, and I went to the Sun Centre for a meeting. Before it could start, we heard of widespread disturbances, so the school was closed immediately and the children taken back to their homes. At this point I drove back to the college and encountered many cars driving with their headlights on in memory of the deaths. When I arrived at the college the students were in a state of great anxiety and Nasser, the psychologist, reported that the downtown area was "like a war zone." Consequently, we closed the college at 9:30 a.m. and returned home.

Our area seemed like a scene from Beirut. There were burning tires and barricades in many intersections and a pall of acrid smoke hung over the neighborhood. Several people told us that the entire Gaza Strip was under curfew, but there were crowds of people in the streets spreading rumors and panic. Periodically cars hurtled up and down Ittalatini Street overflowing with young men who waved Palestinian flags and shouted *Allahu akbar*. These scenes continued for perhaps two hours.

The Israeli army gradually began to increase its grip on the situation. Although many burning tires and barricades remained, we became aware of helicopters and spotter planes flying overhead, and one or two Jeeps were seen on Ittalatini Street. Eventually most people went home and later the soldiers announced we were under curfew until further notice. The Gaza Strip has been closed to the media and the telephone lines have been cut off. Once more, we have been virtually isolated from the outside world.

At 11 a.m. we listened to the BBC World Service and were told that seven people had been killed and five others seriously wounded. Their assailant was said not to be a soldier but a mentally-disturbed young man wearing his brother's army uniform. The killer is now under arrest.

Continued at 8:30 p.m.

We have just had an update on the situation from the radio. It seems that seven people were killed and 11 wounded in the Rishon Le-Ziyyon incident. In the ensuing disturbances in the West Bank and Gaza Strip, it was reported that another six people have been killed and more than 200 wounded. It is difficult to assess the validity of this information, given that the Gaza Strip and many places in the West Bank are off limits to the media. As I write this I can hear, out there in the darkness, the sound of many voices shouting *Allahu akbar*.

Rhona and I believe that today's events clearly illustrate the weaknesses of the Palestinian resistance to the military occupation. Early this morning, with the army unprepared and at a disadvantage, they could have staged a mass demonstration in the centre of the town perhaps taking over the town hall. Instead, almost everybody seemed to rush home to their families. The small gangs of young men who took to the streets stayed close to their homes, threw stones at the soldiers for an hour or so, and then went inside. As usual, half the population — women — did not participate. The older people are mostly afraid, so they hurried home, locked their doors, and waited for the soldiers to lift the curfew. The Palestinians will never achieve nationhood without a radical change in attitudes and behaviors.

May 25th 1990

Yesterday it was necessary for us to try to leave Gaza even though we were entering our sixth day under curfew. We had to retrieve 12 boxes of college library books which had arrived at Ben Gurion Airport in Tel Aviv. They were donated by Canadian students. The customs people will only deal with Gazan residents on certain days of the week and yesterday was one of them. although the Gazans are not allowed to retrieve their goods, in typical Israeli fashion, they must still pay for them to be stored in the customs warehouse! Consequently, we felt the need to get to the airport as soon as possible to deal with this matter.

Fortunately, Hatem has a curfew pass for one of his drivers, and so this morning Emad came to take us to the airport. We also took the precaution of taking Tom Oakland with us because he has an American passport. Tom sat in the front of the car with Emad, while Rhona and I were in the back seats.

At 7:15 a.m. Gaza was like a ghost town. The streets were completely deserted. On the way to the Eretz Checkpoint we were stopped three times by the soldiers. Emad showed his pass, Tom flashed his passport, and on each occasion we were waved through the roadblock. They hardly glanced at Rhona and me in the back.

We accomplished what we could at the airport and then went on to the Canadian Embassy in Tel Aviv to pick up our mail. As we were leaving, we bumped into the Ambassador who invited us into his office as he wanted to hear our impressions of the situation in Gaza. The new Charge D'Affaires was also present during the interview.

Rhona and I described what we had seen and gave our opinions. We said that our part of Gaza had been out of Israeli control only for an hour or so. The reaction to the killings in Rishon Le-Ziyyon was strong but totally predictable — burning tires, barricaded streets, and stone throwing. There were no new strategies, little cooperation between the people, and even less large-scale organization. We concluded by pointing out that this type of resistance will always be contained with little effort by the IDF.

It was obvious from the face of the Ambassador and Charge D'Affaires that they did not like what we were saying. In true diplomatic style, their facial expressions never changed. When we challenged them on this, they told us they had an observer in Gaza immediately after the killings in Rishon Le-Ziyyon, and this person reported there were many violent confrontations between the soldiers and the *shabab*. I have no doubt this was true.

Why then is there something of a discrepancy between perceptions? Possibly it is due to the difference between experienced and inexperienced observers. A new person in Gaza may see the situation as violent and out of control, whereas we would see it in the context of daily life in Gaza. In other words, we are now able to predict the outcome of a particular incident with a fair amount of accuracy. I suspect that when people know the outcome of an incident, they rate it as being less violent than would a less-experienced observer. In spite of the wishful thinking of some people, we believe there is little chance that we are witnessing "the beginning of the end" of the Israeli occupation of Gaza and the West Bank.

Another issue is the Israeli control of information emanating from the Gaza Strip. It is possible that the Embassy observer had seen events of which we were completely unaware. Our problem is that as the curfew continues, we become more and more isolated from other parts of the community. We have information only about the events we see or hear from our apartment. This seems to be a deliberate policy of the occupying forces. The media have been barred from the Gaza Strip, and for several days, the curfew has not been mentioned on Israeli radio or television.

Last evening, as we were re-entering the Strip, we saw a convoy of cars leaving. We noticed that one of them was flying the tricolor and realized we were witnessing the end of a much-publicized visit by a French cabinet minister. His car stopped just outside the Gaza Strip and was immediately surrounded by media people who, earlier in the day, were not allowed to enter the area with him. Later, we heard on the radio that the minister had said Gaza was like a ghost town with only a few women wandering around seeking food for their children.

Within five minutes of leaving the French minister, we entered the city of Gaza — and what a sight met us! There were burning tires everywhere, and between the large mosque in Tufah and the big hill on El-Waehda Street, six or seven roadblocks controlled by dozens of *shabab*. It was necessary for us to stop at each one and seek permission to pass. The atmosphere was very tense as angry and hostile faces pressed against the windows looking for any clues which might indicate we were Israeli settlers. If they had thought we were anything but international aid workers, I think we would have been dragged out of the car and killed. Fortunately, Emad was able to convince them of our identities, and we were allowed to proceed.

At the bottom of Omar El-Mukhtar Street, we saw the Israeli army preparing to deal with this resistance. There were about 200 soldiers with personnel carriers organizing to move in on the barricades. We seemed to be witnessing the prelude to some violent clashes, and I was happy to leave the area.

Why hadn't the French minister seen all this activity? Probably because he was being escorted around the quieter parts of the Gaza Strip by an Israeli officer.

Soon after we reached home, we heard the curfew was to be lifted for a period of two hours. At this point, people went out on the street and some burning tires and barricades re-appeared. The soldiers stayed away from our neighborhood. A half an hour before the curfew was re-imposed, the streets were once again empty. The *shabab* had become bored and gone home.

May 27th 1990

We are under curfew for the eighth consecutive day. This is the longest curfew since we have been in Gaza. Many families are beginning to run out of food, and those with small children are existing under very difficult conditions. The situation is quiet and we expect to be let out shortly. We have heard that the people in Breiyuj, Nusseirat, and Mughazi Camps were released today, and if they do not cause trouble, the curfew on the rest of the Gaza Strip will be lifted tomorrow.

On the radio this morning several interesting items caught my attention. First, in Tel Aviv there was a large Peace Now rally which was attended by tens of thousands of people. Next, there was a demonstration by Israeli Arabs who are supporting their compatriots in the Occupied Territories. Finally, Canada has offered to be part of a UN peacekeeping force in the Gaza and the West Bank. Unfortunately, there is little chance of the Israeli government either being influenced by the demonstrations or agreeing to the proposal about a peace-keeping force.

June 11th 1990

Today we were stoned on our way home from the new college building. We were driving along Ittalatini Street when an army Jeep suddenly pulled out in front of us and another one came up quickly from behind. At this point the *shabab* decided we were Israeli settlers being escorted by the army, so they let fly with a barrage of rocks. I pulled over immediately, and we jumped out of the car. This action convinced the *shabab* that we were armed Israelis, so they fled into a maze of narrow streets and alleys. While these are common occurrences in Gaza, they are always unnerving because a person could be badly injured either by a stone or flying glass from a broken window.

June 15th 1990

Gaza has been very quiet since the curfew which followed the murders at Rishon Le-Ziyyon. We have been able to work every day and the programs are progressing well. It seems that long curfews really dampen the spirit of the intifada. Perhaps the loss of a week's income forces many families to put all their efforts into earning money to buy essential foods and medicines. Unless there are any other major incidents, I expect this period of relative calm to continue until the schools re-open in September.

Children And Politics 7

"*Shalom*!" the boy calls out as we walk by. It is a common encounter with the children of Gaza, and, following pre-briefing advice, we have so far ignored it. But there is something naggingly ignorant about the behavior that prompts us to explore it further.

We have been given a variety of explanations. The children think all foreigners in Gaza are Israelis, or they are trying to trick you into revealing that you are an Israeli, or they do it for no reason at all...take your pick. Whatever the reason, it is hard to imagine the children of Poland or France going around shouting greetings in the language of their German occupiers during the Second World War.

We discuss the matter with our students and explain that, from our point of view, it is a matter of education and awareness that one does not go around using the language of the oppressor. They agree, but we have already noted the reluctance on the part of the adult population to interfere with the behavior of male children in Gaza. Even when children have misbehaved in destructive ways, the word *shartir* (clever) is still used in any reprimand, so the boys get mixed messages, and the delinquency usually continues. The leaflets from the underground leadership seemed to be the most successful vehicle for changing their behavior, and were usually obeyed when new behavior was mandated.

Today we have hit upon a new strategy. After the boy's greeting in Hebrew, we stop dead in our tracks and face him, saying, "*Shu haada? Inta Yehudi*?" (What's this! Are you Jewish?). This is something totally unanticipated, and the boy's mouth drops open in surprise, the cocky grin completely wiped off his face.

"No! No! I am Palestinian!" he cries with fervor.

We shake our heads and say no, if he were Palestinian, he would speak Arabic, and *Shalom* is not Arabic.

"I am not Jewish, I am Palestinian!" He is worried now because other people and children are in the street, and he knows how quickly false rumors about affiliations and collaboration can spread in Gaza. "*Salaamu alleykum, Salaamu alleykum*!" he now shouts, and we tell him he is a clever boy.

Several days later as I am getting out of my car outside our gate, a figure rides by on a rickety bicycle. Wobbling, the rider slows down and turns his head. "*Salaamu alleykum*!" he calls out cheerfully. I look up and call back,

"Ah! *Inta Falastini! Hamdulillah*!" (Ah! You are a Palestinian. Thank God!)

The cocky grin is back on his face, but it has been a lesson well learned.

Palestine, Farewell

I was ready to leave, there was no doubt in my mind about that. I'd had enough of the erratic daily life of curfews, strikes, mayhem and chaos. Enough of having to act out a public role of female docility and obedience to Peter; enough of the brutality of both sides: stoning, tear-gas, and bullets. The whole situation seemed futile in terms of the Palestinian people achieving any semblance of autonomy, and it was one big mess heading nowhere. But it was the people I had come to know and love who made leaving so difficult. Part of me felt guilty at having the freedom to walk away from it all. The other part figured I'd done what I could, albeit in a minor, insignificant way in the grand scheme of things. Mostly, I was just dreadfully tired.

As we made our final visits to the families and friends we had known, each goodbye felt like a small, painful amputation. Clasping us in their arms, kissing us many times on the cheeks, the message was always the same: "Don't forget us. Tell the Canadian people that we want to live in peace. Tell them our story."

Then there were all the "last time" things: last visit to the farm, last shawirma sandwich, last meal for Biss, last Arabic lesson...a hundred goodbyes. I found myself trying to look carefully at everything so that the memories would last — the moon shining through the leaves of the palm tree in the garden, the view of the Mediterranean Sea from the roof, the sand dunes heading down to Jabalia Camp, men sitting around an early-morning fire made in a tin out on the street, the three mysterious horses who would appear on the median on strike days. I wanted to hold on to all of it.

The students also became aware of our diminishing time with them. They understood that we had a family in Canada but said that after two years they were now our family and we should stay and bring our Canadian relatives to Gaza. Some of them insisted that we were abandoning them and would forget all about them once we returned to Canada.

In the final week Mitch and Roy arrived. Mitch would take over from us, while Roy was there to assist with the transition and lend support. It was good to have them staying with us and to be able to talk about things Canadian and familiar. I introduced Mitch to the local shopkeepers and neighbors and explained the idiosyncrasies of the apartment. He began to take over the lecturing at the college, and the students, predictably, responded warmly to him and made him feel welcome. They had a new father now.

For three weeks beforehand, Peter and I had been working, each in our own private way, on the speeches we would make at the farewell gathering. Peter got help with his speech from Nasser, the psychologist-administrator at the new college. I got help with mine from Salah, though it inevitably developed into total family participation.

I wrote down in English the phrases I wanted to say, and Salah translated them into classical Arabic for me and also tape-recorded the whole speech so that I could listen and imitate. Salah was always very polite, but obviously had some reservations about my ability to deliver in classical Arabic. That made two of us. I thought I'd never get it right.

Each evening I would listen and repeat the lines until, the evening before our departure, I felt ready for Salah to listen to me. First, Mellika called me downstairs to get ready. Chairs were placed in the courtyard which was illuminated by the verandah lights. The evening air was pleasant and warm. Umm Kamal made her way slowly from the living room, down the steps to the tiled yard, and placed herself in front of me. The old *Haga* followed behind, and then Wasfia and the three children. I explained that I had come to recite to Salah, but they told me he was still busy in his office and they would help prepare me for when he was ready to come. They knew I was stalling!

It was a critical but supportive audience. Every slightly incorrect inflection was noted and corrected: Umm Kamal pronounced the phrases quietly to me; Karma, Ahmed, and Rami shouted at me; Mellika was very critical and not at all sure that some of the phrases captured the best Arabic expressions of gratitude. There was much discussion and debate and many changes made. Throughout the rehearsal, however, the feeling was one of family. Their honor was at stake. If they hadn't prepared me well, it would be their fault, and they wanted people to be proud of me and their tutelage. It felt just fine.

Salah appeared in the courtyard and was provided with a chair. The family assured him I was doing very well and that it was perfect. I felt very nervous for I knew Salah would be more honest. However, I made it through to the end, and was rewarded with his warm approval and admiration. Everyone assured me that I was ready for the performance the next day.

In the morning, we made our farewell visits to Lababidi School and the Sun Centre to say goodbye to the children and teachers with whom we had worked. Then we returned to the college. The students had set up a long table in the common area, with cakes and pop, and everyone was sitting around waiting for us to arrive. As we came in, Bishara placed a beautiful garland of fresh flowers around my neck, and we took our places at the head table.

Majid began the proceedings by speaking on behalf of the older cohort of students, and was followed by Sakher who always seemed to compensate for his physical disability by delivering rousing, emotional speeches. And then it was my turn.

It took three attempts to get started. I thought I would never make it to the end, for I was overwhelmed by the affection and respect that filled the room. As I read the lines, I tried to look at the faces around me. There was Nirmeen, a brilliant student in English. She was trying to raise people's consciousness about thc hazards of in-breeding, by distributing leaflets she had written. There was Hanan, struggling to keep going while helping her family by selling *falafel* in the streets of Jabalia after a day of studying. Here was Hamdi who would have been a professional soccer player in any other country in the world. Here were the twins, Maha and Manal who did daily battle with a father who refused to let them further their education abroad.

Each face had a story and a memory for me, and I had loved them all despite the times when I felt driven to distraction by their seemingly erratic behavior. Each of them in their own way was trying to make changes in a culture that remains very resistant to new ideas. Each of them faced daily violations of human rights. Functioning in the face of such adversity takes more courage than most Canadians can ever imagine.

I became aware of Peter touching my arm, asking if I needed help, for I had started to cry. I kept going. There was cheering when I said that we hoped to return one day to a free Palestine; and then I closed with appropriate blessings.

After the speeches came the eating and the hugs and handshakes and a good deal of sadness as we said goodbye to each person individually. I found it especially hard to leave the young women. They had far more hardship ahead of them than the young men.

Back home we whisked Biss over to Fadi's house, taking a quick farewell of our hardy little feline companion. Fadi and I took him up to the roof where he soon found a comfortable niche behind a metal screen which he seemed to remember from his previous visits. I scratched him under the chin one last time, gave him a kiss, told him to be good and then ran quickly downstairs.

Back at the apartment, Emad was waiting with the minibus that would take us to Tel Aviv. The suitcases were already inside. It only remained for me to say goodbye to the family downstairs, one last time. Umm Kamal was sobbing as I hugged her and told her

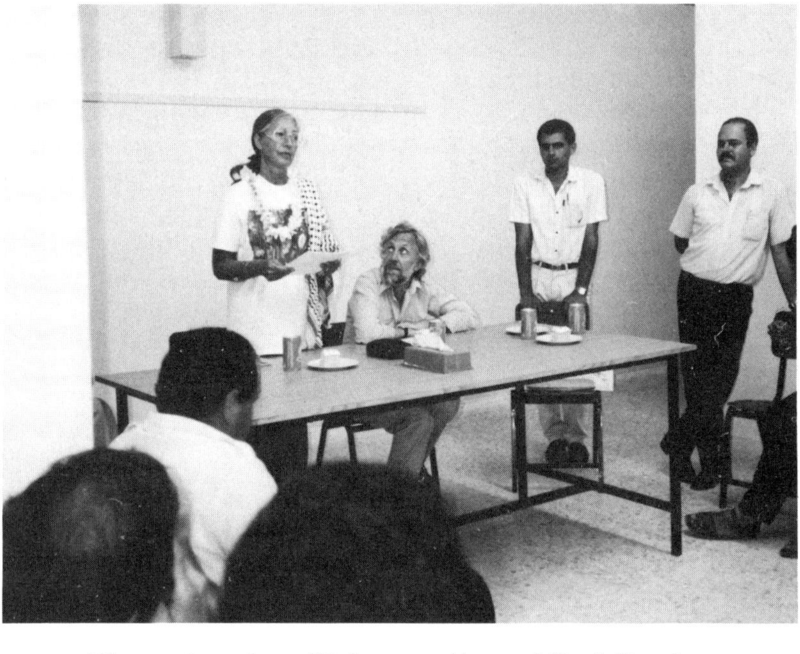

Rhona struggles with her emotions while delivering a farewell speech in classical Arabic.

I would return one day for sure. She said she would watch every day in the hope that she would see me coming down the street. The old *Haga* kissed me on both cheeks and blessed me. Mellika, my dear sister for two years, was too distraught to come out of her bedroom. I understood.

I ran to join Peter at the gate. Roy and Mitch were waiting there to see us off. We climbed into the bus, and Emad drove quickly away. I waved to Mitch and Roy until we turned the corner toward the central prison and they were out of sight. Then I settled down on the seat to take in my last drive through Gaza.

The streets were as busy as ever. Jeeps were still driving the wrong way down one-way roads, Omar had closed the restaurant for the day, and the supermarket had shut down permanently. We drove beneath the "Welcome to Gaza" sign for the last time. Further along the road to the checkpoint we passed the familiar icon of Gaza — a donkey-cart, with a baby donkey trotting alongside its harnessed mother. The children were still playing in the garbage-strewn streets. Nothing had changed, not even my crying at some of these everyday sights.

We passed the checkpoint without incident. I removed the scarf, took out my sunglasses, and looked back for one last time, saying my own farewell to a people and country for whom I see little hope in the political and national arena. It had been wonderful. It had been dreadful. It had been the most challenging thing I had ever done in my life, and I was leaving the richer for having lived with a people whose generosity and determination will remain forever in my heart.

Farewell, Palestine, farewell.

POSTSCRIPT

We left Gaza in the middle of July, 1990. Two weeks later, Saddam Hussein invaded Kuwait and threw the Middle East into turmoil. Most Palestinians support the Iraqi leader whom they see as championing the cause of Arabs from poor countries who are subjected to the oppression of their oil-rich brethren in Kuwait, Saudi Arabia, and the United Arab Emirates. Bowing to pressure from the United States, the Canadian Armed Forces subsequently abandoned its long-held role as peacekeeper and joined the military forces preparing to fight against Iraq. As a result of this action, the Canadians who replaced us were recalled to Canada as it was felt that Gaza and the Middle East had become too dangerous for foreign civilian personnel. Consequently, the educational programs operated by the University of Calgary and Mount Royal College have ground to a virtual standstill. We do not know when the programs will resume, thus allowing our students to graduate and bring their much-needed rehabilitation skills to the ignorance, poverty, and squalor of one of the poorest and most densely-populated places on earth.

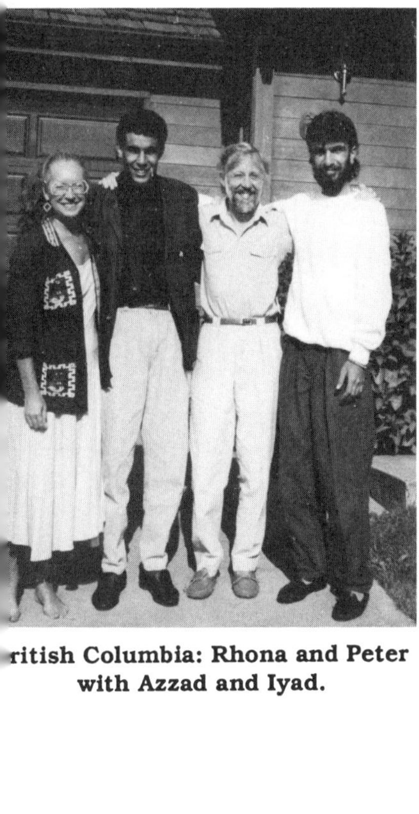

ritish Columbia: Rhona and Peter with Azzad and Iyad.

Toward the end of August 1990, Jenann, Iyad, and Azzad travelled from Calgary to Vancouver to spend the weekend with us. It was wonderful to see them as ordinary young people enjoying the pleasures of a west-coast summer weekend. Jenann was en route to Princeton where she will do graduate work in philosophy. Iyad is struggling to upgrade his English at Mount Royal College, while Azzad has applied for landed immigrant status. He has based his case on the proposition that he is a political refugee and presently awaits a ruling from Immigration Canada. In spite of their current varied activities, we believe all three of them will return to Gaza at some time in the future to further the cause of the Palestinian people.

Printed in Canada